45p

AND HOW THEY ARE USED

POULTRY	MEAT	VEGETABLES		SALADS
Stuffings	Liver Chopped meat Ragouts Stews Meat pies Meat sauces	Cauliflower Onions Peas Spinach String beans	Tomatoes Turnips Squash/Marrow Zucchini/Courgettes	Greens Tomato Cole-slaw
Fricassee Parboiling	Pot roast Stews	Cooked tomatoes		

	Roast pork
	Liver
	Kidneys
		Broccoli
		Brussels
		  sprouts
		Cabbage
			Red
			  cabbage
			Potatoes
				Tips of
				  fresh leaves
				  with greens

Broiled chicken
Most chicken
  dishes
Stuffings
	Stews
	Gravies
	With butter
	  on steak
		Artichoke
		  hearts
		Beets
		Broccoli
			Carrots
			Celery
			Eggplant
				Greens
				Potato

	Hamburger Sauces	Cabbage Carrots Celery	Peas Potatoes	Greens Potato

	Broiled
	  chops
	Many meats
	Some veal
	  dishes
		Avocado
		Beans
		Beets
			Eggplant
			Parsnips
			Potatoes
				Cucumber
				Potato
				Manv

Duck Turkey Stuffings	Marinades Roasts Stews Sausages Sauces	Brusse sprou Cabbag Eggplar Mushro		

Marinades	Marinades
	Lamb
	Stews
	Stuffings
	Spanish, Italian
	  and Mexican
	  dishes
		Broccoli
		Mushroo
		Zucchini/Courgettes		

Almost
  all
	Marinades
	Stews
		Chopped
		  on almost
		  all
				Greens
				Potato
				Vegetable

Stuffings	Lamb marinade
	Pork
	Roast lamb
	Roast veal
	Stuffings
		Beans: baked,
		  string
		Eggplant
			Spinach
			Zucchini/Courgettes
			Boiled
			  potatoes	

Fresh with
  duck and
  geese
Stuffings
	Head cheese
	Pork
	Roasts
	Stews
	Sausage
	Stuffings
		Cabbage
		Carrots
		Fresh with
		  string
		  beans		

Almost all
  poultry
  dishes
	Stews
	Most
	  meat
	  dishes
		Cabbage
		Green
		  pepper
		Mushrooms
			Peas
			Tomatoes
				Greens
				Tomato
				Vegetable

Stuffings	Marinades
	Roasts
	Stews
	Croquettes
	Meat loaf
		Brussels
		  sprouts
		Cabbage
		Carrots
		Peas
			Squash/Marrow
			Sweet
			  potatoes
			Sliced raw
			  tomatoes
				Fresh in
				  green
				  salads

D0996986

NEW
CASSEROLE TREASURY

NEW
CASSEROLE TREASURY

Lousene Rousseau Brunner

THE COOKERY BOOK CLUB

To my husband EDMUND DE SCHWEINITZ BRUNNER
Who has cheerfully played the role of guinea pig
for all my recipe testing

NEW CASSEROLE TREASURY. Copyright © 1970 by Lousene Rousseau Brunner.
This edition published 1972 by The Cookery Book Club by arrangement with Harper
& Row, publishers, New York, U.S.A. Printed by Hazell Watson & Viney Ltd.,
Aylesbury, Bucks.

CONTENTS

COLOUR ILLUSTRATIONS

Photographs by John Cross

GUIDE TO METRIC MEASURES

Here are a few equivalent measurements which, though approximate, are sufficiently accurate for cooking purposes.

1 oz.	=	28 grammes
4 oz.	=	112 grammes
8 oz.	=	225 grammes
1 lb.	=	450 grammes
2 lbs. 3 oz.	=	1 kilogramme
$\frac{1}{4}$ pint	=	140 grammes
$\frac{1}{2}$ pint	=	280 grammes
1 pint	=	0.568 litres
$1\frac{3}{4}$ pints	=	1 litre

FOREWORD

New Casserole Treasury is an enlarged, revised and illustrated edition of my earlier collection of casserole recipes which has been so successful since its publication six years ago.

It is a collection of more than four hundred of the many hundreds of casserole recipes which could be assembled. They have come from many countries, from great chefs and from peasant kitchens. Their ingredients run the gamut from truffles and *pâtés* to cabbage and beer.

There is a section on soups and chowders, and one on desserts that lend themselves to casserole preparation and service. Many dishes are included that call for flaming, either early in their preparation or at the table. Wines and liqueurs lend their magic to many of the casseroles, as do herbs, especially fresh herbs, now featured in so many gardens. Many delightful buffet casseroles are included.

Many of these recipes make use of so-called 'convenience foods', especially frozen vegetables and tinned soups. In a few recipes ready-mixed ingredients are suggested. But it has been no part of my intention to recommend short cuts in cooking at the expense of that careful and painstaking preparation which is the essence of good cooking. One of the principal advantages of casserole cookery is that it usually makes it possible to do all the drudgery early in the day, thus making the preparation of the evening meal a relatively painless process.

I have tried to make the directions explicit enough for even the most inexperienced cook to follow. Cooking times, oven temperatures, and number of servings are clearly stated. However, these will depend to some extent upon the material of the casserole (clay, glass, stainless steel, copper, porcelain-coated cast iron, etc.), its size and shape, and the depth of the food in it.

It is my hope that *New Casserole Treasury* will bring new eating pleasure to many homes.

Lousene Rousseau Brunner

NOTES ON THE RECIPES

1. A useful ingredient in practically all casserole dishes except desserts is monosodium glutamate (MSG), better known by such trade names as 'Accent'. It is not listed here because it would appear in almost every recipe. I use it as I use salt and pepper. A little experimenting will provide a guide to quantities to use—it can vary from a shake to a teaspoonful.

2. Oven temperatures indicated always mean that the oven should be *preheated* to that temperature.

3. Many of these casseroles can be cooked on top of the stove as easily as in the oven. However, this will mean a somewhat shorter cooking time and more careful watching to prevent overcooking and scorching. Obviously, soufflés and custards must always be baked in the oven.

4. Where casseroles do not have their own close-fitting lids, lids can be readily improvised with heavy-duty foil.

5. If you do much casserole cooking, keep certain basic supplies on hand. Frozen chopped onions and green peppers, for example, save time with no sacrifice of flavour whatever. Chicken stock cubes keep indefinitely on the shelf and produce in an instant a most satisfactory chicken stock—an ingredient frequently needed. Grated Parmesan cheese is called for repeatedly, and keeps well in the refrigerator. Tinned condensed cream of mushroom soup and cream of celery soup are often called for. Chopped and split almonds are required repeatedly, and keep well in the refrigerator. If you do not grow your own herbs, keep small jars of dried herbs on hand, replacing them every few months. Packaged cornflake crumbs are often more flavourful than bread crumbs and keep perfectly.

SOUPS

BORSCH

1 lb. chuck
2 quarts water
2½ lbs. beetroot, peeled and grated
    coarsely
2 carrots, scraped and cut in thin strips
1 large onion, cut in fine strips
1 large tomato or 2 medium, skinned and
    chopped

1 tablespoon butter or margarine
4 oz. finely shredded cabbage
1 small bay leaf
2 tablespoons vinegar
1 tablespoon sugar
1 teaspoon salt
½ teaspoon fresh-ground pepper
    Sour cream

THIS is probably the best known of all Russian dishes, and certainly one of the best liked. There are innumerable recipes for it, all including beetroot, cabbage, and sour cream. This is an excellent way of making it.

1. Cover the meat with 2 quarts of water, salted, and cook, covered, over low heat, for at least 2 hours. Skim the top several times to remove the scum and fat. Remove the meat and strain the stock.

2. In a heavy casserole put the carrots, onion, tomato, and all but 3 tablespoons of the beetroot, which will be used later.

3. Add enough stock just to cover, and the butter. Cover and simmer about 20 minutes.

4. Add the cabbage, bay leaf, 1 tablespoon of the vinegar, sugar, salt, pepper, and all but a cupful of the remaining stock. Mix well, cover, and simmer 20 minutes more.

5. Add the reserved stock to the grated beetroot kept back at the beginning, with the remaining tablespoon of vinegar. Bring to a boil, simmer a few minutes, and strain the red liquid into the soup pot to give it the proper red colour. Put a large dollop of sour cream on top of each serving. Makes 8 large plates or 10 smaller bowls.

BOUILLABAISSE (for 12)

5 lbs. mixed fish (fresh haddock,
 whiting, eel, sole, etc.)
1 crab
1 live lobster (about 1½ lbs.)
2 pts. mussels
 Salt and pepper
¼ pt. olive oil
3 large onions, chopped

1 clove garlic
1 oz. minced parsley
1 oz. chopped celery tops
3 tomatoes, peeled, seeded, and slightly
 mashed
1½ teaspoons crumbled saffron
 Dry white wine

A TRUE French bouillabaisse calls for varieties of fish not available in Britain, but you can make a good substitute with what we have available—and many kinds of fish can be used.

1. Cut all the fish into 2-inch chunks, sprinkle with salt and fresh-ground pepper, and let stand while the rest is being prepared.

2. Cut the crab in two, clean, dust with salt, and add to the fish.

3. The lobster *must* be alive. With a sharp cleaver or hatchet cut it up in 2-inch hunks. Wash the pieces in water to which a little lemon juice or vinegar has been added. Add to the fish.

4. The mussels can either be shelled or they can have just the top half of the shell removed— the latter method is the usual one. Set these aside separately.

5. Make this 'soup' in a large stew pot or porcelain-coated casserole. Heat the olive oil in it and add the onions, garlic, parsley, celery, and tomatoes.

6. Cook this 4–5 minutes, stirring constantly, and then stir in the saffron. Add all the fish and seafood except the mussels. Cover, but just barely, with half water and half dry white wine. Bring to a fast boil and keep boiling for 8–10 minutes. Add the mussels, reduce the heat and boil 5 minutes longer.

If you have made this in a stew pot, transfer to a large casserole for serving. Serve in big soup plates in which you first place two or three thick pieces of slightly dry French bread. Do not remove lobster, crab, or mussel shells when you serve. You can't be dainty in eating bouillabaisse. Serves 12.

Serve with warm fresh rolls and follow with a green salad.

CORN CHOWDER

1-lb. tin sweet corn or fresh corn cut off
  the cob
3 slices bacon cut in strips
1 medium onion sliced
4½ oz. diced or thinly sliced potato
  Salt and pepper to taste
1 tablespoon sugar

1¼ pts. boiling water
1 large tin evaporated milk or
  ¾ pt. rich milk scalded
2 egg yolks stirred with a fork
1 tablespoon butter
  Chopped parsley or chives

1. Make this chowder in a large casserole. Fry the bacon in it until it is *almost* crisp. Add the onion and potato and sauté lightly—do not brown.

2. Stir in the sweet corn and seasonings. Add the boiling water, cover, and bake about 45 minutes in a 350° oven, or cook on top of the stove over the least possible heat for 30–35 minutes, stirring occasionally. Add the milk and continue to cook until it is very hot.

3. When you are about ready to serve stir a little of the hot mixture into the egg yolks and stir all back together. Add the butter, dust the top with parsley or chives, and serve at once. Serves 4–5 as a main course, or 8 as a first course.

As a main course, serve with warm French bread or salty rolls, and a green salad with vegetables added.

CRABMEAT CHOWDER BOSTON STYLE

½ lb. fresh, frozen, or tinned crabmeat
1 tin condensed cream of mushroom soup
1 tin condensed cream of celery soup
¾ pt. top milk
8 oz. cooked potatoes diced quite small

2 tablespoons minced or grated onion
6 oz. cooked peas
1 tablespoon lemon juice
  Salt and pepper
2 tablespoons minced parsley

THIS is really a meal in itself, and needs nothing but hot rolls or French bread and a green salad to make a hearty lunch.

    Flake the crabmeat carefully, being sure to remove all the membranes, but leaving much of it in lumps. Combine all the ingredients except parsley in a heatproof tureen or large casserole, cover, and heat 20–25 minutes in a 325° oven. Stir well and sprinkle with parsley before serving. Or make in a heavy casserole on top of the stove, but stir occasionally to keep it from lumping. Serves 4 generously.

CREAMED CRAB SOUP

1 lb. fresh-cooked, frozen, or tinned
  crabmeat
3 tablespoons butter
  Grated rind of 1 lemon
1 tablespoon flour
1 teaspoon Worcestershire sauce
  Pinch mace (optional)
2 chopped hard-boiled eggs

3 mushrooms chopped
3 stalks celery chopped
1 spring onion or shallot minced
1¾ pts. milk scalded
½ pt. cream scalded
  Salt and pepper to taste
¼ pt. dry sherry

THIS crab soup, when made from all fresh ingredients, is especially good. Like the others, it is hearty enough for a main dish. Note, though, how differently it is made.
1. Mash 2 tablespoons butter, lemon rind, flour, Worcestershire sauce, mace, and eggs to a paste. Mix with the crabmeat (which has been carefully picked over).
2. Heat the remaining tablespoon butter in a large casserole on top of the stove and lightly sauté the mushrooms, celery, and spring onion or shallot. Stir in the scalded milk and cream and the crabmeat mixture. Season to taste, cover, and heat to just under boiling in a 300° oven—about 20–25 minutes. Stir two or three times while it is heating.
3. Add the sherry just before serving. Serves 6 large plates or 8 bowls.

If this is the main luncheon course, serve also a large green salad with French dressing and crisp rolls.

CRABMEAT AND SWEET CORN CHOWDER

½ lb. crabmeat flaked, fresh, frozen, or
  tinned
1¼ lbs. fresh grated sweet corn or cream-
  style sweet corn
2 thin slices onion, or 1 tablespoon
  minced or grated

1 pt. rich milk scalded
1 pt. thin white sauce
  Salt and pepper to taste
  Grating of nutmeg
2 egg yolks slightly beaten
1 tablespoon butter

THIS is a smooth, velvety chowder. The crab-corn combination is intriguing.
1. Put the sweet corn, onion, and milk in the top of a double boiler and cook over hot water for 20–25 minutes. Force through a sieve or a food mill into a casserole, or give it about 20 seconds in a blender.
2. Make the white sauce with 1 tablespoon butter or margarine, 1 tablespoon flour, and 1 pt. milk. Season to taste with the salt, pepper, and nutmeg. Stir into the mixture in the casserole, cover, and bake in a 300° oven 20 minutes or until heated almost to boiling.
3. Uncover and stir in the crabmeat. Add a little of the soup to the egg yolks and stir them quickly into the soup. Heat a few minutes, add the butter, and serve at once. Or the whole chowder can be made on top of the stove, though it has to be watched more carefully. Serves 6 large plates or 8 bowls or small plates.

If you make this your main luncheon course, serve with crisp rolls and a vegetable salad.

CURRIED CHICKEN SOUP

1 lb. cooked chicken cut up coarsely
2 oz. butter or margarine
1 medium onion minced
1 tart apple peeled and chopped
1¼ pts. chicken broth
1 tablespoon curry powder or to taste

¼ teaspoon dried thyme or 1 teaspoon
  fresh, chopped
  Salt and pepper to taste
2 oz. raisins
2 oz. salted peanuts coarsely chopped
4 oz. cooked hot rice

A CURRIED soup is rather unusual, and this is an exceptionally good one. Like all the soups in this section it is hearty enough for the main course of a luncheon or Sunday supper.

Put the butter in a heavy casserole and heat on top of the stove. Simmer the onion and apple in it lightly, but do not brown. Add remaining ingredients except peanuts and rice, cover, and bake half an hour in a 350° oven.

When ready to serve stir in the peanuts and check the seasoning. Put a tablespoon of the cooked rice in each soup plate and ladle the soup over. Serves 4.

FRENCH PEASANT SOUP

2 tablespoons butter or margarine
2 medium carrots chopped rather coarsely
1 small white turnip peeled and chopped
2 leeks (white part only) chopped
2 small onions chopped
4 oz. chopped cabbage
1 stalk celery chopped

¼ teaspoon sugar
  Salt and pepper
1 quart chicken broth, consommé, or water
1 medium potato chopped
3 oz. green peas
3 oz. cut green beans
  French bread

1. Heat the butter in a heavy casserole and add the carrots, turnip, leeks, onions, cabbage, and celery. Sprinkle with sugar, salt and pepper to taste. Cook about 10 minutes, over medium heat, stirring often.

2. Cover the casserole, turn the heat down as far as possible, and simmer half an hour, stirring frequently.

3. Add half the liquid. Increase the heat a little, and when it is boiling stir in the potato, peas, and beans.

4. Turn the heat down again and simmer another half hour. Add the remainder of the stock and continue to simmer another half hour.

5. When you are ready to serve, toast enough half-inch slices of French bread to cover the soup. Butter the toast, lay on top of the soup, and put the whole casserole under the grill for 2–3 minutes, or until the toast is sizzling. Serves 6.

HEARTY TURKEY SOUP

½ lb. diced cooked turkey
1¼ pts. turkey or chicken broth
2 oz. butter or margarine
2 tablespoons chopped onion
1 teaspoon curry powder
8 oz. diced potatoes
3 oz. diced carrots
3 oz. celery sliced diagonally

Salt and pepper to taste
1 8-oz. packet frozen French beans
1 teaspoon minced fresh oregano or
 ½ teaspoon dried
1 tablespoon minced parsley
14½-oz. tin evaporated milk or ¾ pt. thin
 cream
1 tablespoon flour

THIS is one of the most delectable soups you can imagine—far better than the usual after-the-turkey soup. It is one of the heartiest soups I know, and needs nothing but French bread or rolls, crisped in the oven, to accompany it, with a tossed green salad to follow.

1. Melt the butter in a good-sized casserole on top of the stove and cook the onion until it is just transparent. Stir in the curry powder and cook a minute or two longer.

2. Stir in the potatoes, carrots, celery, broth, seasoning to taste, and bring to a boil. Transfer to a slow oven, 300°, and bake 10 to 15 minutes. Or cook entirely on top of the stove, with low heat.

3. Stir in the French beans, turkey, oregano, and parsley and continue baking about 15 minutes, or until the vegetables are barely tender, but still a little crisp.

4. Combine milk and flour and stir in gently until well blended. The soup should be slightly thickened. Check seasoning. Serves 4 hungry people amply or 6 if more food is to follow.

LENTIL SOUP

8 oz. dried lentils
1 lb. veal shank
2 oz. chopped onion
2 teaspoons salt
½ teaspoon pepper

3 pts. boiling water
3 tablespoons lemon juice
1 teaspoon Worcestershire sauce
1 oz. chopped parsley

LENTIL soup can be so delicious that it seems a pity more people are not familiar with it.

1. In a large casserole put the veal shank, the lentils, onion, salt, pepper, and water. Cover and put in a 275° oven for about 1½–1¾ hours, stirring occasionally.

2. Remove the veal shank from the casserole, cut off the meat, and cut it up. Return it to the casserole with the lemon juice, Worcestershire sauce, and parsley. Continue to bake 10 minutes more. Serves 8 in bowls or 6 in large plates.

It is nice to serve this soup, like many others, with a large spoonful of sour cream on top, dusted with paprika.

HOTPOT CHOWDER

12 oz. sweet corn cut off the cob or whole
   kernel sweet corn tinned or frozen
12 oz. celery chopped
½ green pepper cut in strips
1 onion sliced thin
6 oz. chopped tomatoes, tinned or fresh
1 tablespoon salt
¼ teaspoon pepper

½ pt. cold water
2 oz. butter or margarine
2 tablespoons flour
¼ teaspoon paprika
1½ pts. milk scalded
2 oz. grated sharp Cheddar cheese
1 pimento sliced thin

THIS is a very old recipe for a most unusual kind of creamed vegetable soup. Like the other soups in this section it is practically a meal in itself.

1. Start the casserole on top of the stove. Put in it the sweet corn, celery, green pepper, onion, tomatoes, salt and pepper, and water. Bring it just to a boil, turn down the heat, cover, and simmer for 15 minutes.

2. Knead the butter, flour, and paprika together and stir into the hot milk. Then stir this mixture into the casserole, cover, and bake in a slow oven, 300°, 15 to 20 minutes. Add the cheese and pimento just before serving, continuing to bake just until the cheese is melted. Serves 6 generously.

Serve with croûtons or French bread. Follow with a green salad.

LAMB AND LENTIL SOUP LUNCHEON

1 lb. ground lamb shoulder
1 lb. lentils
4 pts. cold water
2 tablespoons salt
¼ teaspoon fresh-ground pepper
4 oz. butter
1 lb. chopped tomatoes, fresh or tinned
1 large onion minced

2 tablespoons fresh chopped dill or 2
   teaspoons dried
3 medium cloves garlic crushed
1 bay leaf
1½ teaspoons salt
1 egg beaten slightly
   Flour
1 tablespoon salad oil
2 oz. elbow macaroni

THIS looks like a lot of ingredients, but actually the dish is a simple one, and all except the last step can be done early in the morning.

1. Wash the lentils well and put in a large casserole with the water, the 2 tablespoons salt, ¼ teaspoon of the pepper, butter, tomatoes, onion, dill, garlic, and bay leaf. Stir well, cover, and put in a slow oven, 275°, for 1¾–2 hours.

2. While this is cooking combine the ground lamb with the 1½ teaspoons salt, the remaining ¼ teaspoon pepper, and the egg. Shape into 24 small balls and roll in flour. Heat the salad oil in a heavy frying-pan and brown the lamb balls well on all sides.

3. If you have cooked the casserole early, heat it about 20 minutes before you are ready to serve, and stir in the lamb balls and the macaroni. Continue to bake, checking seasoning before serving. Serves 8 in large plates or about 12 in bowls.

FISH CHOWDER

1 lb. fresh or frozen fish fillets, preferably cod or haddock, or a larger chunk with bone in
2 quarter-inch slices salt pork diced small
3 medium onions sliced

3 medium potatoes diced
¾ pt. water
¾ pt. creamy milk
1 teaspoon Worcestershire sauce
Salt and pepper

FOR generations this has been a North American classic. Make the chowder in a heavy casserole on top of the stove, or make it in a stew pot and transfer it to a casserole to serve at the table.

1. Put the salt pork in the casserole and cook until crisp. Take out the pieces and reserve. Add the onions and cook gently until transparent but not browned at all. Add the potatoes and cook 3–4 minutes.

2. At the same time, put the fish into a saucepan with the water, bring to a boil, lower the heat, and simmer 10–15 minutes, or until the fish will flake with a fork. A chunk of fish will, of course, take considerably longer than fillets.

3. Add the fish and water to the casserole (lifting out the bone, if any) and simmer until the potatoes are soft—5–10 minutes.

4. Stir in milk and season to taste with Worcestershire sauce, salt, and pepper. Scatter salt pork on top. Serves 4 in large plates.

FRENCH ONION SOUP

1 lb. onions sliced thin
3 tablespoons butter or margarine
1 oz. grated Parmesan cheese

4 tins condensed beef consommé
Salt and pepper
4 slices French bread toasted on one side

ONION soup is a universal favourite, but the tinned variety can't compete with a good home-made onion soup, and it is simple to make.

1. Heat 2 tablespoons of the butter in a large casserole on top of the stove and sauté the onions until they are soft and barely beginning to brown.

2. Add the undiluted consommé and salt and pepper to taste. Go slow with the salt until you taste it. Cover and bake in a 350° oven for 30 minutes. Check in about 15 minutes, and if the soup is too bland—not 'beefy' enough—add a little concentrate of beef, such as Maggi, Bovril, or the like.

3. Spread the hot toast (on the untoasted side) with the remaining butter and gently lay on top of the casserole. Cover with cheese and brown under the grill. Serve with a bowl of extra cheese. Serves 6 in large plates or 8 in bowls.

PETITE MARMITE

1 boiling fowl, cut up
2 veal bones
5 pts. water
Pinch thyme
1 small bay leaf
3 medium onions
2 cloves
Salt and pepper

3 carrots
1 stalk celery
2 leeks (white part only)
1 small white turnip
4 oz. chopped cabbage
Grated cheese
Croûtons

THIS is a classic of French cookery, such a staple of French homes that the wonderful French soup pot is usually called a *marmite*. It you do not have a *marmite*, make the soup in a stew pot or a large heavy casserole. The porcelain-lined iron ones are perfect for such soups.

1. Put in the pot the pieces of fowl, veal bones, water, thyme, bay leaf, one of the onions stuck with the two cloves, and salt and pepper to taste. Bring the water to a boil, turn the heat down to the merest simmer, cover, and cook for anywhere from 4–12 hours. (The latter is the French way.)

2. Remove the chicken pieces, cool the soup, strain it, and skim off as much fat as you can. Skin and bone the chicken.

3. Chop all the vegetables quite fine. Add to the soup with good-sized hunks of the chicken. Simmer until the vegetables are tender, correcting the seasoning.

4. Serve from the casserole into individual bowls, topping each one with a little cheese and crisp croûtons. Serves 10.

ROMAN BEAN SOUP

½ lb. pink or pinto beans
1 carrot minced
1 medium onion minced
1 stalk celery minced
2 tablespoons salad oil
2 cloves garlic crushed
2 tablespoons chopped parsley

6 oz. peeled, seeded, and chopped
  tomatoes, or 1 small tin
Salt and pepper to taste
¼ teaspoon rosemary
4 oz. hot rice
Grated Parmesan or Romano cheese

1. Soak the beans overnight in water to cover well. In the morning drain them, put in a good-sized heavy casserole, cover generously with fresh water, add the carrot, onion, and celery, and bake, covered, in a very slow oven, 275°, about 2½ hours, or until the beans are medium soft. This can be done on top of the stove instead, over the lowest possible heat, using an asbestos plate if necessary. Stir occasionally. If it seems rather thick, thin with water.

2. In a heavy frying pan heat the oil and sauté the garlic, parsley, and tomatoes, until the tomatoes are soft.

3. Add this mixture to the casserole as soon as the beans are ready, and season to taste with salt and pepper and rosemary.

4. Simmer the soup 30 minutes longer. Remove about a cup of beans and set aside. Strain the rest and put the solid part through a food mill, or add a little of the liquid and blend 30–40 seconds. Put it all together again in the casserole, add the reserved beans and the rice, check seasoning and reheat. Serve with a bowl of grated cheese. Serves 4.

VEGETABLE CHOWDER

6 large potatoes diced small
5-6 medium onions chopped
4 stalks celery cut in ½-inch pieces
½ green pepper chopped
1 cup chopped salted peanuts
1 tin condensed tomato soup
1 tin cream-style sweet corn
1 tin green pea soup
¾ pt. milk

1 1-lb. packet frozen runner beans partly
  thawed
½ teaspoon dried basil or 1½ teaspoons
  fresh, chopped
1 teaspoon minced parsley
½ teaspoon dried marjoram or 1½ teaspoons
  fresh, chopped
Salt to taste

This is a wonderful solution for a simple but hearty meal, especially since it can be put together in the morning and requires no attention in cooking.

If you combine the ingredients hours in advance, reserve the salted peanuts until you put the soup on to cook. Otherwise, mix everything together in a large heavy casserole and simmer about 30 minutes, or until the potatoes and celery are tender. Serves 12.

Serve with warm French bread and a salad tossed in French dressing.

COUNTRY VEGETABLE SOUP

2 potatoes sliced
2 tablespoons salad oil or margarine
2 leeks well cleaned and sliced (white part
  only)
2 onions sliced
2 carrots sliced
2 tomatoes sliced
1 white turnip sliced

1 clove
1 sprig parsley
  Salt and pepper to taste
2 pts. consommé or chicken broth plus
  1 pt. water, or 3 pts. water
¼ pt. sour cream
1 egg yolk slightly beaten

THIS is an old family recipe, and it makes a soup so different from the usual vegetable soup as to be a most welcome change. Make it on top of the stove in a heavy casserole that can go directly to the table.

1. Heat the oil in the casserole and lightly sauté all the sliced vegetables until they are almost but not quite tender.

2. Add the clove, parsley, salt and pepper, and the liquid, a pint at a time. Simmer 45 minutes to an hour over the lowest possible heat, stirring occasionally.

3. Strain the soup and put the thick part through a food mill or a coarse sieve, or purée it in a blender.

4. Combine again with the liquid, reheat, and stir in the sour cream and egg yolk, well mixed, just before serving. Serves 6 generously.

Serve with French bread or rolls, and a salad of runner beans, cucumber sliced without peeling, and mixed greens.

NOTES

MEATS

BEEF

BAKED ALASKA MEAT LOAF

2 lbs. lean chuck, ground
2 eggs slightly beaten
2 scant teaspoons salt
$\frac{1}{8}$ teaspoon pepper
6 oz. soft bread crumbs
2 oz. minced onion
$\frac{1}{2}$ teaspoon dried oregano or 1$\frac{1}{2}$ teaspoons
  fresh, chopped

$\frac{1}{2}$ teaspoon dried sweet basil or
  1$\frac{1}{2}$ teaspoons fresh, chopped
2 tablespoons minced parsley
3 lbs. fresh mashed potato
2 egg yolks
Paprika
Parmesan cheese (optional)

THIS is a sort of cross between a regular meat loaf and a shepherd's pie, but to my mind better than either and more appealing to the eye.

1. Blend well in a mixing bowl the meat, eggs, salt and pepper, crumbs, onion, and herbs. Pack firmly into a round ovenproof bowl and bake 1 hour and 20 minutes at 400°.

2. Drain off the liquid which will accumulate and invert the bowl on a wire rack to drain completely. Pat the loaf dry with paper towels and slide it onto a shallow casserole or a Pyrex pie plate somewhat larger than the loaf.

3. In the meantime prepare the mashed potatoes. Beat them until they are fluffy and beat in the egg yolks.

4. Frost the meat loaf thickly with the potatoes. Sprinkle with paprika and grated Parmesan cheese (if you use it) and set the loaf back in the oven 25–30 minutes, or until the surface is golden. Serves 6 amply.

Serve with green peas mixed with tiny white onions.

BEEF AND BURGUNDY CASSEROLE

3 lbs. lean chuck or rump steak cut in
  2-inch cubes
4 tablespoons butter or margarine
2 tablespoons bacon fat
2 tablespoons flour
2 teaspoons salt
½ teaspoon fresh-ground pepper
1 bay leaf
½ teaspoon dried sweet basil or
  1½ teaspoons fresh, chopped

1 clove garlic crushed
½ teaspoon dried oregano or 1½ teaspoons
  fresh, chopped
1 lb. tiny white onions peeled and
  parboiled or 1-lb. tin
1 large or 2 small tins baby carrots
½ pt. Burgundy or other dry red wine
1 tablespoon sugar
¾ pt. Madeira
3 tablespoons brandy

THIS is one of the most delectable of all the casseroles I have ever served. It makes a highly successful main dish for a party.

1. Heat 2 tablespoons of the butter and the bacon fat in a large, heavy frying-pan, and brown the beef well on all sides. Arrange in a large casserole.

2. Add to fat in the pan the flour, salt, pepper, bay leaf, basil, oregano, and garlic, and stir until the flour begins to brown.

3. Drain liquid from vegetables and, if necessary, add water to make ¾ pint *scant*. Stir this into the pan and keep stirring until it thickens.

4. Add the Burgundy, stir until the sauce is smooth and thickened somewhat, and pour over the meat in the casserole. Cover and bake about 3 hours in a 300° oven.

5. Melt the remaining 2 tablespoons butter in the pan and stir in the sugar. When this has melted add the drained vegetables and stir them frequently until they are slightly browned. Add them to the casserole with the Madeira and continue to cook, covered, 30 minutes longer.

6. Stir in the brandy just before serving. Serves 8.

Serve with a wild rice casserole (see Index), a large green salad tossed in French dressing, sliced tomatoes, and warm French bread.

French peasant soup

BARBECUED MEAT LOAVES

Loaves

1 lb. ground lean beef
1 egg lightly beaten
4 tablespoons fine bread crumbs or
  cornflake crumbs
1 tablespoon minced parsley

3 tablespoons water
2 tablespoons chopped onion
2 tablespoons prepared horseradish
1 teaspoon salt
$\frac{1}{8}$ teaspoon pepper

Sauce

$\frac{1}{4}$ pt. chili sauce
3 tablespoons ketchup
1 teaspoon Worcestershire sauce

$\frac{1}{2}$ teaspoon dry mustard
Dash Tabasco

COMBINE all the ingredients for the meat loaves, mix well, and shape into 4 oblong loaves. Place these in a greased shallow casserole, not touching.

Combine the sauce ingredients and spread over the tops and sides of the loaves. Bake in a 350° oven about 45 minutes, basting the loaves two or three times with the drippings which accumulate. Serves 4.

Serve with fluffy mashed potatoes and thinly sliced buttered carrots.

BARBECUED BEEF STRIPS

2 lbs. topside $\frac{1}{2}$-inch thick, cut in strips
  $1\frac{1}{2}$ by 3 inches
3 tablespoons prepared mustard
  Flour
4 tablespoons cooking oil
1 teaspoon crushed garlic
3 oz. minced onion
3 oz. chopped green pepper

1 oz. chopped celery leaves
1 oz. minced parsley
8-oz. bottle tomato sauce
3 tablespoons cider or tarragon vinegar
$\frac{3}{4}$ pt. water
2 tablespoons brown sugar
$\frac{1}{2}$ teaspoon salt
$\frac{1}{4}$ teaspoon cayenne pepper

THIS is a spicy and flavourful dish, especially welcome on a cold night.
1. Put the mustard in a large bowl, add the strips of beef, and stir until they are well coated. Roll lightly in flour and brown well in a heavy frying-pan in hot oil. Spread them in a 1½-quart casserole.
2. Add all the remaining ingredients to the fat remaining in the pan, stir well, and let simmer about 10 minutes, stirring frequently.
3. Pour this mixture over the steak strips in the casserole, cover tightly, and bake 2–2¼ hours in a 300° oven. Stir two or three times while baking, and if it seems dry add a little more water. Serves 5–6.

Serve with buttered noodles and cut green beans.

Ingredients for lamb and aubergine casserole

BEEF CASSEROLE WITH POTATO TOPPING

1 lb. leftover cooked beef cut in ½-inch cubes
2 tins condensed green pea soup
3 oz. sliced mushrooms sautéed in a little butter or margarine
¼ pt. milk
1 teaspoon chopped parsley

½ teaspoon dried sweet basil or ¼ tablespoon fresh, chopped
1 small onion chopped
Salt and pepper
1¼ lbs. fresh hot mashed potatoes
6 oz. cooked peas (optional)
1 egg well beaten
2 tablespoons melted butter or margarine

THIS casserole is almost a meal in itself, though you need an additional vegetable with it.
1. In a 2-quart casserole place the meat, soup, mushrooms, milk, herbs, and onion. Season to taste. (The mixture will blend better if you warm the soup first and stir in the milk.) Bake 25 minutes, covered, in a 350° oven.
2. Make fresh mashed potatoes and stir in the peas and egg. Spread evenly over the casserole and sprinkle the melted butter over. Increase the heat to 425° and bake 10 minutes more. Serves 6.

Serve with sliced tomatoes and cole slaw.

SPECIAL BEEF AND RICE CASSEROLE

3 lbs. boneless chuck cut in 1½-inch cubes
12 slices bacon cut in ½-inch strips
2 large onions sliced
8 oz. raw rice
½ pt. dry red wine
1 pt. consommé
1 clove garlic crushed

½ teaspoon dried thyme or 1 sprig fresh
1 teaspoon chopped parsley
1 small bay leaf
½ teaspoon saffron crumbled (optional)
10 oz. chopped fresh tomatoes (or tinned)
4 oz. grated Parmesan cheese
Salt and pepper to taste

THIS is truly a special casserole, the wine giving it delightful flavour. (If you do not want to use wine, use 1½ pints consommé.)
1. Cook the bacon in a large heavy frying-pan. When it is crisp take it out and spread it on the bottom of a large casserole.
2. In the accumulated fat brown the beef cubes well and transfer them to the casserole.
3. Brown the onions lightly in the fat remaining in the pan and stir in the dry rice. Stir constantly until the rice is starting to brown and set aside for the moment.
4. Add to the casserole the wine, consommé, garlic, thyme, parsley, bay leaf, and saffron. Cover and bake 1 hour in a 325° oven.
5. Skim off any fat accumulated and stir the rice mixture and tomatoes into the casserole. Cover again and bake an additional hour. Check a couple of times to be sure there is enough liquid for the rice to absorb; you may have to add a bit more consommé.
6. Just before you are ready to serve check the seasoning and stir in the cheese. Heat long enough to melt the cheese. Serves 6.

Serve with only a large dressed green salad, to which you have added a grated carrot, thin tomato wedges, and sliced cucumbers (not peeled).

BEEF AND MACARONI

1 lb. lean ground beef
8-oz. packet macaroni cooked
2 tablespoons butter or margarine
2 tablespoons chopped green pepper

½ pt. sour cream
3 tablespoons onion soup mix
½ pt. milk
1 oz. crumbs, bread or cornflake

1. Melt the butter in a heavy frying-pan and in it sauté the beef and green pepper, stirring until the green pepper is soft and there is no more red in the meat.
2. Mix the sour cream and onion soup mix, heat just to the boiling point, and whip with a rotary egg beater. Stir in the milk gradually.
3. Combine this mixture with the meat and the macaroni, cooked according to package directions, and pour into a 3-pint casserole. Top with crumbs and dabs of butter and bake about 20–25 minutes at 350°, covered.
4. Just before serving remove cover and brown under the grill. Serves 6–8.

Serve with buttered baby carrots and sliced tomatoes.

BEEF WITH DUMPLINGS

2 lbs. lean chuck cut in 1-inch cubes
2 tablespoons flour
1½ teaspoons salt
¼ teaspoon pepper
3 tablespoons salad oil

3 medium onions, each stuck with 1 clove
4 carrots cut in thin strips lengthwise
¾ pt. consommé
1 tablespoon vinegar
3 tablespoons chopped chives

Dumplings

8 oz. flour
4 oz. suet finely grated (or packet)
½ teaspoon baking powder

½ teaspoon salt
Cold water

1. Shake up the flour, salt, and pepper in a paper bag and dredge the pieces of meat by shaking them in it, a few at a time.
2. Heat the oil in a large heavy casserole and brown the meat well, adding the onions as the meat starts to brown. Stir in the carrots, consommé, and vinegar. Cover and bake the casserole 45 minutes at 350°.
3. Shortly before the casserole is ready make the dumplings. Mix all the dry ingredients together and add enough cold water to make a firm dough. Turn on to a floured board and knead lightly until free from cracks. Uncover the casserole, drop the dumplings by spoonfuls on top, replace the cover at once, and continue to bake 30 minutes more. Sprinkle with chives. Serves 4–5.

Serve with chopped spinach into which slightly sautéed mushrooms and a dash of nutmeg have been stirred, and with sliced tomatoes and cucumber sticks.

BEEF AND AUBERGINE CASSEROLE

1½ lbs. lean chuck ground
  1 medium aubergine sliced in ½-inch
    slices
    Salt and pepper
  2 tablespoons chopped onions
  5 tablespoons salad oil

3 oz. flour
½ teaspoon dried oregano or 1½ teaspoons
  fresh, chopped
8-oz. tin tomato sauce or tomato soup
  Mozzarella cheese

1. Wash the aubergine and slice it without peeling. Salt each slice and pile them up for 15 or 20 minutes to take out the bitterness.
2. Mix the chuck, 1 teaspoon of salt and a little fresh-ground pepper, and the onions. Form into 8 patties, handling the mixture as little as possible.
3. Heat 2 tablespoons of the oil in a heavy frying-pan and brown the patties on both sides. Arrange four of them on the bottom of a medium casserole and put the others on a plate for the moment.
4. Pat the aubergine slices dry with paper towels, dip them in the flour, and brown them lightly in the rest of the oil.
5. Arrange half of the slices on top of the beef patties in the casserole and sprinkle them with the oregano. Spread 1 tablespoon tomato sauce on each. Cover with the remaining patties, the remaining aubergine, and the remaining oregano. Pour the remaining tomato sauce on top and cover completely with slices of cheese.
6. Bake 30 minutes at 350°, or until the cheese is golden and bubbly. Serves 4–5.

BEEF WITH HORSERADISH SAUCE

2 lbs. stewing steak cut in 1½-inch cubes
2 tablespoons butter or margarine
1 large onion sliced thin
1 teaspoon curry powder
½ teaspoon ground ginger
1 teaspoon sugar
1 tablespoon Worcestershire sauce

½ teaspoon salt
¼ teaspoon pepper
¾ pt. water
½ pt. sour cream
2 tablespoons horseradish cream
1 teaspoon minced parsley

THIS is a rather highly flavoured casserole, but perfectly delicious. Even people who like their food pretty bland take to it.
1. Brown meat cubes well in hot butter in a heavy frying-pan and arrange in a medium-sized casserole.
2. Add the onion, curry powder, ginger, sugar, Worcestershire sauce, salt, pepper, and water. Cover and bake in a slow oven (300°) 2½–3 hours, or until the meat is fork tender.
3. When you are ready to serve stir in the sour cream, horseradish cream, and parsley. If you prefer the sauce somewhat thicker, thicken it with flour and butter or margarine kneaded together. Serves 4–5.

BEEF AND MUSHROOM CASSEROLE

2 lbs. topside sliced thin and cut in strips
   $1\frac{1}{2}'' \times 3\frac{1}{2}''$
6 oz. dried mushrooms soaked an hour or
   more in dry red wine
1 oz. flour
$1\frac{1}{2}$ teaspoons salt

$\frac{1}{8}$ teaspoon fresh-ground pepper
2 tablespoons salad oil
$\frac{1}{2}-\frac{3}{4}$ pt. consommé
6 oz. chopped onions
Sour cream if desired

1. Put the flour, salt, and pepper in a paper bag, and shake the pieces of meat in it, a few at a time, to dredge them lightly.

2. Heat the oil to sizzling in a heavy frying-pan and brown the meat strips well on both sides. Arrange them in a medium casserole, add half of the consommé, cover, and bake in a 300° oven. After 30 minutes begin to watch, and add more consommé as needed.

3. After an hour's cooking stir in the chopped onions, raw, cover again, and continue to cook.

4. About 15 minutes before you are ready to serve stir in the mushrooms and cover again. The overall cooking time for this casserole is about 2 hours, and there should be next to no liquid left at the end of that time. Serves 4–5.

Serve with noodles, buttered green peas, and warm French bread.

BEEF AND NOODLES

1 lb. lean beef, ground
$\frac{1}{4}$ lb. medium noodles cooked
1 tablespoon butter or margarine
1 tablespoon salad oil
2 medium onions chopped
1 teaspoon salt
$\frac{1}{4}$ teaspoon pepper

$\frac{1}{4}$ teaspoon dried thyme or $\frac{3}{4}$ teaspoon
   fresh, chopped
1 tin condensed cream of mushroom soup
2 eggs beaten
3 tablespoons milk
3 oz. grated Cheddar cheese

1. Heat butter and oil together in a heavy frying-pan and sauté the onions lightly. Move them to a bowl temporarily, while you brown the meat in the fat remaining in the pan.

2. Break up the meat into rather loose chunks as it cooks. Add salt, pepper, and thyme. When the meat loses its colour but is not browned, stir the cooked onions back in.

3. In a good-sized casserole make layers of $\frac{1}{3}$ of the noodles, $\frac{1}{2}$ of the meat, and $\frac{1}{2}$ of the soup. Repeat the layers, with the last $\frac{1}{3}$ of the noodles as the top layer.

4. Mix the beaten eggs with the milk and pour over the casserole. Top with cheese and bake in a 350° oven 35–40 minutes, or until golden brown and bubbly. Serves 8.

Serve with shredded green cabbage cooked slowly, covered, in a heavy frying-pan, in butter, and sliced buttered beetroot.

BEEF WITH OLIVES

3 lbs. chuck cut in 1½-inch cubes
6 oz. pitted green olives
2 oz. flour
  Salt and pepper
3 tablespoons salad oil
12 little white onions peeled
1 clove garlic crushed

½ teaspoon dried thyme or 1 teaspoon
  fresh, chopped
¾ pt. condensed consommé
2 oz. chopped parsley
1 tablespoon butter or margarine
1 tablespoon flour

1. Put the 2 oz. flour, about 2 teaspoons salt, and pepper in a paper bag and dredge the beef cubes in it. Brown them in the hot oil and transfer to a large heavy casserole.
2. In the fat remaining in the pan lightly sauté the onions and garlic. Add the thyme and the consommé and pour over the meat in the casserole, scraping up all the brown bits in the pan.
3. Cover the casserole and bake about an hour in a slow oven, 300°.
4. Stir in the olives and parsley, cover again, and bake about 45 minutes longer, or until the meat is fork tender.
5. Knead the butter and remaining flour together and stir in to thicken the sauce. Check the seasoning before serving. Serves 6–8.

Serve with buttered thick noodles and buttered baby Brussels sprouts.

BEER-BRAISED ROUND OF BEEF

2-lb. slice of topside
¾ teaspoon salt
¼ teaspoon pepper
2 tablespoons flour
3 tablespoons butter or margarine
1 clove garlic crushed
1 large onion sliced thin

¾ pt. beer
¼ pt. water
1 sprig parsely
1 sprig thyme
1 stalk celery cut in 3 or 4 pieces
1 bay leaf

COOKING with beer, as so much of the Flemish cooking is done, is almost always a highly successful way to add flavour to a dish, even for people who strongly dislike beer alone.
1. Mix the salt, pepper, and flour and pound it into the meat with the blunt side of a butcher's knife or the edge of a saucer.
2. Heat 1 tablespoon of the butter in a heavy frying-pan and brown the meat quickly on both sides. Remove it to a shallow casserole.
3. Add the remaining butter to the pan and lightly sauté the garlic and onion.
4. Stir in the beer and water and bring to a boil. Pour over the meat in the casserole, add the parsley, thyme, celery, and bay leaf, cover, and bake in a 275° oven about 1½ hours, or until tender. (Use aluminium foil to make a cover.)
5. Drain the liquid into a saucepan and thicken it a bit if you prefer. Pour back over the meat and heat another 5 minutes if the meat has cooled. Serves 4–6.

Serve with small parsley-butter potatoes and runner beans with butter and a tablespoon of thick cream.

SPECIAL BŒUF BOURGUIGNON

2 lbs. chuck or rump cut In $\frac{1}{4}$-inch slices
2 tablespoons salad oil
2 large slices salt pork
$\frac{1}{2}$ lb. thin-sliced carrots
　Salt and pepper
2 medium onions chopped coarsely

1 clove garlic crushed
2 shallots minced (or spring onions)
$\frac{1}{2}$ lb. mushrooms chopped
$\frac{1}{2}$ bottle good Burgundy
4 tablespoons cognac

BŒUF BOURGUIGNON differs from the one found in most cookbooks, but is equally delicious. I find it less trouble to make, too. Make it in a heavy casserole that can be started on top of the stove, like the French *petite marmite* or the newer porcelain-coated iron or stainless steel casseroles.

1. Pour oil in the bottom of the casserole and lay in one slice of pork. Add the carrots in an even layer and cover with $\frac{1}{3}$ of the beef. Sprinkle with salt and pepper.

2. Cover this layer of meat with half the onions, garlic, shallots, and mushrooms. Repeat layers. Add the rest of the beef and lay on top the remaining slice of salt pork.

3. Pour over the Burgundy and cognac and season with additional salt and pepper.

4. Place the casserole over high heat until it begins to simmer and then place in a 250° oven for 3–3$\frac{1}{2}$ hours, or until the meat is fork tender. Check occasionally to be sure it is barely bubbling. Remove the top slice of salt pork before serving. Serves 6.

Serve with mixed vegetables (runner beans, sweet corn, green peas, asparagus, or any other combination), a plain green salad, and warm French bread.

BŒUF EN DAUBE NIÇOISE

3-lb. piece of topside
½ lb. carrots cut in 1-inch pieces
1 tablespoon chopped fresh oregano or
  1 teaspoon dried

1 tablespoon chopped parsley
1 tablespoon chopped fresh sweet basil or
  1 teaspoon dried
  Bacon
3 tomatoes skinned and chopped

Marinade

½ pt. salad oil
1 medium onion chopped
4 shallots cut up
4-inch piece of celery
1 carrot split lengthwise and crosswise
¼ pt. dry red wine
6 whole peppercorns

2 cloves garlic split
1 bay leaf
1 tablespoon fresh thyme or 1 teaspoon
  dried
1 tablespoon fresh marjoram or 1 teaspoon
  dried
2 sprigs parsley

THIS is rather like a French pot roast, and is so good that it is worth the trouble to make it.

1. Combine the marinade ingredients in a saucepan and simmer gently 15 to 20 minutes. Cool and pour over the beef in a large bowl. Marinate the meat 12–24 hours, part of the time in the refrigerator. Pierce the meat with a long-tined fork once in a while to let the marinade penetrate. Turn it 2 or 3 times.

2. Lay the meat in a casserole with about ½ pint of liquid from the marinade. Arrange the carrots and herbs around it and cover the top surface with bacon slices.

3. Cover the casserole first with brown paper and then with the casserole lid. Bake in a 275° oven about 2½ hours.

4. Add the tomatoes and continue baking another half hour. Remove the bacon, but slice the meat in the casserole at the table. Serves 6–8.

Serve with buttered noodles and asparagus with a sauce made of melted butter, lemon juice, and fine bread or cornflake crumbs.

CHILI CON CARNE CABELL

3 lbs. lean beef ground
1 lb. black beans cooked
  Salad oil
2 medium onions chopped
1 green pepper chopped
1 clove garlic chopped
1 small tin tomato purée

1 teaspoon celery salt
1 teaspoon Worcestershire sauce
$\frac{1}{2}$ teaspoon dry mustard
  Pinch cayenne
  Pinch cumin seed (optional)
1 tablespoon chili powder
  Salt and pepper to taste

THE usual chili is made with red kidney beans. The use of the regular Mexican black beans here makes this an outstanding dish for chili fanciers.

1. To cook the beans soak them overnight in plenty of water and simmer them next day in just enough fresh water to cover, with a generous teaspoon of salt. When they are almost soft so that you can crush one between your fingers, remove them from the stove but do not drain.

2. Heat the oil in a large heavy casserole on top of the stove and brown the chopped vegetables and garlic very lightly, stirring often.

3. Stir in the beef and cook until there is no more red in it, stirring with a fork and leaving the meat in small chunks, about the size of an olive.

4. Add the beans with the water in which they were cooked, and all the remaining ingredients.

5. Cover and bake in a 300° oven about 25 minutes, or simmer gently on top of the stove, covered, for 20 minutes. Check seasoning before serving. Serves about 10, but this depends upon the number of servings per person!

Serve with plenty of hot fluffy rice and French bread, and a large salad tossed in French dressing.

BŒUF À LA BARONNE

$2\frac{1}{2}$-lb. slice of topside
  Boiling water
1 bay leaf
3 small onions
3 tablespoons capers

1 sprig parsley
$\frac{3}{4}$ pt. dry red wine
$\frac{1}{2}$ teaspoon salt
$\frac{1}{8}$ teaspoon pepper
  Flour-and-water thickening (if desired)

1. Put the beef in a pan just about its size, pour over boiling water just to the surface of the meat, cover, and simmer 30 minutes at extremely low heat.

2. Transfer the meat and the liquid to a shallow casserole a little larger than the meat.

3. Add the bay leaf, onions, capers, parsley, wine, salt, and pepper. Cover (with aluminium foil if you do not have a lid which fits), and bake at 375° about 1 hour, or until tender.

4. Drain the liquid into a saucepan and thicken it slightly with flour-and-water paste if you prefer it that way. Pour back over the casserole. Serves 6.

Serve with fluffy hot rice or buttered noodles to soak up the rich sauce, warm French bread, and baby carrots with butter and parsley stirred in.

BURGUNDY MEAT BALLS

¾ lb. ground lean chuck
2 oz. cup bread or cornflake crumbs
1 small onion minced
1 egg beaten
¼ pt. thin cream
1¼ teaspoons salt
3 tablespoons salad oil

1 tablespoon flour
¾ pt. consommé or half water and half
    consommé
½ pt. Burgundy or other dry red wine
⅛ teaspoon pepper
¼ teaspoon sugar
    Gravy browning

1. Mix the meat, crumbs, onion, egg, cream, and ¾ teaspoon of salt. Shape into small balls and brown in a heavy frying-pan in the hot oil. Don't crowd the pan. Transfer the meat balls to a medium casserole as they are ready. (If the meat balls seem too soft as you shape them either add more crumbs or roll them in flour.)
2. Stir the flour into the fat left in the skillet and blend in the consommé, wine, ½ teaspoon salt, pepper, sugar, and just enough gravy browning to give the sauce a good colour—a few drops. Cook until smooth, stirring constantly.
3. Pour the sauce over the meat balls in the casserole and bake 30 minutes in a moderate oven, 350°. Stir two or three times. Serves 6.

Serve with something to absorb the fine sauce—hot fluffy rice, buttered noodles, or spaghetti with cheese.

CANNELON OF BEEF

¾ lb. cooked roast beef (rare)
½ lb. cooked ham
1 medium onion peeled
2 stalks celery
1 tablespoon chopped parsley
¼ teaspoon dried thyme or ¾ teaspoon
    fresh, chopped
¼ teaspoon dried sweet basil or ¾
    teaspoon fresh, chopped

¼ teaspoon sweet marjoram or ¾
    teaspoon fresh, chopped
1¼ teaspoons salt
1 egg beaten slightly
1 tin condensed tomato soup
1 tablespoon butter or margarine
3 oz. minced onion
3 medium tomatoes peeled and chopped
½ teaspoon vinegar

These little individual meat loaves look tempting and taste delicious.
1. Put the beef, ham, peeled onion, and celery through the meat grinder. Mix in the parsley, thyme, basil, marjoram, ¾ teaspoon salt, egg, and 3 tablespoons of the soup. With your hands shape into six oblong meat loaves, and place them in a shallow, lightly greased casserole large enough to take them without touching.
2. Put the casserole in a moderate oven—350°—for 25 minutes.
3. While it bakes make the sauce. Heat the butter in a frying-pan and lightly brown the minced onion. Add the chopped tomatoes and simmer a few minutes. Then stir in the remaining soup, the remaining ½ teaspoon salt, and the vinegar. Cook until smooth and pour over the meat loaves. Continue to bake them about 10 minutes more. Serves 6.

FLEMISH CARBONNADES OF BEEF

3–4 lbs. of lean chuck or topside cut in
    1½-inch cubes
2 oz. butter or margarine
2 lbs. onions sliced
    Flour
1 teaspoon salt

4–6 tablespoons beef fat, butter,
    margarine, or oil
1 teaspoon fresh-ground pepper
2 cloves garlic
1 pt. beer
1½ tablespoons cognac

As in so many Flemish dishes, the distinctive flavour here comes from the beer.

1. Melt the 2 oz. butter in a large heavy frying-pan and sauté the onions until they are just beginning to brown, stirring frequently. Transfer them to a large casserole—a large, old-fashioned bean pot is fine for this dish.

2. Roll the cubes of beef in flour to coat them well.

3. Heat the beef fat, or whatever fat you are using, in the frying-pan and brown the meat well on all sides. Don't crowd the pan, or the meat won't brown well. As the pieces are browned move them to the casserole.

4. When all the meat is in the casserole add the salt, pepper, and garlic. Pour a little of the beer into the pan to clean out all the brown bits and add to the casserole. Stir the contents of the casserole well and add enough beer just to cover.

5. Cover the casserole tightly and bake it in a very slow oven, 275°, about 3 hours, or until the meat is fork tender. If you like a thicker sauce thicken it somewhat with flour and butter kneaded together. Stir in the cognac just before serving. Serves 8–10.

Serve with parsley-butter new potatoes or little potato balls scooped out of large potatoes and sautéed gently in a heavy frying-pan, and steamed broccoli with a butter-lemon-bread-crumb sauce. A green salad tossed in French dressing goes well with this meal.

GOURMET BEEF STROGANOFF

2 lbs. fillet of beef sliced as thin as possible and cut in strips or squares	¾ pt. consommé
Salt	¼ pt. sour cream
3 tablespoons butter	2 tablespoons tomato purée
2 tablespoons flour	½ lb. sliced mushrooms
	3 tablespoons grated onion

THIS is truly a gourmet dish, a perfect choice for a party.
1. Salt the meat and let it stand a couple of hours in the refrigerator before you need it.
2. Melt 2 tablespoons of the butter in a heavy frying-pan and blend in the flour. Let it cook a moment and blend in the consommé. Cook until it begins to thicken, stirring constantly. Strain into a casserole heavy enough to cook on top of the stove.
3. Stir in the sour cream and tomato purée alternately over medium heat, stirring constantly.
4. Meantime, sauté the sliced mushrooms lightly in the remaining butter, take them out and add to the casserole.
5. In the fat remaining in the pan quickly brown the meat and onion, very lightly.
6. Pour the meat into the casserole, stir just enough to blend, and simmer over the lowest possible heat 20 minutes. *Do not overcook.* Serves 6.

Serve with fluffy hot rice or plain boiled wild rice, buttered green peas, and a dressed salad of mixed greens, along with plenty of French bread.

FRENCH BEEF CASSEROLE

2-lb. slice of topside, cut thick	1 sprig of thyme, dried or fresh
2 tablespoons butter or margarine	¼ pt. dry red wine
1 small carrot minced	6 fluid oz. consommé
2 shallots or spring onions minced	½ teaspoon cornflour
1 small bay leaf	Pepper and salt to taste

THIS is a typically French stew, with all the flavour that implies.
1. Grill the steak under high heat until it is nicely browned on both sides. Divide into serving portions and arrange in a shallow casserole. Save the juice accumulated in the grill pan.
2. Melt butter in a saucepan and lightly sauté carrot and shallots. (Use a couple of slices of onion if neither shallots nor spring onions are available.)
3. Add the steak juice, the bay leaf, thyme, wine, and consommé and pour over the casserole. Cover tightly and bake in a slow oven, 300°, 1½–2 hours, or until the meat is fork tender.
4. With a sharp-tined fork lift out the pieces of meat to a bowl for a moment and strain the sauce into a saucepan. Return the meat to the casserole and the casserole to the oven while you thicken the sauce with the cornflour mixed to a thin paste with a little water.
5. Season the sauce to taste, pour over the casserole, and continue to cook about 10 minutes more, uncovered. Serves 4–5.

Serve with parsley-butter new potatoes and buttered French or runner beans. A green salad is really called for, too.

HAMBURGER PIE

1 lb. chopped lean beef
3 oz. diced bacon
3 oz. minced onions (or 1 oz. dehydrated
  onions soaked 20 minutes in 3
  tablespoons water)
½ pt. water
2 teaspoons salt

1 saltspoon pepper
1 teaspoon prepared mustard
1 teaspoon minced parsley
4 tablespoons ketchup
1 tablespoon flour
Pastry for double-crust pie

1. Fry the bacon a few minutes but not until it is crisp. Add onions and cook until they are lightly browned.

2. Stir in the beef and cook until the beef is lightly browned, stirring often to break it up.

3. Add the water, salt, pepper, mustard, parsley, and ketchup, and bring to a brisk boil.

4. Mix the flour into a smooth paste with water and stir into the meat mixture, continuing to stir until it is fairly thick.

5. Line a 9-inch pie plate with your favourite pastry, pour in the mixture, and cover with the rest of the pastry. Slash to let steam escape and bake 40 minutes in a 425° oven, or until the top is golden brown. Serves 5–6.

MEAT BALLS STROGANOFF

1 lb. ground lean beef
1 teaspoon salt
¼ teaspoon pepper
3 tablespoons ketchup
1 tablespoon Worcestershire
  sauce
2 oz. minced onion

2 oz. bread or cornflake crumbs
12 fluid oz. evaporated milk
2 tablespoons flour
2 tablespoons vegetable oil
1 tin condensed cream of mushroom soup
1 tablespoon vinegar
1½ teaspoons Worcestershire sauce

1. Mix the beef, salt, pepper, ketchup, the 1 tablespoon Worcestershire sauce, onion, and crumbs, together with ⅓ of the evaporated milk. Mix well and shape into 16 meat balls.

2. Roll the meat balls in the flour and brown in the hot oil in a heavy frying-pan. Arrange in a medium casserole and pour off any fat remaining in the pan.

3. Mix the rest of the evaporated milk, the soup, the vinegar, and the 1½ teaspoons of Worcestershire sauce. Blend well and add to the pan. When it is hot pour over the meat balls and bake 10 minutes in a 350° oven or finish on top of the stove over very low heat. Serves 4.

With this good sauce, serve buttered noodles or fluffy rice and buttered baby carrots sprinkled with chopped parsley.

HAMBURGER POTATO ROLL

1 lb. ground chuck
1¼ lbs. seasoned mashed potato
1 medium onion chopped
1 small clove garlic crushed
1 tablespoon dripping
1 egg lightly beaten
2 slices bread, crusts removed
1 teaspoon salt

¼ teaspoon dried oregano, rosemary, or
  basil, or ¾ teaspoon fresh, chopped
  Fresh-ground black pepper
2 tablespoons dry bread crumbs
1 tablespoon minced parsley or green
  pepper (optional)
3 rashers bacon (optional)

THIS recipe has appeared a number of times in the press because it is so frequently requested. Try it once and you can understand its popularity.

1. Sauté the onion and garlic lightly in hot dripping, remove from the heat, and mix in the beef and egg.

2. Soften the sliced bread in water a few minutes, squeeze out the water, and add the bread to the meat, along with the salt, oregano, and pepper. Mix well.

3. Spread out a piece of waxed paper and sprinkle it with the crumbs. Turn the beef out on the crumbs and pat it into a rectangle about ½ inch thick.

4. Beat the mashed potato with the parsley and spread it over the meat.

5. Roll up the meat by lifting the paper along the long side of the rectangle, as you would roll a Swiss roll. Lift the roll carefully into a shallow casserole, greased if the meat is quite lean. Place bacon on top.

6. Bake about 1 hour in a moderate oven, 350°. Serve with gravy made from the pan drippings or with mushroom or tomato sauce. Serves 5–6.

Serve with buttered baby carrots and fried tomatoes.

MOUSSAKA OF BEEF

1 lb. lean ground beef
6 fluid oz. salad oil
3 medium onions chopped
1 tablespoon minced parsley
4 tablespoons water
1 tablespoon tomato purée
2 teaspoons salt

$\frac{1}{2}$ teaspoon fresh-ground black pepper
1 large or 2 medium aubergines
2 egg whites well beaten
1$\frac{1}{2}$ oz. bread or cornflake crumbs
$\frac{1}{2}$ pt. medium white sauce
4 oz. grated Parmesan cheese

MOUSSAKA is a famous dish in the Middle East. The Turkish and Armenian versions are usually made with lamb, the Greek with beef, though either can be used. This is a delightful version with beef, far simpler than the traditional dish.

1. Heat a little of the oil in a heavy frying-pan and brown the meat lightly. Add the onions, parsley, water, tomato purée, salt, and pepper. Simmer over the lowest possible heat for about 25 minutes, stirring occasionally.

2. Meantime, cut the aubergines in $\frac{1}{4}$-inch slices and sauté lightly in the rest of the oil.

3. Add the egg whites and crumbs to the meat mixture and blend until they are absorbed.

4. In a medium casserole, broad rather than deep, make alternate layers of aubergine slices and meat mixture, ending with aubergine.

5. Pour over the white sauce (made with 1 oz. butter or margarine, 1 oz. flour, $\frac{1}{2}$ pint milk, and seasoning to taste) and top with the cheese.

6. Bake in a medium oven, 350°, for half an hour, or until well browned. Serves 6.

Serve with one of the vegetable casseroles at the beginning of the vegetable chapter and a large dressed salad. If you can get it, the flat Armenian bread, crisped in the oven a moment, is a nice accompaniment.

JAPANESE MEAT BALLS

1 lb. ground lean beef
1 oz. fine bread or cornflake crumbs
1 large chopped onion
1 teaspoon salt
⅛ teaspoon pepper
¼ pt. evaporated milk
2 tablespoons butter or margarine

2 9-oz. tins bean sprouts
1¼ oz. cornflour
3 tablespoons
4 fluid oz. soy sauce
3 medium onions thin-sliced
6 oz. thin-sliced mushrooms
4 oz. shredded raw spinach

1. Mix well the beef, crumbs, chopped onion, salt, pepper, and milk, and shape into 12 balls.
2. Melt butter in a heavy frying-pan and brown the balls well on all sides, over medium heat.
3. Drain the bean sprouts but save the liquid; if necessary add water to make 12 fluid ounces.
4. Mix the cornflour and water into a smooth paste.
5. Stir the bean-sprout liquid into the pan with the meat balls and add the cornflour, stirring constantly until it is smooth and thickened. Add the soy sauce.
6. Turn the mixture into a 4-pint casserole, cover, and bake 25 minutes in a 350° oven, or until the sauce is clear.
7. Remove from oven, stir in the bean sprouts, sliced onions, mushrooms, and spinach. Cover and continue cooking about 10 minutes longer. Serves 6.

SHEPHERD'S PIE FLORENTINE

1 lb. ground lean beef
2¼ teaspoons salt
¼ teaspoon fresh-ground pepper
2 tablespoons minced onion
1 oz. cornflake or bread crumbs
2 eggs
1 1-lb. packet frozen chopped spinach

8 fluid oz. water
8 fluid oz. milk
1 packet instant mashed potato (4-serving size)
1 tablespoon butter or margarine
¼ teaspoon garlic salt
Thin-sliced Cheddar cheese

1. Combine beef, 1 teaspoon of the salt, pepper, 1 tablespoon of the onion, the crumbs, and one egg. Mix lightly and pat gently into a 9-inch pie plate, covering the bottom and sides.
2. Bake this shell 15 minutes in a 425° oven. Pour off any fat that has accumulated.
3. Heat the spinach in a heavy frying-pan over low heat, covered, turning it often until it is completely thawed. Press out as much water as you can with a spatula.
4. In a saucepan bring the water to a boil, add milk, and beat in the instant potato, butter, garlic salt, remaining 1¼ teaspoons salt, the rest of the onion, and the other egg.
5. Fold in the spinach and pour into the cooked meat shell.
6. Cover the top with slices of cheese and put back in the oven for 10 minutes, or until cheese is melted and golden. Serves 6.

Serve with crisp cole slaw and fresh bread rolls.

TURKISH MEAT BALLS

1 lb. ground lean chuck
½ lb. ground lean lamb
½ lb. ground lean pork
2 large garlic cloves crushed
2 oz. chopped parsley
1 teaspoon dried oregano or 1 tablespoon
   fresh, chopped
1 small bay leaf

2 oz. pine nuts
1 teaspoon salt
¼ teaspoon fresh-ground pepper
   Dash cayenne pepper
1 egg beaten lightly
2 tablespoons salad oil
¼ pt. condensed consommé
¼ pt. tomato purée

HAVE the butcher grind the meats together. Mix with the garlic, parsley, oregano, crumbled bay leaf, pine nuts, salt and pepper, cayenne, and egg. Form this mixture into small balls, about the size of a walnut, and brown quickly in hot oil in a heavy frying-pan. Shake the pan to keep them from sticking and to keep them well rounded. Transfer them to a rather shallow casserole.

Mix the consommé and tomato purée, clean out the brown particles in the pan with it, and pour over the meat balls. Bake an hour in a 350° oven, covering the casserole for the first half of the period. Serves 6–7.

SAUERBRATEN

4–6 lb. beef shoulder or rump roast,
   larded with strips of salt pork or
   bacon 2″ × ¼″
   Pepper
1 large clove garlic cut
   Mild cider vinegar
1 medium onion sliced

2 small bay leaves
1 teaspoon peppercorns
2 oz. sugar
2 tablespoons salad oil
   Flour-and-water paste
8 fluid oz. sour cream
   Salt

THIS is one of the classics of German cooking, and is widely popular in this country. Have the butcher lard the meat, or do it yourself by making gashes every 2 inches or so in the meat with a sharp-pointed knife and forcing the lardoons into the holes.
1. Rub the meat well with pepper and the cut clove of garlic and put in a large bowl.
2. Heat to the boiling point equal parts of vinegar and water, the onion, bay leaves, peppercorns, and sugar. Pour over the beef. There should be enough liquid to more than half immerse the meat. Cover the bowl and put in the refrigerator for anywhere from two to ten days—the longer the better. Turn the meat once a day.
3. Drain the meat, saving the marinade. Heat the oil to sizzling in a stew pot or heavy casserole and sear the meat well on all sides.
4. Add marinade to a depth of 1½–2 inches. Salt the meat, cover it, and bake 2–3 hours in a slow oven, 275°. Add more of the marinade if it becomes dry, but this is not likely to happen if the cover is tight.
5. Lift the meat from the casserole carefully and set aside for a moment while you thicken the gravy with flour-and-water paste, stir in the sour cream, and correct the seasoning.
6. Return the sauerbraten to the casserole.
7. Slice at the table, or, if you prefer, slice it before returning to the casserole. Serves 10–12.

Serve with boiled potatoes and red cabbage.

SWISS STEAK WITH HORSERADISH SAUCE

3-lb. slice of rump steak
2 teaspoons salt
   Fresh-ground black pepper
1 clove garlic cut
   Flour

Salad oil
4 fluid oz. water
1 large onion sliced
4 fluid oz. sour cream
1 tablespoon horseradish

THIS is really a delicious version of the popular Swiss steak.

1. Prepare the steak as usual, seasoning it well with salt and pepper, rubbing it with the cut clove of garlic, and pounding in all the flour it will take. (Use the edge of a saucer or the dull side of a butcher's knife.) Treat both sides like this and brown the meat well in sizzling salad oil—the least amount that will keep it from sticking to the frying-pan.

2. Transfer the steak to an oval casserole—a shallow one—and add only the water and the onion. (See note below.) Under no circumstances increase the amount of water.

3. Cover the casserole tightly—with aluminium foil if you do not have a fitted cover—and bake in a slow oven, 275°, about 2 hours, or until the meat is very tender.

4. When it is done lift the steak onto a platter, using two spatulas, long enough to pour what sauce has accumulated into a small saucepan; or drain sauce off by holding back steak with a spatula. Return the steak in the casserole to the oven while you stir the sour cream and horseradish into the sauce until it is smooth. Pour over the casserole and serve at once. Serves 6.

Note: If you prefer, cut the meat into serving portions before you lay it in the casserole. This makes it easier to use a round casserole with a fitted cover, and you can then drain off the sauce more easily.

Serve with fluffy mashed potatoes, buttered green beans, and sliced ripe tomatoes.

SAVOURY CORNED BEEF

12-oz. tin corned beef, chopped
9 oz. cooked potatoes diced small
1 tablespoon prepared mustard
3 oz. soft (fresh) bread crumbs
2 tablespoons minced onion
2 tablespoons minced green pepper

1 tablespoon butter or margarine melted
$\frac{1}{8}$ teaspoon fresh-ground pepper
  Garlic salt
8 fluid oz. milk
2 eggs beaten slightly

THIS is a simple way to make a corned beef casserole. It can also be made in a ring mould, and the centre filled with vegetables.

1. Blend well the corned beef, potatoes, mustard, bread crumbs, onion, green pepper, butter, and pepper. Check seasoning—the chances are that you will not need salt with corned beef, but sometimes you do. If so, use garlic salt.

2. Shake the eggs and milk in a jar and stir into the corned beef mixture.

3. Arrange in a greased casserole or, as suggested above, in a greased 1-quart ring mould. Bake in a 350° oven about 30 minutes, or until a knife inserted in the centre comes out clean. A ring mould will take only 20 minutes. Serves 6.

Serve with one of the tomato casseroles given in this book (see Index) and diced cucumbers in sour cream. If you make this into a ring, unmould on a hot platter and fill the centre with creamed onions.

GYPSY HASH

2 large tins corned beef hash
  ($1\frac{1}{2}$ pts.)
1 large onion minced
1 small clove garlic crushed
4 fluid oz. sour cream

2 eggs well beaten
3 tablespoons dry red wine
$\frac{1}{4}$ teaspoon fresh-ground pepper
$\frac{1}{4}$ teaspoon nutmeg
  Fine bread or cornflake crumbs

THIS is a very old recipe, but as good as any modern one.
   Blend well all the ingredients except the fine crumbs. You may need to add a little salt, but the corned beef is likely to be salty enough. Spread in a fairly shallow greased casserole and top with a thin sprinkling of crumbs. Bake 20–25 minutes in a 350° oven, or until the centre is firm to the touch. Serves 6.

Serve with runner beans and buttered sweet corn.

BARBECUED TONGUE

1 fresh or smoked beef tongue
2 teaspoons salt

1¼ oz. flour
1 tablespoon butter, margarine, or salad oil

Barbecue Sauce

1 tablespoon flour
1 tablespoon prepared mustard
8 fluid oz. condensed tomato soup
1½ oz. chopped onion
1½ oz. chopped celery
½ teaspoon powdered cloves

1 teaspoon salt
¼ teaspoon fresh-ground pepper
2 tablespoons Worcestershire sauce
2 tablespoons vinegar
4 fluid oz. water

IF you do not want to go to the trouble of cooking a tongue you can use this barbecue sauce with a tinned whole tongue.

1. If you start with a fresh or smoked tongue, cover it with water, add the salt, and simmer from 2–4 hours, or until tender. Use only half the salt if the tongue is smoked.
2. Plunge the tongue immediately into cold water for several minutes and peel off the skin. Remove and discard the root end.
3. Dust the meat with flour, brown it delicately in the hot butter, and lay in a casserole.
4. To make the barbecue sauce, mix the flour and mustard, stir in the remaining ingredients, bring to a boil in a small saucepan, and pour over the tongue.
5. Bake in a moderate oven, 350°, for 30–40 minutes, basting often. Serves 8–10, depending upon size of tongue.

Serve with fluffy hot rice and French beans.

BLACKBERRY TONGUE

1 cooked tongue (tinned or fresh)
3 oz. raisins
8 fluid oz. water

3 tablespoons lemon juice
8 fluid oz. blackberry jelly

IF you cook the tongue yourself, see the directions in the recipe for Barbecued Tongue.

1. Place the cooked tongue in a greased casserole.
2. Simmer the raisins in the water about 10 minutes. Drain and mix with the lemon juice and jelly in a small saucepan. Heat over very low heat until the jelly is melted.
3. Pour over the tongue in the casserole and bake, uncovered, 45 minutes in a 325° oven.
4. Serves 8–10, depending upon size of tongue.

Serve with fluffy mashed potatoes and buttered broccoli.

SPICED OX TONGUE MARYLAND

1 fresh or smoked ox tongue weighing
  about 4 lbs.
¾ pt. milk
3 strips lemon peel about ½″ × 2″

1 teaspoon ground cinnamon
2 teaspoons brown sugar
½ teaspoon black pepper
¾ pt. dry white wine

FOR those who like spicy foods this is a wonderful way to cook a tongue.

1. Lay the smoked tongue in a small fish-kettle or pan and pour milk over it. Add enough water to cover the tongue and let it soak for an hour or two to remove the salt. (This is unnecessary if you start with a fresh tongue.)

2. Pour off the milk and water, cover the tongue with cold water, bring to a boil, and simmer, covered, 3–4 hours, or until the meat is tender. Let it cool in the stock.

3. Skin the tongue, remove the root end, and slice about ¼ inch thick. Arrange the tongue slices in a large shallow casserole.

4. Mix remaining ingredients and pour over the tongue.

5. Cover and bake in a moderate oven, 375°, 35 minutes. The tongue should have absorbed most of the wine by this time. If not, uncover the last 15 minutes. Serves 6–8.

Serve with mashed potatoes and sweet corn, together with a green salad tossed in French dressing.

TONGUE WITH FRUIT SAUCE

12-oz. tinned tongue, whole
2 oz. brown sugar
2 tablespoons flour
½ teaspoon dry mustard

½ pt. apricot juice
3 tablespoons vinegar (scant)
2 oz. seedless raisins

A QUICK and easy way to convert a tinned tongue into a delicacy.

1. Slice the tongue thin (save the gelatine) and arrange the slices, overlapping, in a shallow casserole.

2. Mix the sugar, flour, and mustard in a saucepan and stir in the remaining ingredients, including the gelatine from the tongue. Cook a minute or two, stirring constantly, until the sauce thickens.

3. Spread it over the tongue and bake in a 350° oven 15 minutes, or until well heated and bubbling. Serves 4.

Serve with herb-flavoured rice and butter beans.

AVIGNON PANCAKE ROLLS

Pancake batter (your favourite or a mix)	½ teaspoon Worcestershire sauce
¼ lb. cooked ham diced fine	1 teaspoon dry mustard
1½ oz. butter or margarine	1 large tin sliced mushrooms, drained
1½ oz. flour	2 tablespoons brandy
8 fluid oz. chicken stock	2 tablespoons chopped parsley
8 fluid oz. rich milk	4 tablespoons grated Cheddar
Salt and pepper to taste	

MANY delightful dishes are made with rolled-up thin pancakes. This is a good example.
1. Make the pancake batter first, quite thin, and let it stand while you make the filling.
2. Melt the butter in a medium saucepan, blend in the flour, and slowly stir in the stock and milk. Keep stirring until you have a smooth, velvety, thick sauce. Season it well with salt and pepper, Worcestershire, and mustard. Let it simmer on very low heat for about 10 minutes.
3. Remove the sauce from the stove and measure out ¼ pint. To the remaining sauce add the mushrooms, ham, and brandy. Let it cool while you make the pancakes—about 5 inches in diameter, 18 in all.
4. Spread a tablespoon of the ham-mushroom mixture in the centre of each pancake and roll up. Place, seam side down, close together in a buttered shallow casserole.
5. Mix the rest of the sauce (the ¼ pint you reserved) with the parsley and spread it evenly over the pancakes. Bake 30 minutes in a 325° oven.
6. Five minutes before the dish is ready, sprinkle with grated cheese and brown under the grill. Serves 6.

Serve with buttered green peas and a salad of cooked vegetables (sliced or baby carrots, sweet corn, green beans, etc.).

BAKED HAM WITH GINGER PEARS

1 slice ham, about 2½ lbs.	Grated rind of 1 lemon
3 fresh pears, preferably Bartlett	2 oz. preserved ginger chopped
8 fluid oz. water	8–10 cloves
4 oz. sugar	3 oz. brown sugar
Juice of 1 lemon	

1. Combine water, sugar, lemon juice and rind, and ginger in a saucepan and simmer 5 minutes. Add pears, peeled, halved, and cored, and simmer 5 minutes longer.
2. Lay the ham in a large but shallow casserole. Stick with cloves, and pat the brown sugar on top. Pour 3 tablespoons of the pear syrup around it.
3. Bake 20 minutes in a 350° oven, basting 2 or 3 times.
4. Arrange the pear halves around the ham with another 3 tablespoons of the pear syrup, and bake 20 or 25 minutes longer. Serves 6.

Serve with baked potatoes and green beans.

GERMAN HAM AND VEAL PÂTÉ

2 slices cold boiled ham ½-inch thick
2 slices cooked veal (leftover) ½-inch thick
  Pastry for 2-crust pie
4 tablespoons butter, margarine, or lard
2 tablespoons minced parsley

2 shallots minced or one tablespoon
  minced onion
4 oz. mushrooms chopped (tinned or fresh)
2 large eggs or 3 small
  Salt and pepper

1. Use your favourite recipe for the pastry. Roll out about ⅔ of it and line a 3-pint casserole with it, leaving a little rim around the edge.
2. Cut both meats into ¼-inch cubes.
3. Mix the meat trimmings with the butter or lard, shallots, parsley, and mushrooms. Grind this mixture very fine, beat in the eggs, and season to taste.
4. Fill the casserole with alternate layers of mixed ham and veal and the butter-mushroom mixture.
5. Cover with pastry gashed several times to allow steam to escape. Seal to lining pastry by moistening and pinching together.
6. Bake 1½ hours in a slow oven, 300°, or until the crust is golden. Serve hot or cold. Serves 4. (Can be doubled for larger casserole.)

Serve with red cabbage and buttered carrots if hot, with a mixed vegetable salad if cold.

HAM, BROCCOLI, AND CHEESE PIE

1 lb. cooked ham cut in ½-inch dice
1 1-lb. packet frozen broccoli or 1 lb. fresh,
  trimmed weight
½ lb. shredded Swiss cheese
3 tablespoons chopped onion

¾ pt. milk scalded
3 eggs beaten slightly
  Salt and pepper
  Unbaked 10-inch pastry shell

1. If you use fresh broccoli, clean it well and cut off all the flowerets. Chop the stems coarsely. Cook separately in boiling water, the flowerets 5 minutes, the stems 10 minutes. If you use frozen broccoli, cook according to packet directions, drain, and cut off the stems, chopping them coarsely also.
2. In the unbaked pie shell spread half the ham, the broccoli stems, the broccoli flowerets, and the cheese. Repeat the layers and spread the chopped onion on top.
3. Gradually stir the milk into the beaten eggs, add the seasonings (go slow on salt!), and pour carefully on top of the filled pie.
4. Bake in a 450° oven 10 minutes, lower the heat to 325°, and bake 25–30 minutes longer, or until the centre is firm. Serves 4–6.
Note: You can make the pie more attractive-looking by reserving 2 tablespoons of the cheese and sprinkling it on top of the pie before baking.

Serve with herb-flavoured rice and a green salad.

HAM WITH CAULIFLOWER

1¼ lbs. ground cooked ham
2 small heads cauliflower broken into
  flowerets
3 oz. grated Parmesan cheese
2 egg yolks
12 fluid oz. sour cream

2 tablespoons minced onion
1 tablespoon minced parsley
1 teaspoon paprika
Salt
Butter or margarine

1. Simmer the cauliflower flowerets in boiling salted water barely to cover for about 5 minutes. They should still be crisp. Drain.

2. In a greased casserole make alternate layers of cauliflower and ham, pressing them slightly together. Sprinkle each layer with part of the cheese, using 2 oz.

3. Beat the egg yolks with the sour cream. Stir in the onion, parsley, paprika, and a little salt if the ham is mild.

4. Pour this mixture over the casserole, spread with the remaining 1 oz. cheese, dot with butter, and bake in a 375° oven 20 minutes or until golden brown. Serves 5–6.

Serve with buttered noodles or a rice casserole. (See Index.)

HAM CASSEROLE WITH SHERRY

2 lbs. ground cooked ham
2 eggs well beaten
2 tablespoons chopped green pepper
4 fluid oz. thick sour cream
½ lb. cooked rice
2 tomatoes peeled and chopped or an
  8-oz. tin

1 teaspoon prepared mustard
1 teaspoon Worcestershire sauce
4 fluid oz. sherry
1 tablespoon grated or finely minced onion
2 tablespoons buttered bread or cornflake
  crumbs
Paprika

BLEND well all the ingredients except crumbs and paprika and spread in a well-greased medium casserole. Sprinkle the top with buttered crumbs and paprika. Bake 30 minutes in a 350° oven. Serves 6.

Serve with buttered baby carrots sprinkled with parsley and a green salad with French dressing.

HAWAIIAN HAM CASSEROLE

1 lb. cooked ham cut in ½-inch dice
2 tablespoons butter or margarine
8½-oz. tin pineapple chunks drained
3 tablespoons brown sugar
1 tin condensed onion soup

Salt and pepper
4 large sweet potatoes boiled, peeled, and
sliced thick, or 10½-oz. tin
3 oz. chopped pecans

1. Heat butter in a heavy casserole and lightly brown the ham in it.
2. Stir in the pineapple chunks, 1 tablespoon of the brown sugar, and the onion soup. Season to taste. Cook just until it reaches the boiling point and remove from the heat.
3. Arrange the sweet potato slices on top of the ham-pineapple mixture, overlapping a little.
4. Mix pecans and remaining brown sugar and spread over the potatoes. Bake ½ hour at 400°. Serves 4.

Serve with buttered baby Brussels sprouts and corn on the cob.

HAM JUBILEE

1 slice ham—about 2½ lbs.
2 10-oz. tins pitted black cherries
¼ teaspoon each ground cloves, curry
powder, cinnamon, dry mustard

1 tablespoon vinegar, preferably wine
vinegar
8 fluid oz. blackcurrant jelly
4 fluid oz. orange juice
1 oz. grated orange rind

1. Combine in a saucepan the juice from the cherries, the spices, vinegar, jelly, and orange juice. Bring to a low boil. Remove from the stove and stir in the grated orange rind and the cherries.
2. Arrange the ham slice in a casserole a little larger than the ham but rather shallow. (Trim off some of the fat edge first and slash remaining fat several times to prevent the ham from humping up.)
3. Bake 30 minutes in a 350° oven.
4. Pour the syrup over the ham and continue to bake 30 minutes longer. Serves 4–5.

SPICY HAM LOAF

1 lb. lean ham ground
½ lb. lean pork ground
1 tin condensed tomato soup
3 oz. chopped onion
2 oz. fine dry crumbs
1 oz. minced celery

2 tablespoons minced parsley
1 egg slightly beaten
¼ teaspoon dry mustard
Dash fresh-ground pepper
2 teaspoons prepared horseradish

1. Mix thoroughly the meats, ¼ pt. of the soup, the onion, crumbs, celery, parsley, egg, mustard, and pepper (no salt). Shape into a firm loaf and put it in a shallow casserole.
2. Bake the loaf about 1¼ hours in a 350° oven. Hold the loaf back firmly with a spatula and drain off all the fat.
3. Heat the remaining soup in a small saucepan, stir in the horseradish, and pour over the loaf. Bake a few minutes longer before serving. Serves 6.

HAM CASSEROLE WITH RAISINS AND PINEAPPLE

1½ lbs. diced cooked ham
3 oz. dark or golden raisins
5 oz. pineapple chunks
1 medium onion sliced and separated into rings
1 small green pepper sliced in rings
½ pt. pineapple syrup (from tin of chunks)

4 tablespoons vinegar
3 oz. brown sugar
1 tablespoon cornflour
2 teaspoons dry mustard
¼ teaspoon salt
1 teaspoon Worcestershire sauce
1 tablespoon soy sauce

1. Put ham in casserole and arrange onion and green pepper rings over it. Arrange pineapple and raisins on top.

2. In a small saucepan heat the pineapple syrup and vinegar. Mix the sugar, cornflour, mustard, and salt. Add this to the hot liquid and stir until it thickens.

3. Add the Worcestershire and soy sauces and pour over the casserole.

4. Bake 45 minutes at 350°. Serves 5–6.

HAM CASSEROLE WITH NOODLES AND SESAME SEEDS

1½ lbs. diced cooked ham
8-oz. packet medium noodles cooked
2 tablespoons toasted sesame seeds
2 tablespoons butter or margarine

¾ pt. rich white sauce or 1½ tins condensed cream of chicken soup
3 tablespoons buttered crumbs

SESAME seeds give this casserole a special flavour.

1. Cook the noodles according to packet directions, drain, and stir the butter in at once.

2. Toast the sesame seeds in the 400° oven where you will bake the casserole, 8–10 minutes.

3. Make the white sauce, if you use that instead of the soup, with 1½ oz. margarine, 1½ oz. flour, and ¾ pt. top milk, with salt and pepper to taste.

4. Mix the ham and sesame seeds with this sauce.

5. In a medium casserole make alternate layers of the noodles and the ham-cream sauce, making 2 layers of each.

6. Top with buttered crumbs and bake 20 minutes in the 400° oven. Serves 6.

Serve with cole slaw and purée of spinach.

HAM-AND-LEEK PIE WITH CHEESE

¾ lb. cooked ham diced small (or two
   4½-oz. tins devilled ham or 12 slices
   bacon cooked crisp)
1⅞-oz. packet dry cream of leek soup-mix
10 oz. coarsely grated Swiss cheese
12 fluid oz. milk
12 fluid oz. single cream

4 eggs well beaten
1 teaspoon dry mustard
1 teaspoon salt (scant)
¼ teaspoon pepper
3 tablespoons bread or cornflake crumbs
2 tablespoons Parmesan cheese
   Unbaked 10-inch pie shell

1. Make the pie crust with 8 oz. flour, using your favourite recipe, and chill it while you make the filling.

2. Blend the soup mix with the milk in a saucepan and bring to a boil, stirring constantly. Cool a little, stir in the cream, and refrigerate until cold.

3. Mix well the eggs, mustard, salt and pepper, and blend in the soup mixture as soon as it has cooled.

4. If you use cooked ham, spread it on the bottom of the pie shell and add the crumbs to the soup mixture. If you use devilled ham or bacon, mix it with the crumbs and spread on the bottom of the shell. In either case, cover with the Swiss cheese.

4. Pour the milk-soup mixture over the cheese carefully, top with the Parmesan cheese, and bake at 375° about 50 minutes, or until a knife inserted in the centre comes out clean. Serves 8.

Serve with warm French bread or fresh rolls and a mixed vegetable salad.

BRAISED HAM STEAK IN WINE

1 slice ham 2 inches thick
   Whole cloves
1½ oz. brown sugar

1 teaspoon cornflour
6 fluid oz. dry red wine

ONE of the simplest possible ways of producing a delicious ham casserole.

1. Trim the fat from the ham, leaving not more than ¼ inch around it. Slash this a number of times. Insert a dozen or so cloves in the fat around the outside and in fat pockets in the ham itself. Lay the ham in a shallow casserole.

2. Mix sugar and cornflour, spread evenly over the ham, and bake uncovered in a slow oven, 300°, about 30 minutes.

3. Add the wine to the casserole and continue to bake another 30–40 minutes, basting frequently with the wine. Serves 6.

Serve with potatoes baked in the oven with the ham. Broccoli spears go well with this dinner.

HAM STEAK FLAMBÉ

1 slice of ham 1 inch thick
1½ oz. brown sugar
¾ teaspoon dry mustard

1 tablespoon orange juice
3 tablespoons Grand Marnier or Curaçao
   liqueur warmed slightly

NOT only good to eat but spectacular to see, as all flambé dishes are.

1. Trim excess fat from the edge of the ham and lay in a shallow casserole.

2. Mix the brown sugar, mustard, and orange juice into a thin paste and spread half of it in a thin layer on the ham.

3. Put under the grill, about 3 inches down, under medium heat if your grill can be regulated. If not, put it about 5 inches from the heat. Grill about 10 minutes.

4. Turn the steak, spread with the remaining sugar mixture, and continue grilling about 5 minutes.

5. Just as you are ready to serve pour over the warmed liqueur and ignite. Serve flaming. (It is often easier to light liqueur in a pan or ladle and pour it blazing over the food.) Serves 4.

Serve with buttered noodles garnished with poppy seeds and split almonds, and a green salad with tomato wedges and cucumber slices added.

HAM AND SPAGHETTI PARMA

1 lb. cooked ham diced
8-oz. packet spaghetti cooked
3 oz. grated Parmesan cheese
3 oz. butter or margarine
1 large mushroom sliced
2 tablespoons minced or grated onion
1¼ oz. flour

¾ pt. thin cream or top milk
6 fluid oz. dry white wine
2 oz. sliced green olives
1 pimento cut in thin strips
¼ teaspoon dried oregano or ¾ teaspoon
   fresh, chopped
⅛ teaspoon fresh-ground pepper

1. Cook the spaghetti as directed on the packet, but be careful not to overcook it—it should be *al dente*, as the Italians say.

2. Drain and immediately toss it with 2 oz. of the cheese. Spread it out in a large shallow buttered casserole and keep barely warm.

3. Melt butter in a large frying-pan and cook the mushroom and onion in it, over medium heat, 3–4 minutes. Skim out of the pan and set aside.

4. Into the fat remaining in the pan blend flour and gradually stir in the cream. When it thickens stir in the wine, cooked mushroom and onion, ham, olives, pimento, oregano, and pepper.

5. Spoon this mixture carefully over the spaghetti in the casserole, sprinkle with the remaining cheese, and grill 4–6 inches from the heat until golden. Serves 6–8.

Serve with warm French bread and a salad made with separated leaves of chicory and cooked beetroot diced and tossed in French dressing.

48

SPICED HAM BALLS

1 12-oz. tin pork luncheon meat ground
3 oz. uncooked oatmeal
1 egg beaten

4 fluid oz. milk
1 teaspoon Worcestershire sauce
1 tablespoon prepared mustard

Sauce

1 tablespoon flour
2 oz. brown sugar or maple syrup

¼ pt. water
2 tablespoons vinegar

1. Mix thoroughly the meat, oatmeal, egg, milk, Worcestershire sauce, and mustard. Shape into small balls and lay in a shallow casserole.

2. Bake these ham balls 30 minutes in a 350° oven.

3. While the casserole is baking, combine the sauce ingredients in a saucepan and cook slowly until thick.

4. When the casserole has baked 30 minutes pour the sauce over and continue baking 15 minutes longer. Serves 5–6.

SOUFFLÉ STRASBOURG

6 oz. ground ham
4 oz. purée of foie gras
1 tablespoon chopped truffles
   (optional)
1½ oz. butter or margarine

1½ oz. flour
¾ pt. milk
   Salt and pepper
3 eggs separated

1. Make a white sauce of the butter, flour, and milk, seasoning it to your taste. Stir in the ham, foie gras, and truffles. Cool somewhat.

2. Stir in the well-beaten egg yolks and fold in the whites, beaten until they are stiff but not dry.

3. Pour gently into a buttered soufflé dish and bake in a 350° oven 50 minutes. Serves 4–5.

A delicate soufflé like this calls for something light to accompany it, such as tiny green peas, sliced ripe tomatoes, and a simple salad of mixed greens.

HAM AND WHOLEMEAL SOUFFLÉ

¾ pt. milk
½ oz. butter or margarine
1½ oz. wholemeal
1 teaspoon salt
4 eggs separated

4 oz. shredded Cheddar cheese
1 teaspoon dry mustard
1 teaspoon Worcestershire sauce
1 teaspoon grated onion
½ lb. finely diced cooked ham

1. In a medium saucepan combine milk, butter, wholemeal, and salt. Cook gently, over low heat, about 5 minutes, stirring constantly until it thickens. Remove from heat and cool slightly.
2. Gradually stir in the well-beaten egg yolks, then the cheese, onion, mustard, Worcestershire sauce and ham.
3. Beat the egg whites until stiff but not dry and fold them gently into the soufflé mixture. Turn into a buttered two-quart casserole or soufflé dish, and bake uncovered in a slow oven, about 300°, or until a knife inserted in the centre comes out clean. Serve at once, before it has time to fall. Serves 4 amply.

TOAST SANDWICH WITH HAM AND PINEAPPLE

4 slices pumpernickel
4 thin slices baked or boiled ham—
 leftover, tinned, or the kind you buy
 ready sliced
2 large slices Swiss cheese
2 eggs

¼ pt. thin cream
¼ teaspoon salt
2–3 oz. butter or margarine
2 slices tinned pineapple
2 tablespoons brown sugar
 Raspberry jelly

Now that pumpernickel is widely available, this is a good combination for a luncheon sandwich.
1. Top each slice of pumpernickel with 2 slices of ham, or one slice if you get large slices. Put one slice of cheese over the ham, and top with another slice of pumpernickel. If desired you can spread each slice of ham with a thin dab of mustard. Set these sandwiches aside until you are ready to serve.
2. Beat the eggs lightly, blend in the cream and salt, and pour into a large soup plate or shallow casserole.
3. Holding the sandwiches carefully with two forks, dip each of them into the egg mixture, letting them stay there a minute or so to moisten them well. Have most of the butter bubbling in a large heavy frying-pan and carefully place the sandwiches in it. When the under side is lightly browned, turn the sandwiches carefully with two spatulas or forks and brown the other side.
4. Glaze the pineapple. Add the little butter left over from the sandwiches to a small pan and heat to bubbling. Put the brown sugar on a plate. Dip the pineapple slices in the brown sugar and sauté in the butter until glazed on both sides. Serve with a helping of jelly. Makes two sandwiches.

LAMB

BLANQUETTE OF LAMB

3 lbs. boned shoulder of lamb cut in
   1¼-inch cubes
5 tablespoons butter, margarine, or salad
   oil
18 small white onions (tinned will do)

½ lb. mushroom caps, halved or quartered
   if large
4 fluid oz. Madeira or sherry
1 tablespoon flour
12 fluid oz. thin cream
   Salt and pepper to taste

A FLAVOURFUL combination, and a fine buffet dish for a party.

1. Heat 4 tablespoons of the butter in a heavy frying-pan and brown the lamb slightly. As the pieces are browned arrange them in a medium casserole. Cover the casserole and bake 20 minutes in a 300° oven.

2. In the fat remaining in the pan sauté lightly first the onions and then the mushrooms, adding each to the casserole as they are ready. (If you use tinned onions add them later, with the sauce.)

3. Pour the Madeira into the pan, scrape up all the brown particles, and add this to the casserole.

4. Blend the remaining tablespoon of butter and the flour in a medium saucepan and cook over medium heat. Slowly stir in the cream and keep stirring until the sauce is somewhat thickened. Season to taste.

5. Add this to the casserole at the end of the 20 minutes it has cooked. Stir gently to blend ingredients, cover again, and bake 30 minutes longer. Serves 6.

Serve with herb-flavoured or curried rice, warm French bread with sesame seeds added to the garlic butter, and mixed sweet corn and French beans.

LAMB CHOP CASSEROLE

4 thick best end of neck chops
2 tablespoons flour
¾ teaspoon salt
⅛ teaspoon pepper
2 tablespoons butter, margarine, or salad oil
8 small white onions
2 medium carrots diced small
1 oz. diced celery

4 fluid oz. red-currant jelly
4 fluid oz. condensed consommé
½ teaspoon dried chervil or 1½ teaspoons fresh, chopped
½ teaspoon dried oregano or 1½ teaspoons fresh, chopped
1 small bay leaf
3 tablespoons orange juice

1. Shake the flour, salt, and pepper together in a bag and dredge the chops in it.
2. Heat the butter in a shallow casserole large enough to hold all the chops flat and brown them on both sides.
3. Add all remaining ingredients except the orange juice, cover the casserole, and bake one hour in a 375° oven, basting several times.
4. Add the orange juice and bake 15 minutes more, uncovered. Serves 4.

Serve with riced potatoes and asparagus with butter-lemon-juice-bread-crumb sauce.

GREEK LAMB CASSEROLE

3 lbs. stewing lamb cut in 1-inch cubes
3 tablespoons salad oil
2 oz. chopped onion
1½ lb. tin tomatoes
2 teaspoons salt
¼ teaspoon dried thyme or ¾ teaspoon fresh, chopped
¼ teaspoon dried oregano or ¾ teaspoon fresh, chopped

¼ teaspoon dried sweet basil or ¾ teaspoon fresh, chopped
1 large or 2 medium carrots diced small or sliced thin
1 or 2 leeks (white part only)
12 small white onions peeled or 1 medium tin
8 oz. okra (optional)
1 teaspoon lemon juice

1. Brown the meat well in hot oil in a heavy frying-pan and transfer to a medium casserole with a slotted spoon.
2. In the fat remaining in the pan cook the chopped onion until soft but not browned and add to the casserole.
3. Pour the tomatoes into the pan and stir to pick up all the browned particles. Add herbs and salt and pour over the casserole. Cover and bake 1 hour in a 325° oven.
4. Remove cover and stir in carrots, leeks, and onions. (If you use tinned boiled onions do not add them until later.) Cover again and bake 25 minutes longer.
5. Uncover and add the okra (if used) and lemon juice. If you use boiled onions add them at this time also. Bake 15 minutes longer, uncovered. Serves 6.

Serve with baked potatoes, cole slaw, and buttered baby Brussels sprouts.

Greek lamb with jacket potatoes

LAMB CHOPS FARM STYLE

6 best end of neck chops cut rather thick
3 tablespoons flour
2 teaspoons salt
⅛ teaspoon fresh-ground pepper

2 tablespoons butter, margarine, or salad oil
2 tablespoons water
1 tin condensed cream of mushroom soup

1. Shake up the flour, salt, and pepper in a paper bag and dredge the chops in it.

2. Heat the butter in a large heavy casserole or frying-pan and brown the chops well. Arrange in a shallow casserole.

3. Stir the water into the soup until well mixed and pour over the casserole.

4. Bake at 375° one hour, uncovered, or until chops are tender. Serves 6.

Serve with a baked rice casserole (see Index) and sliced courgettes gently sautéed in butter, covered, about 8–10 minutes.

LAMB WITH AUBERGINE

1 lb. ground raw lamb
1 medium aubergine cut in ½-inch slices
    (unpeeled)
2½ oz. butter or margarine, or 4 tablespoons
    salad oil
1 small chopped onion

½ teaspoon salt
    Dash fresh-ground pepper
8-oz. bottle tomato sauce
1 oz. grated Parmesan cheese
    Mozzarella cheese sliced

1. Heat the fat in a heavy frying-pan and brown the aubergine slices lightly on both sides. Arrange some of them as a layer on the bottom of a medium casserole and reserve the rest on a plate. You may have to add a bit more fat to brown all the aubergine.

2. In any fat remaining in the pan put the lamb, onion, and seasonings. Cook until the lamb is lightly browned, stirring several times.

3. Spread the lamb on top of the aubergine layer in the casserole. Arrange the remaining aubergine slices on top, cut in halves or quarters.

4. Pour tomato sauce over, sprinkle Parmesan cheese on top, and bake 20 minutes in a 350° oven.

5. Arrange mozzarella cheese slices to cover top of casserole and bake 10 minutes more, or until cheese is bubbly. Serves 6.

Serve with buttered noodles and a green salad tossed in French dressing.

LAMB 53

American fish casserole

LAMB WITH BEANS

2 lbs. boned lamb cut in good-sized
  chunks, 1½-2 inches
8 oz. dried butter beans
4 slices bacon diced
3 oz. chopped onion
1 tablespoon flour
¾ pt. chicken broth
  Salt and pepper to taste
½ clove garlic crushed

½ teaspoon dried thyme or 1½ teaspoons
  fresh, chopped
½ teaspoon dried oregano or 1½ teaspoons
  fresh, chopped
½ teaspoon dried marjoram or 1½
  teaspoons fresh, chopped
4 oz. spring onions chopped
8 tiny white onions or 1 small tin whole
  boiled onions

1. If you use old-style beans soak them overnight, drain, cover with fresh cold water, bring to a boil, and simmer until tender (when the skin cracks if you put a bean in a spoon and blow on it). If you use the newer quick-cooking beans follow packet directions in cooking. Drain beans, but save water in which they were cooked.

2. In a heavy frying-pan sauté the bacon and chopped onion together lightly and put in a medium casserole with the cooked beans.

3. In the fat left in the pan brown the lamb pieces lightly and transfer to the casserole.

4. Stir the flour into the fat left in the pan, adding a bit of butter or margarine if necessary to make a smooth paste.

5. Add the chicken broth slowly, season to taste, and add to the casserole with the garlic, herbs, chopped spring onions, whole onions, and enough of the bean water to come about ¾ of the way up.

6. Cover and bake 2 hours in a 300° oven. If sauce is too thin at this time, thicken with flour-and-water paste. Serves 4.

Serve with spaghetti tossed well with Parmesan cheese and French beans well buttered.

LAMB AND MACARONI

1 lb. cooked lamb diced rather small
8-oz. packet shell macaroni cooked
1 tin condensed cream of celery soup
4-oz. tin sliced mushrooms with liquid

½ teaspoon dried rosemary, basil, or
  oregano, or 1½ teaspoons fresh, chopped
  Salt and pepper to taste
2 oz. grated Parmesan cheese

1. Cook the macaroni according to packet directions. Be sure not to overcook it. Drain.

2. Combine lamb, soup, mushrooms, herb, and seasonings. Add the cooked and drained macaroni and mix well.

3. Pour into a medium casserole, buttered, and sprinkle with cheese.

4. Bake 35 minutes in a 350° oven. Serves 5–6.

DE LUXE LAMB HASH

1 lb. cold roast lamb chopped rather fine, not ground
5 tablespoons brandy
1 garlic clove cut in half
½ teaspoon dried oregano or 1½ teaspoons fresh, chopped
1 teaspoon chopped parsley

1 generous teaspoon meat glaze
1 tin condensed consommé
2 tablespoons butter or margarine
1 good-sized onion sliced thin
6 oz. fresh bread crumbs slightly packed
Salt

1. Pour the brandy over the lamb, stir to be sure it is all moistened, and let stand an hour.
2. Add the garlic clove, herbs, and meat glaze to the consommé and let it stand until the meat is ready to use. Remove the garlic clove at that time.
3. Heat the butter in a frying-pan and lightly sauté the onion.
4. Add consommé and bread crumbs to the meat, and add the onion. Let stand briefly, until the liquid is all absorbed by the bread. Check seasoning and add a little salt if needed. Spread in a rather shallow casserole.
5. Bake 15 minutes in a 350° oven and then brown under the grill. Serves 4–5.

Serve with asparagus Hollandaise and French beans.

SWEDISH LAMB SHANKS

4 lamb shanks
2 tablespoons salad oil
1 teaspoon paprika
1 large onion sliced
8 oz. sliced mushrooms
½ pt. water or ¼ pt. each water and dry white wine

1 tablespoon prepared horseradish
¾ teaspoon mixed herbs: rosemary, parsley, sweet basil, and oregano
1 teaspoon salt
¼ teaspoon fresh-ground pepper
8 fluid oz. sour cream

1. Heat oil in a heavy frying-pan. Sprinkle the lamb shanks with paprika and brown them in the oil, along with the onion and mushrooms.
2. When the lamb is browned on all sides transfer it to a large casserole. Add the water or water-wine mixture to the pan, scrape up all the brown particles, and add this to the casserole, along with the horseradish, herbs, and salt and pepper.
3. Cover and bake in a 325° oven 1½ hours, or until lamb is fork tender.
4. Remove the shanks and cut off the meat.
5. Stir the sour cream into the casserole, return the meat to it, and just reheat to serving temperature. Serves 4.

Serve with buttered noodles and buttered beetroot.

LAMB AND SPAGHETTI PARMESAN

1 lb. ground lean lamb
6 oz. spaghetti cooked and drained
3 tablespoons butter or margarine
4 medium onions chopped
5-oz. tin tomato purée
½ pt. warm water
½ teaspoon cinnamon

⅛ teaspoon nutmeg
  Salt and pepper
1 oz. grated Parmesan cheese
3 eggs
1 tablespoon flour
¾ pt. milk

1. Heat 2 tablespoons of the butter in a medium casserole and brown the lamb and onion.

2. Stir in the tomato purée and water, cinnamon, nutmeg, and salt and pepper to taste.

3. Cover and bake 25–30 minutes in a slow oven, 300°.

4. Combine the cheese and one of the eggs, beaten with a fork. Stir this into the drained spaghetti and spread on top of the lamb mixture in the casserole.

5. Melt the remaining tablespoon of butter, blend in the flour, and slowly stir in the milk. Cook until thickened, stirring constantly. Season to taste.

6. Beat the other two eggs well. Stir a little of the hot white sauce into them and stir back into the sauce. Simmer a couple of minutes but do not let it boil.

7. Pour the sauce over the spaghetti in the casserole, increase the heat to 400°, and bake 15 minutes more. Serves 4.

LAMB STEAKS WITH VEGETABLES

4 lamb steaks ¾-inch thick
2 cloves garlic crushed
8 oz. sliced mushrooms
1 large chopped green pepper
2 large chopped onions
2 medium tomatoes sliced

1 teaspoon salt
¼ teaspoon fresh-ground pepper
2 teaspoons paprika
½ teaspoon dried rosemary or 1½ teaspoons
  fresh, chopped
3 tablespoons dry sherry

SPREAD crushed garlic on the steaks and arrange them in a fairly shallow casserole that will hold them in one layer.

Arrange the remaining ingredients on top of the steaks, and bake in a 325° oven 40 minutes, or until the steaks are very tender. Cover for the first 25 minutes, then remove cover. Serves 4, or more if the steaks are very large.

Serve with riced potatoes and a plain green salad.

LAMB STEW WITH WINE

2 lbs. lean lamb shoulder cut in 1½-inch
   cubes
2 medium onions sliced
1 medium clove garlic, peeled
12 fluid oz. dry white wine

Seasoned flour
2 tablespoons salad oil
¼ pt. water
1 teaspoon chopped parsley

THE wine gives this stew a lot of flavour, particularly because it is used for marinating.
1. Put the lamb in a deep bowl with onions and garlic and stir well. Pour the wine over it, cover, and let marinate 2–3 hours, or put in the refrigerator overnight.
2. Drain the meat cubes well (save the marinade) and roll them in seasoned flour or shake them in a paper bag. (Use 1 oz. flour, 2 scant teaspoons salt, and ¼ teaspoon pepper.)
3. Heat oil in a heavy frying-pan, brown the meat, and remove to a medium casserole.
4. Add water and parsley to the leftover marinade and pour over the casserole.
5. Cover and bake 1½ hours in a 325° oven, or simmer an hour over very low heat on top of the stove. Serves 4–5.

Note: *If you want to make this a complete meal, add vegetables when you put the casserole in the oven: carrots and celery sliced, a dozen little white onions, and 2 good-sized potatoes diced or 15–20 small potato balls. Otherwise, serve with little new potatoes and buttered green beans.*

LAMB TERRAPIN

1¼ lbs. cooked lamb cut in small slices or
   diced
1 tablespoon butter, margarine, or salad oil
1 tablespoon flour
½ teaspoon dry mustard
½ pt. condensed consommé or ¼ pt.
   consommé and ¼ pt. dry red wine

¼ pt. cream or top milk
1 tablespoon Worcestershire sauce
2 hard-boiled eggs chopped
4 oz. sliced mushrooms lightly sautéed
2 oz. buttered crumbs
1 teaspoon minced parsley

LEFTOVER lamb should meet a royal welcome if dressed up in this way, especially if you use the wine.
1. Melt the butter in a medium casserole on top of the stove, stir in flour and mustard, and blend in the consommé gradually, stirring constantly.
2. Cook 2–3 minutes and then stir in the cream, Worcestershire sauce, eggs, mushrooms, and meat.
3. Top with buttered crumbs and parsley mixed.
4. Bake the casserole 20–25 minutes in a moderate oven, 350°, uncovered, until it is bubbly and golden. Serves 5–6.

Serve with buttered noodles, buttered Brussels sprouts, and sliced ripe tomatoes topped with chopped chives and French dressing.

LAMBROSIA

2 lbs. stewing lamb cut in medium cubes
1 oz. flour
1 teaspoon curry powder or to taste
3 teaspoons salt
$\frac{1}{4}$ teaspoon pepper

2 tablespoons butter or margarine
$\frac{3}{4}$ pt. water (or $\frac{1}{2}$ chicken broth or white wine)
8 medium carrots cut in strips
1-lb. tin boiled whole onions

Topping

4 oz. fine sifted flour
6 oz. flour
2 teaspoons baking powder
$\frac{3}{4}$ teaspoon salt

4 oz. shortening
6 oz. tinned or cooked frozen whole-kernel sweet corn
$\frac{1}{4}$ pt. milk

THIS dish is well named, especially if you use boned lamb or bone it yourself.

1. Combine the flour, curry powder, salt, and pepper in a paper bag and shake the lamb pieces in it. Brown well in hot fat and put in a medium casserole.

2. Pour the water or broth into the frying-pan, scrape out the browned particles, and add to the casserole.

3. Cover the casserole and bake 30 minutes in a 325° oven.

4. Add the carrots and bake 25 minutes more.

5. Remove the casserole from the oven and stir in the onions. Increase oven heat to 425°.

6. For the topping, sift together the flours, baking powder, and salt. Cut in the shortening until the mixture is uniform. Stir in the sweet corn (drained if you use tinned). Add the milk all at once and stir just enough to dampen the mixture.

7. Drop on top of the casserole by tablespoonfuls and bake 25 minutes. Serves 5–6.

Serve with French beans to which sliced and lightly sautéed mushrooms have been added.

NOISETTES D'AGNEAU

8 fillets cut from saddle of lamb, 1½
  inches thick
1½ tablespoons clarified butter
  Salt and pepper
3 tablespoons dry sherry
3 tablespoons dry vermouth

½ pt. veal or chicken stock
1 tablespoon butter
1 truffle peeled and minced (optional)
½ pt. Soubise sauce
  Grated Parmesan cheese

THIS is a delectable French dish, something to make for very special people.

To clarify butter melt it, preferably over hot water, and after it settles pour it carefully through a fine cloth or folded cheesecloth wrung out in warm water. This filters out the scum.

1. Heat the clarified butter in a heavy frying-pan. Season the fillets and brown them lightly on both sides.

2. Add the sherry and vermouth and cook until the wines are greatly reduced.

3. Add the stock and cook slowly over low heat until the sauce becomes slightly thickened. Transfer fillets and sauce to a shallow serving casserole.

4. Cream the other butter with the truffle and place a nut-sized piece on each chop.

5. Top with Soubise sauce. (This is a white sauce strongly flavoured with onion. Make the sauce with 1 tablespoon butter, 1 tablespoon flour, and ½ pt. top milk. Boil 2 small chopped onions in water 5 minutes. Drain, add more water, just to cover, and cook until they are soft. Drain well and press through a sieve into the white sauce. Season to taste.)

6. Sprinkle the Soubise sauce topping of the fillets with a generous coating of Parmesan cheese, put under the grill, and grill until golden brown. Serves 4.

This is a rich dish, and needs only something like fat asparagus stalks with butter-lemon-juice-bread-crumb dressing and a salad of chicory with French dressing.

ROQUEFORT LAMB CHOPS

4 loin chops cut 2 inches thick
¼ lb. Roquefort cheese crumbled
1 clove garlic cut
  Salt and pepper

2 teaspoons Worcestershire sauce
½ tin condensed consommé or ½
  consommé and ¼ red wine

1. Trim the chops of excess fat and rub well all over with the cut garlic. Sprinkle with salt and pepper.

2. Mix cheese and Worcestershire sauce and spread on the chops. Lay them in a shallow casserole just large enough to hold them.

3. Pour the consommé around the chops and bake 45 minutes in a 350° oven, basting occasionally. Serves 4.

Serve with roast potatoes and baked apples, if your oven can take 3 casseroles. If not, substitute sliced green beans for the apples.

LAMB CHOPS BERMUDA

6 best end of neck chops cut 1½ inches thick
Salt and pepper
1 tablespoon butter, margarine, or salad oil

6 medium onions sliced
¾ pt. chicken stock or water
12 tiny new potatoes sliced
2 teaspoons chopped parsley

1. Season the chops well and brown in hot butter in a large heavy frying-pan or directly in the casserole in which they will be baked, if you have one large enough. Drain off excess fat.
2. Add the onions and stock or water to the casserole and bake 25–30 minutes in a 325° oven, covered.
3. Add the potatoes and parsley to the casserole, check seasoning, cover again, and continue to bake 25–30 minutes longer, or until potatoes are tender. Serves 6.

Serve with young courgettes, sliced but not peeled, and sautéed gently in unsalted butter until done—8–10 minutes.

PORK

CALIFORNIA PORK CHOPS

6 loin or rib pork chops 1 inch thick
Salt and pepper
1 oz. flour
Salad oil
2 oranges peeled and sliced
5 tablespoons brown sugar
2 teaspoons cornflour

¼ pt. chicken stock, white wine, or water
½ pt. orange juice
½ teaspoon dried marjoram or 1½ teaspoons fresh, chopped
2 medium onions sliced
2 tablespoons chopped parsley

ORANGES and pork make a delightful combination, and this recipe makes the most of it.
1. Trim excess fat from chops and melt the pieces in a heavy frying-pan. Skim out and discard the scraps when they are brown.
2. Season the chops to taste, roll lightly in the flour, and brown well in the hot fat, adding a little oil if there is not enough fat from the pork fat pieces.
3. Arrange the browned chops in a large shallow casserole, preferably one that will enable you to crowd them in one layer.
4. Sprinkle the orange slices with 3 tablespoons of the brown sugar and let them stand.
5. Blend the cornflour with the stock or wine, the orange juice, marjoram, and the rest of the brown sugar. Pour this mixture over the chops in the casserole and arrange the onions on top.
6. Sprinkle the onions with parsley, cover, and bake 1 hour in a 350° oven.
7. Arrange the orange slices on top and bake 15 minutes more, uncovered. Serves 6.

Serve with creamy mashed potatoes and buttered French beans, along with a plain salad tossed in French dressing.

CARBONNADES OF PORK

3 lbs. shoulder of pork, boned
2½ oz. flour
¼ teaspoon fresh-ground pepper
6 tablespoons butter, margarine, or salad
  oil

3 lbs. medium onions sliced
½ teaspoon dried thyme or 1½ teaspoons
  fresh, chopped
1 small bay leaf
1 pint beer

1. Trim off excess fat from the pork, cut in 2-inch cubes, and shake in a paper bag with the flour, 2 teaspoons salt, and the pepper. Shake off excess flour, leaving a thin coating on the meat.
2. Melt the fat trimmings in a heavy casserole and skim out the pieces when they are brown. Brown the pork cubes well in the fat.
3. In a frying-pan melt the butter and lightly brown the onions in it. Salt sparingly. Stir in the thyme, bay leaf, and beer and pour over the pork in the casserole.
4. Cover and bake 1½–2 hours in a slow oven, 300°.
5. If the sauce is too thin for your taste, drain it into a small saucepan and thicken slightly with either flour-and-water paste or *beurre manié* (flour and butter kneaded together). Return the sauce to the casserole. Serves 6–8.

Serve with fluffy rice and baked apples.

CHINESE PORK PIE

1 lb. cold roast pork cut in 1-inch dice
1 clove garlic crushed
1 leek minced (white part only) or
  1 tablespoon minced onion
2 tablespoons butter or margarine
¾ pt. leftover pork gravy
  Salt and pepper
1 small bay leaf crushed

2 cloves
1 medium carrot sliced thin
½ cup sliced water chestnuts
6 oz. tinned bean sprouts
1 apple pared and chopped
1½ lbs. hot mashed sweet potatoes
1 tablespoon brown sugar
2 teaspoons butter or margarine

1. Sauté garlic and leek or onion in hot fat until lightly brown. Stir in pork cubes and brown lightly.
2. Add gravy, seasonings, and carrot. If gravy is pretty thick thin it out a bit with water or dry white wine.
3. When the gravy comes to a boil stir in water chestnuts, bean sprouts, and apple. All this can be done in a medium casserole, but if it has been done in a frying-pan pour into a casserole now and put in a moderate oven, 350°, for 10 minutes.
4. Remove casserole from the oven and carefully top with hot mashed sweet potatoes, adding them by small tablespoonfuls and then smoothing over to make a solid top. Sprinkle with the brown sugar, dot with butter, and bake 10 minutes more. Serves 6.

Serve with glazed carrots and a green salad tossed in French dressing.

FLANDERS PORK AND APPLES

2 lbs. pork shoulder or loin sliced ½-inch
    thick
12 small white onions
1 tablespoon flour
¼ pt. dry white wine
¼ pt. chicken broth or condensed
    consommé

Salt and pepper to taste
1 teaspoon dried oregano and rosemary
    mixed or 1 tablespoon fresh, chopped
1 teaspoon minced parsley
1 lb. tart cooking apples peeled and
    quartered

1. Trim fat off the pork slices and melt in a heavy frying-pan. Skim out the brown particles, and sauté in the fat the pork and onions. Remove to a medium casserole.
2. If there is much fat left in the pan pour it out and measure back 1 tablespoon. Stir in the flour and slowly add the wine and broth, stirring until the sauce is smooth and thick.
3. Season the sauce to taste with salt and pepper, add the herbs, and pour over the casserole. Cover tightly and bake 2 hours in a slow oven, 300°. (If your casserole lid does not fit tightly cover the casserole first with heavy brown paper and then put on the lid.)
4. When the casserole has baked 1½ hours stir in the apples, cover again, and finish baking. Serves 6.

Serve with mashed potatoes and buttered runner beans.

FRENCH MEAT PIE

1 lb. lean pork shoulder ground
½ lb. lean veal shoulder ground
¾ teaspoon salt
½ teaspoon dry mustard
½ clove garlic crushed
1 small bay leaf crumbled

¼ teaspoon dried marjoram or ¾ teaspoon
    fresh, chopped
¼ teaspoon dried thyme or ¾ teaspoon fresh,
    chopped
Pastry for 10-inch 2-crust pie

1. Mix the ground meats (have the butcher grind them together) with salt, mustard, garlic, and bay leaf. Brown in a hot, dry frying-pan 2–3 minutes, stirring constantly.
2. Cover, reduce heat, and simmer over lowest possible heat about 25 minutes, stirring occasionally.
3. Stir in marjoram and thyme, correct seasoning, and cool a little.
4. Roll out just over half the pastry to ⅛ inch thickness and line a 10-inch pie plate with it. Spread the meat mixture evenly in it. Roll out the remaining pastry and lay over the meat.
5. Seal the edges by moistening and pinching together to form a rim and gash the crust several times to permit steam to escape.
6. Bake the pie 40–45 minutes in a hot oven, 425°, or until pastry is golden. Serve hot or cold. Serves 6–8.

If hot, serve with buttered beetroot cut in thin strips and fresh corn on the cob or buttered sweet corn. If cold, serve with hot mixed vegetables and a green salad.

PORK CHOPS IN CIDER

6 loin pork chops cut 1 inch thick
2 tablespoons butter, margarine, or salad oil
6 fluid oz. cider
4 fluid oz. water
3 medium onions chopped fine

$\frac{1}{2}$ teaspoon dried sweet basil or 1$\frac{1}{2}$ teaspoons fresh, chopped
$\frac{1}{2}$ teaspoon dried sweet marjoram or 1$\frac{1}{2}$ teaspoons fresh, chopped
Salt and pepper to taste
Paprika

1. Heat the butter in a large heavy casserole and brown the chops well on both sides. (If you do not have a casserole large enough to take them all do them three at a time and arrange in 2 overlapping layers.)
2. Pour over the chops the cider and water and spread over the chopped onions, pushing them into the spaces where you can.
3. Sprinkle with herbs, salt and pepper, and paprika, cover, and bake 45 minutes to an hour in a 350° oven. Serves 6.

Note: If you want a thicker sauce than this provides, drain off the liquid into a small sauce-pan, thicken it to taste with flour-and-water paste, and pour back on the chops.

Serve with hot fluffy rice and buttered carrots.

PORK CHOPS NIÇOISE

6 pork chops 1 inch thick
4 medium ripe tomatoes, peeled, seeded, and chopped
3 small cloves of garlic crushed
1 medium green pepper minced

1 teaspoon dried basil or 1 tablespoon fresh, chopped
Salt and pepper
3 oz. ripe olives pitted or cut off pits

THIS is a different way of cooking pork chops that should prove popular for its Mediter-ranean flavour.
1. Remove excess fat from chops, melt in a heavy frying-pan, skim out the browned pieces, and brown the chops well in the fat, on both sides. Arrange in a rather shallow casserole large enough to hold them in one layer.
2. Mix the remaining ingredients, except the olives, season to taste, and spread over the chops. Cover and bake 35 minutes in a slow oven, 325°.
3. Stir in the olives and bake 10 minutes longer, uncovered. Serves 6.

Serve with plenty of fresh hot rice, buttered and mixed with a lot of coarsely chopped parsley. Buttered green peas and a dressed green salad will complete the meal.

PORK NORMANDY

1½ lbs. pork shoulder cut in 1-inch cubes
   Salt and pepper
2 medium onions chopped
1 clove garlic crushed

¾ pt. apple sauce
2 tablespoons tomato purée
¼ teaspoon dried rosemary or ¾ teaspoon
   fresh, chopped

As in other recipes in this section, the flavour of the pork is brought out by apples.
1. Remove what excess fat you can from the pork and melt it in a heavy casserole. Remove the browned bits and brown the pork cubes well on all sides in the fat. Season with salt and pepper and arrange in a medium casserole.
2. In the fat remaining in the pan brown the onion and garlic very lightly.
3. Stir in the apple sauce, tomato purée, and rosemary, season to taste, and spread over the meat in the casserole.
4. Cover and bake in a 350° oven about 50 minutes. Uncover and continue baking 15–20 minutes longer. Serves 4–6.

Serve with buttered noodles and buttered broccoli.

ORANGE-GLAZED STUFFED PORK CHOPS

4 double loin pork chops   Salt and pepper

Stuffing

2 oz. seasoned crumbs
2 teaspoons minced parsley
1 teaspoon grated orange peel

½ teaspoon salt
½ teaspoon Worcestershire sauce
¼ teaspoon pepper

Glaze

¼ pt. orange juice
4 tablespoons brown sugar

4 tablespoons orange marmalade
2 tablespoons cider vinegar

1. Trim off excess fat from the chops, wipe them, and cut a pocket in each one clear to the bone—or have the butcher cut the pocket.
2. Mix the stuffing ingredients in a small bowl and fill the pockets in the chops. Fasten the edges together with several toothpicks and secure them by running a piece of twine in and out and tying it around the back of each chop.
3. Salt and pepper the chops lightly and arrange them in a casserole which will hold them comfortably.
4. Put the casserole in a 375° oven, bake it for 15 minutes, turn the chops, and bake 15 minutes more.
5. Mix the glaze ingredients and simmer, uncovered, 10 minutes while the chops are baking. Pour over the chops and bake an additional 30 minutes, basting with a baster every 10 minutes. Serves 4.

Serve with riced potatoes, buttered baby Brussels sprouts, and a green salad.

PORK CHOPS WITH WHITE WINE

6 loin pork chops 1 inch thick
¾ teaspoon dry mustard
1 teaspoon salt
½ teaspoon fresh-ground pepper

4 tablespoons butter or margarine
1 large onion sliced
6 fluid oz. dry white wine

1. Blend the mustard, salt, and pepper and season the chops with the mixture.
2. Heat 2 tablespoons of the butter in a heavy frying-pan and brown the chops well on both sides. Remove them to a casserole, preferably one that will hold them in a single layer.
3. Add remaining butter to the pan and sauté the onion until soft but not brown. Spread over the chops and fill spaces with them.
4. Clean out the pan with the wine and pour over the chops. Cover and bake 1 hour in a 325° oven.
   The sauce is very good as it is but, if you prefer, drain the liquid from the casserole into a saucepan and thicken slightly with flour-and-water paste. Serves 6.

Serve with rice or sweet corn, and a dressed green salad.

SOUTH SEAS PORK

2 lbs. pork loin cut in 1-inch cubes
1 tablespoon flour
1½ tablespoons cornflour
6 tablespoons soy sauce
4 fluid oz. salad oil
1 green pepper sliced
2 medium onions sliced thin
1 carrot sliced thin

4-oz. tin bamboo shoots
8½-oz. tin pineapple chunks
2 oz. sugar
2 tablespoons vinegar
3 tablespoons tomato sauce
6 fluid oz. condensed consommé
   or ½ water and ½ consommé
Salt and pepper

THIS is a delectable casserole, spicy and mouth-watering.
1. In a good-sized bowl put the flour, half of the cornflour, and 1 tablespoon of the soy sauce. Mix them well. Add the meat cubes and stir until the flour mixture is evenly distributed on them.
2. Heat the oil in a heavy frying-pan and brown the pork pieces all over. Arrange in a medium casserole.
3. Drain off the remaining oil and measure back 2 tablespoons into the pan. In this sauté lightly the green pepper, onions, carrot, bamboo shoots, and pineapple. Stir in the sugar, the rest of the soy sauce, vinegar, tomato sauce, consommé, and salt and pepper to taste.
4. Add this mixture to the pork in the casserole, cover, and bake 30 minutes in a 350° oven.
5. Mix the remaining cornflour with a little water and stir into the casserole. If the sauce is not as thick as you like, add a little more cornflour-and-water paste. Correct seasoning and bake another 15 minutes, uncovered. Serves 4–6.

Serve with corn on the cob and buttered runner beans.

SAUSAGE-APPLE-NOODLE CASSEROLE

1 lb. pork sausages
8-oz. noodles cooked
½ pt. sweetened apple sauce

2 teaspoons lemon juice
⅛ teaspoon nutmeg
2 oz. grated Cheddar cheese

1. Prick the sausages well with a sharp-tined fork, lay them in a pan, and bake in a 400° oven 25 minutes. Turn once or twice to brown evenly. Drain on paper towelling.

2. Stir 2 tablespoons of the pork dripping into the noodles and arrange half of them in a greased medium casserole.

3. Combine the apple sauce, lemon juice, and nutmeg and pour on top of the noodles. Add the rest of the noodles and lay the sausages on top.

4. Sprinkle with cheese and bake 20 minutes at 350°, uncovered. Serves 4–5.

Serve with buttered green peas and warm French bread.

SAUSAGE PUDDING

1½ lbs. country sausage meat
1 tablespoon salad oil
3 eggs
¾ pt. milk
6 oz. flour

¼ teaspoon dried thyme or ¾ teaspoon
   fresh, chopped
   Dash cayenne pepper
¼ teaspoon salt

A REMARKABLY simple and delicious dish, especially for luncheon or Sunday-night supper.

1. Roll the sausage meat into small balls, about the size of a walnut.

2. Heat the oil in a heavy casserole of medium size and brown the sausage balls lightly on all sides. If the sausage meat is unusually fat, drain the fat from the casserole and pour back 1 tablespoon of it.

3. Make a batter by combining the eggs, milk, flour, thyme, cayenne, and salt. Pour over the sausages and bake in a hot oven, 450°, 15 minutes.

4. Lower the heat to 350° and continue to bake 15–20 minutes, or until the pudding is puffy and brown. Serves 5–6.

Serve with mixed vegetables and a plain dressed green salad.

PORK TENDERLOIN IN EGG BATTER

1 lb. pork tenderloin
4 oz. butter or margarine
1 egg beaten

Salt to taste
Flour, bread crumbs, or
wheat germ

THIS is one of the most delightful of pork dishes, but the tenderloin of the pork is scarce and often not available.
1. If you buy the tenderloin in one piece, slice off as many strips as you want to use. Then pound them thin with a wooden mallet, laying them between sheets of butcher's paper or plastic, until they are not more than ¼ inch thick.
2. Cook the slices in half of the butter, just until the meat loses its pinkness; remove from the frying-pan.
3. Melt the remaining butter in the same pan and as soon as it is sizzling, dip each slice of pork loin into the crumbs on both sides and return to the pan to cook. Keep the heat low and continue to cook until the pieces are crisp and brown—10 to 15 minutes at low heat. Serve 2 to a person.

Serve with fluffy mashed potatoes, tiny peas in butter, and warm French bread.

VEAL

BAKED VEAL CUTLETS

2 lbs. veal cutlets ½ inch thick
6 slices bacon
1 egg
2 tablespoons water
2 oz. bread or cornflake crumbs

2 small onions minced
1 teaspoon Worcestershire sauce
2 tins condensed cream of mushroom soup
 Buttered crumbs

1. Wipe the veal and cut it into 8 serving pieces.
2. Cook the bacon in a heavy frying-pan until crisp. Take out and reserve.
3. Combine the egg and water and beat lightly with a fork. Dip the pieces of veal first into this and then into the crumbs.
4. Brown the veal quickly on both sides in the bacon fat left in the pan. Arrange in a casserole, crumble the bacon over it, and scatter the onions on top.
5. Stir the Worcestershire sauce into the soup and pour over the casserole.
6. Top with buttered crumbs and bake, covered, in a 350° oven 30–40 minutes, or until the veal is tender. Serves 8.

Serve with buttered noodles with poppy seeds and split almonds added and buttered whole young green beans.

BALKAN VEAL STEW WITH ALMONDS

2 lbs. shoulder veal cut in 1-inch cubes
2 oz. flour
2 teaspoons salt
$\frac{1}{2}$ teaspoon fresh-ground pepper
3 tablespoons salad oil
1 large onion chopped

$\frac{1}{4}$ lb. mushrooms sliced or 4-oz. tin drained
12 fluid oz. dry white wine
2 tablespoons paprika
3 tablespoons water
8 fluid oz. sour cream
3 oz. blanched and toasted split almonds

1. Put half the flour, half the salt, and the pepper in a paper bag and shake the pieces of veal well in it.

2. Heat the oil in a large frying-pan and brown the veal well on all sides. Remove to a medium casserole.

3. In the fat remaining in the pan brown the onion and mushrooms slightly. Stir in the wine, paprika, and remaining salt. Pour over the casserole and bake 1 hour at 375°, covered.

4. Make a paste of the remaining 1 oz. of flour and the water. Remove the casserole from the oven and thicken the sauce with the paste.

5. Stir in the sour cream and almonds and return to the oven for 5 minutes. Serves 6.

Serve with fresh boiled rice, green peas, and a green salad.

BRAISED VEAL CHOPS À LA CHARTRES

6 veal chops 1 inch thick
2 tablespoons butter, margarine, or salad oil
Salt and pepper

4 tablespoons minced onion
6 oz. fine bread or cornflake crumbs
4 oz. grated Parmesan cheese
8 fluid oz. dry white wine

HERE is an extremely simple way to make veal chops outstanding fare.

1. Melt the butter in a heavy frying-pan, season the chops well, and brown them well on both sides. Arrange in a shallow casserole, preferably in one layer.

2. Sauté the onion lightly in the fat remaining in the pan. Stir in crumbs and cheese. If the mixture seems very dry blend in 1–2 tablespoons of the wine.

3. Pat this mixture carefully onto the chops, heaping it smoothly. Pour in the wine carefully, so as not to disturb the topping.

4. Cover and bake 1$\frac{1}{2}$ hours at 375°. Baste the chops every 15 or 20 minutes and add a little water if they dry out. Serves 6.

Serve with a rice casserole (see Index), buttered runner beans, and a green salad.

BLANQUETTE OF VEAL

2 lbs. of veal fillet cut in 1-inch cubes
12–15 small white onions peeled, or 1-lb. tin
3 medium carrots cut in large pieces
1½ teaspoons salt
Bouquet garni

1 lb. mushrooms (halved or quartered if large)
Juice of 1 lemon
1 tablespoon butter
1 tablespoon flour
2 egg yolks
½ pt. thin cream

1. Cover the veal with water and parboil it 5 minutes. Drain, rinse in cold water, and spread in a medium casserole.

2. Add the onions if raw (add later if tinned), the carrots, 1 teaspoon of the salt, the *bouquet garni*, and 1 quart of water. Bring to a boil on top of the stove and simmer 1–1½ hours, or until tender.

3. Put the mushrooms in a saucepan with ¼ pt. of water, the lemon juice, and the remaining ¼ teaspoon salt. Bring to a boil and remove from the heat at once. Let them stand a few minutes to marinate.

4. When the veal is done, drain the liquid in which it was cooked into a saucepan and boil hard until it is reduced to about ⅓ of the original quantity.

5. In a separate saucepan melt the butter, blend in the flour, and cook until it begins to colour. Blend in both the reduced veal liquid (discard the *bouquet garni*) and the liquid drained from the mushrooms. Cook until smooth and thickened, stirring constantly.

6. Beat the egg yolks slightly with the cream and blend into the sauce. Do not allow it to boil. Add sauce and mushrooms to casserole and check seasoning. Serves 6–8.

Serve with plenty of hot fluffy rice to take up the wonderful sauce, and buttered baby green peas. A green salad and warm French bread will complete an outstanding meal.

EXOTIC VEAL

2 lbs. veal shoulder cut in 1-inch cubes
2 teaspoons gravy browning
2 tablespoons butter, margarine, or salad oil
6 oz. chopped onions
¼ lb. mushrooms sliced or 6-oz. tin
½ pt. water, white wine, or chicken broth
2 tablespoons light brown sugar
3 tablespoons vinegar

1 teaspoon ground ginger
1 teaspoon dry mustard
1 teaspoon salt
¼ teaspoon fresh-ground pepper
1 teaspoon cornflour
1 tablespoon water
2 tablespoons dry red wine
6 oz. moist desiccated coconut (optional)

THIS is a fussy casserole that you might not tackle for an ordinary family dinner, but it is delicious beyond words, and is a wonderful party dish, especially since it can be put together except for the last step even a day ahead.

1. Spread out the cubes of veal on waxed paper and brush all of them with gravy browning, using a pastry brush.

2. Heat the butter in a heavy frying-pan and brown the veal on all sides, a few pieces at a time so as not to crowd the pan. Transfer the pieces to a good-sized casserole as they are browned.

3. In the fat remaining in the pan lightly sauté the onions and mushrooms and spread them over the meat in the casserole.

4. Add the ½ pt. liquid, sugar, vinegar, ginger, mustard, salt, and pepper to the frying-pan. Clean out all the brown particles and pour over the casserole.

5. Cover and bake 1 hour in a 325° oven, or until the meat is very tender.

6. Mix the cornflour with the tablespoon of water and stir in.

7. Add the wine and coconut, and bake 10–15 minutes longer. Serves 5–6, but can be doubled or tripled.

Serve with lots of hot fluffy rice and a salad made of cold cooked vegetables: peas, sweet corn, butter beans, runner beans, asparagus, etc.

CÔTES DE VEAU FOYOT

4 veal cutlets
1 medium onion chopped
3 tablespoons butter or margarine
3 tablespoons dry white wine
3 tablespoons chicken broth

Salt and pepper
1 oz. each (scant) Parmesan and
  Gruyère cheese, grated
Bread or cornflake crumbs

THIS is an adaptation of a classic French dish, from a famous restaurant.

1. Cook the onion slowly in butter until golden. Stir in the wine and chicken broth.

2. Season the veal with salt and pepper. Mix the grated cheeses and roll the chops first in the cheese and then in the crumbs.

3. Put a thin layer of crumbs in a shallow casserole. Lay the cutlets on them and cover with the cooked onion and their liquid. Cook uncovered in a very slow oven, 275°, about an hour, adding a bit of chicken broth occasionally. Serves 4.

Serve with fluffy mashed potatoes and buttered baby green peas.

HUNGARIAN VEAL

1½ lbs. veal fillet cut in 1-inch pieces
1¼ oz. flour
2 tablespoons butter, margarine or salad
  oil
1 clove garlic crushed
2 tablespoons minced onion

1 tablespoon chopped parsley
½ teaspoon salt
½ teaspoon paprika
¼ teaspoon celery salt
½ pt. chicken stock
¼ pt. sour cream

ROLL or shake the veal pieces in flour and brown well in butter in a heavy frying-pan. Add the garlic and onion while the veal is browning. Stir in remaining ingredients except sour cream and pour into a medium casserole. Cover and bake 45–50 minutes in a slow oven, 325°.

Just before serving stir in the sour cream and reheat. Serves 4.

Serve with buttered noodles to which you have added poppy seeds and split almonds. For a vegetable, slice unpeeled courgettes and sauté gently, with a bit of minced onion, in a covered frying-pan, until tender but still crisp, 10–12 minutes.

HUNGARIAN VEAL ROLLS

8 veal cutlets about 5″ × 2½″ × ¼″
¼ lb. lean beef ground
¼ lb. lean pork ground
2 tablespoons bread or cornflake crumbs
3 tablespoons thin cream
1 egg
1½ teaspoons salt
¼ teaspoon pepper
1 tablespoon minced onion

3 tablespoons minced parsley
2 tablespoons butter, margarine, or salad
  oil
4-oz. tin sliced mushrooms
½ pt. condensed consommé and red or
  white wine mixed
6 fluid oz. sour cream
1 teaspoon sugar
1 teaspoon Worcestershire sauce

THIS looks like a lot of ingredients, but is actually an easy casserole to make and an especially good one.

1. Mix the ground beef and pork with the crumbs, thin cream, egg, salt and pepper, onion, and parsley.
2. Trim the cutlets, pounding them between sheets of waxed paper if more than ¼ inch thick.
3. Divide the ground meat mixture among them, roll up, and skewer with toothpicks or tie with twine.
4. Heat the butter in a heavy frying-pan and brown the rolls well. Transfer them to a medium casserole, stir in mushrooms and their liquid, as well as the consommé mixture, cover, and bake 45 minutes in a 325° oven. Remove the cover 15 minutes before the time is up.
5. Remove the rolls from the casserole and unskewer or untie them.
6. Before returning them to the casserole stir into the sauce the sour cream, sugar, and Worcestershire sauce. Reheat. Serves 4.

Serve with buttered noodles to which a tablespoon of poppy seeds have been added, and buttered runner beans.

ROQUEFORT VEAL BIRDS

1½ lbs. veal fillet ¼ inch thick
4 oz. butter or margarine
1 tablespoon minced onion
3 oz. dry bread or cornflake crumbs
1 teaspoon minced parsley
½ teaspoon dried oregano or 1½
  teaspoons fresh, chopped
½ teaspoon dried basil or 1½ teaspoons
  fresh, chopped

½ teaspoon salt
⅛ teaspoon pepper
4 tablespoons finely crumbled Roquefort
  or other blue cheese
3 tablespoons flour
2 tablespoons paprika
½ medium green pepper coarsely chopped
3½-oz. tin sliced mushrooms
¼ pt. chicken broth or water

THERE are many ways of making veal birds. This one, with its delicate blue cheese flavour, is quite unusual.

1. Cut the veal into 6 pieces, about 5 by 3 inches. However, if it has been sliced more than ¼ inch thick, cut it a little smaller, lay the pieces between sheets of waxed paper, and pound them thinner, using a wooden mallet or a rolling pin.

2. Heat half the butter in a frying-pan and cook the onion just until it begins to colour, stirring frequently.

3. Stir in the crumbs, herbs, salt, pepper, and cheese, mixing well.

4. Lay out the pieces of veal and divide the crumb mixture among them, placing it towards one end. Roll up and tie with twine or fasten with toothpicks.

5. Dredge the rolls with flour and brown in the rest of the butter. Arrange in a casserole large enough to take them in one layer but not too deep.

6. Sprinkle with paprika and spread the green pepper and mushrooms on top.

7. Clean out the frying-pan with the chicken broth, and pour over the rolls. Cover and bake 45 minutes in a 350° oven. Serves 6.

Serve with herb-flavoured rice and cole slaw.

TARRAGON VEAL

4 lbs. shoulder veal cut in 1-inch cubes
2 oz. butter or margarine, or 3 tablespoons
  salad oil
2 oz. flour
12 fluid oz. dry white wine
¾ pt. boiling water
2 teaspoons salt
¼ lb. sliced mushrooms lightly sautéed

4 teaspoons dried tarragon or 4
  tablespoons fresh, chopped
2 medium onions chopped
4 egg yolks
8 fluid oz. sour cream
4 tablespoons tarragon vinegar
2 oz. chopped parsley

A HEARTY dish for a buffet meal.

1. Melt butter in a large heavy frying-pan and brown the meat cubes, removing them as they brown, and being careful not to fill the pan too full at a time. Return all the meat to the pan when the last pieces are browned.

2. Sprinkle the flour over, stir well, and when the flour is all absorbed add the wine and water slowly, stirring constantly.

3. Add the salt, mushrooms, tarragon, and onions, cook a moment, and transfer to a large heavy casserole. Cover tightly and bake 2 hours in a slow oven, 275°.

4. Mix the egg yolks with the sour cream. Remove the casserole from the oven briefly and stir in the sour cream mixture and the vinegar.

5. Return to the oven for 5–10 minutes, uncovered, long enough to thicken the sauce. Sprinkle with parsley just before serving. Serves 10–12.

Serve with lots of fluffy hot rice, a large salad with grated carrot, tomato wedges, sliced unpeeled cucumbers, and a sliced avocado, plus greens. Have plenty of warm French bread available.

SAVOURY VEAL

4 lbs. veal cut in 2-inch cubes
$2\frac{1}{2}$ oz. flour
2 teaspoons salt
$\frac{1}{2}$ teaspoon fresh-ground pepper
3–6 tablespoons salad oil
2 large onions chopped
4 medium carrots diced
4 sticks celery cut in diagonal
    $\frac{1}{4}$-inch slices

Bouquet garni
$\frac{3}{4}$ pt. chicken broth
4 fluid oz. dry white wine
4 medium tomatoes skinned and chopped
    or 1 tin Italian-style
1 large clove garlic crushed
2 tablespoons chopped parsley
2 teaspoons grated lemon rind
2 tablespoons lemon juice

This big hearty casserole is a good choice for a buffet dinner.

1. Shake the veal pieces in a paper bag in which you have put the flour, salt, and pepper— a few pieces at a time.

2. Heat half the oil to sizzling in a heavy frying-pan and brown the meat, being careful not to crowd the pan too much at a time. Add more oil as you need it. Arrange the meat in a large casserole.

3. In the same pan sauté lightly the onions, carrots, and celery, and spread them over the meat.

4. Add to the frying-pan the *bouquet garni*, chicken broth, wine, tomatoes, and garlic. Let cook 2–3 minutes and pour over the meat.

5. Cover the casserole and bake $1\frac{3}{4}$ hours in a slow oven, 300°. Uncover the last 20 minutes. About halfway through, check the seasoning and stir.

6. Just before serving stir in the parsley, lemon rind and lemon juice and remove the *bouquet garni*. Serves 10–12.

Serve with plenty of fluffy rice to absorb the good sauce, a dressed green salad, and warm French bread.

VEAL CUTLETS WITH COINTREAU

2 lbs. veal cutlets
    Salt and pepper
2 tablespoons butter, margarine, or salad
    oil

1 tablespoon flour
$\frac{1}{2}$ pt. chicken broth
4 teaspoons Cointreau liqueur
1 tablespoon lemon juice

The Cointreau here performs real magic on the veal.

1. Divide the cutlets into 6 pieces. They should be quite thin, and can be made so by laying the pieces between sheets of waxed paper and pounding them with a wooden mallet or a rolling pin.

2. Season the cutlets and brown them quickly in sizzling fat in a heavy frying-pan. Lay them in a shallow casserole.

3. Stir the flour into the fat left in the pan and brown it lightly. Slowly stir in the chicken broth, Cointreau, and lemon juice. Check seasoning and pour over cutlets.

4. Bake 20 minutes in a 350° oven. Serves 6.

Serve with a rice casserole (see Index), green peas, and a dressed green salad.

VEAL CASSEROLE WITH WHITE WINE

2 lbs. veal fillet cut in strips 2″ × ½″
1 tablespoon salad oil
3 tablespoons butter or margarine
1 tablespoon flour
¾ teaspoon salt
⅛ teaspoon pepper

½ pt. chicken broth
½ pt. dry white wine
2 dozen little white onions, or 1-lb. tin
1 small bay leaf
2 oz. minced parsley
½ lb. small whole mushrooms

1. Heat the oil and 1 tablespoon of the butter in a heavy frying-pan and brown the meat strips well in it. Skim the pieces out with a slotted spoon and arrange them in a medium casserole.
2. Blend the flour into the butter remaining in the casserole, stir in the salt, pepper, and chicken broth, and keep stirring until the sauce is thick and smooth.
3. Add the wine, onions (if raw), bay leaf, and parsley, season to taste, and pour over the casserole.
4. Cover and bake in a 325° oven one hour, or until the meat is very tender. (If you use the tinned little white onions add them about halfway through the cooking.)
5. Melt the rest of the butter in the frying-pan and gently sauté the mushrooms. Stir them into the casserole about 15 minutes before you are ready to serve. Serves 6.

VEAL CHOPS IN CREAM

6 veal chops 1 inch thick
3 tablespoons butter
3 tablespoons warmed brandy (optional)
6 oz. sliced mushrooms
1 tablespoon flour
½ pt. chicken broth or water
1 teaspoon meat glaze

½ pt. thick cream
Salt and pepper
1 small bay leaf
¼ teaspoon dried thyme or ¾ teaspoon fresh
Parmesan cheese
Butter or margarine

1. Brown the chops quickly in hot butter, pour over them the barely warmed brandy, and flame them. (Or light the brandy before you pour it, pouring it flaming.) Arrange the chops in a shallow casserole.
2. In the fat left in the frying-pan sauté the mushrooms lightly. Sprinkle with flour, and gradually add the chicken broth and glaze. Let it come to a boil.
3. Stir in the cream, salt and pepper to taste, bay leaf, and thyme.
4. Pour over the meat in the casserole, cover, and bake in a slow oven, 300°, 1 hour.
5. Sprinkle with Parmesan cheese, dot with butter, and brown under the grill. Serves 6.

Serve with fluffy mashed potatoes and buttered green peas.

VEAL MARENGO

2½ lbs. veal shoulder cut in 1½-inch cubes
3 tablespoons flour
1½ teaspoons salt
2 tablespoons salad oil
2 tablespoons minced onion
6 small white onions
1 clove garlic crushed
20-oz. tin tomatoes, drained

½ pt. chicken broth
½ pt. dry white wine
¼ teaspoon pepper
12 mushroom caps lightly sautéed in
   butter
¼ pt. thick cream or sour cream
1 tablespoon flour
2 tablespoons water

1. Put 3 tablespoons of flour and the salt in a paper bag and shake the veal pieces in it. Brown them on all sides in hot oil and arrange in a good-sized casserole.
2. In the fat remaining in the frying-pan lightly brown the minced onion, the whole onions, and the garlic. Stir in the tomatoes, chicken broth, wine, and pepper. Bring to a boil and pour over the casserole.
3. Cover and bake 1½ hours in a 300° oven.
4. Stir in the sautéed mushroom caps and bake 20–25 minutes longer.
5. Stir in the cream. Transfer the casserole to the top of the stove, over low heat.
6. Mix the 1 tablespoon of flour and water into a paste and stir in to thicken the sauce. Serves 8.

Serve with plain spaghetti mixed with grated cheese and a large green salad mixed with grated carrots and sliced unpeeled cucumber. Warm French bread goes well with this meal.

VEAL ROLLS WITH ANCHOVIES

1 lb. veal cutlets cut as thin as possible
¼ lb. Mozzarella cheese
2-oz. tin anchovy fillets

4 oz. butter
¼ pt. condensed consommé
1 teaspoon chopped parsley

1. Cut the veal into 3″ × 5″ pieces, lay between sheets of waxed paper, and pound thinner with a wooden mallet or a rolling pin.
2. Cut the cheese into as many pieces as you have veal pieces. On each veal piece lay a piece of cheese and an anchovy fillet. Roll up and tie with a string or fasten with toothpicks.
3. Heat half the butter in a heavy frying-pan and brown the rolls lightly in it. Add 2 tablespoons consommé and let the rolls simmer in it about 10 minutes. Arrange in a shallow casserole.
4. Add remaining butter to the skillet and remaining consommé, bring to a boil, and pour over the veal rolls.
5. Bake, uncovered, about 15 minutes in a 325° oven. Serves 4.

Serve with buttered noodles and broccoli with a butter-lemon-crumb sauce.

VEAL CHOPS WITH NOODLES

4 veal chops 1 inch thick
1 egg beaten a little with 1 tablespoon
  water
  Bread or cornflake crumbs

2 oz. butter or margarine, or 3 tablespoons
  salad oil
  Cream sauce
12 oz. hot buttered green noodles
  6 tablespoons grated Parmesan cheese

Cream Sauce

6 tablespoons butter
4 tablespoons flour
1 pt. milk scalded

3 egg yolks lightly beaten
6 tablespoons thick cream whipped

1. With a sharp knife cut the bones from the chops. Lay the meat between sheets of waxed paper and pound to $\frac{1}{8}$-inch thickness with a wooden mallet or a rolling pin.
2. Dip the chops in the egg and then in the crumbs. Cook them to a golden brown in sizzling butter in a heavy frying-pan. They should be very tender.
3. To make the cream sauce, melt the butter, stir in the flour, and gradually add the scalded milk. Season to taste. When the sauce is thick and smooth remove it from the heat and stir in the egg yolks and whipped cream.
4. Spread the cooked noodles in a large casserole. Lay the chops on top and cover with the cream sauce.
5. Top with cheese and grill until well browned. Serves 4.

VEAL SCALOPPINI

1½ lbs. veal fillet
3 oz. grated cheese
3 tablespoons flour
⅛ teaspoon pepper

¼ teaspoon dried marjoram or ¾ teaspoon
  fresh, chopped
4 tablespoons salad oil
¾ pt. condensed consommé

1. Cut the meat into 8 pieces, lay them between sheets of waxed paper, and pound very thin with a wooden mallet or rolling pin.
2. Mix in a large soup plate half the cheese, the flour, the marjoram, and the pepper (salt is usually unnecessary). Coat the veal pieces with the mixture as heavily as you can.
3. Heat the oil in a heavy frying-pan and sauté the veal pieces to a golden brown on both sides, a few at a time.
4. Arrange in a casserole, in 2 layers, and pour over the consommé. Cover and bake 15 minutes in a 325° oven.
5. Sprinkle the casserole with the remaining cheese and put under the grill until well browned, watching carefully to avoid burning. Serves 4.

Serve with spinach noodles and buttered baby carrots.

VEAL MAYACAMAS

1 lb. veal fillet cut ½-inch thick
1-lb. slice ready-to-eat ham ½ inch thick
½ pt. rosé or white wine
2 oz. butter or margarine, or 3 tablespoons
  salad oil
4 carrots cut in 1-inch rounds

¼ lb. mushrooms sliced
2 tablespoons capers
2-oz. tin anchovy fillets
  drained and halved
½ teaspoon rosemary and oregano mixed
½ pt. sour cream

1. Cut the veal in 1-inch squares. Trim fat from the ham and cut it into strips 1½ inches by ½ inch. Put both in a bowl, pour the wine over, and let them marinate at least 1 hour. Drain and save the marinade.
2. Heat the butter in a heavy frying-pan and brown both meats lightly.
3. Add the marinade, carrots, mushrooms, capers, and anchovies, stirring gently.
4. Pour into a medium casserole, sprinkle the herb mixture on top, and bake, uncovered, in a 300° oven 30 minutes.
5. Pour the liquid from the casserole into a saucepan, blend in the sour cream, and thicken with a flour-and-water paste if you so desire. Pour back on the casserole. Serves 6.

VEAL SCALOPPINI WITH SOUR CREAM AND WINE

2 lbs. veal cutlets
3 tablespoons flour
1 teaspoon salt
⅛ teaspoon pepper
2 oz. butter, margarine, or 3 tablespoons
  salad oil
2 medium onions chopped

½ lb. coarsely chopped mushrooms
1 teaspoon dried marjoram or 1 tablespoon
  fresh, chopped
½ pt. dry white wine
½ pt. sour cream
Chopped parsley

1. Cut the veal into small serving portions, lay them between sheets of waxed paper, and pound very thin with a wooden mallet or rolling pin. Shake them well, a few at a time, in a paper bag containing the flour, salt, and pepper. Save the leftover seasoned flour.
2. Heat butter in a heavy frying-pan and brown the veal pieces well on both sides. Arrange them in 2 or 3 layers in a medium casserole or a large shallow one.
3. In the fat remaining in the pan cook the onion and mushrooms until the onion takes on some colour and the mushrooms begin to look transparent. Add to the casserole, with the marjoram.
4. Add the wine, cover, and bake in a 325° oven 25–30 minutes, or until veal is very tender.
5. Remove the casserole from the oven and drain the sauce into a saucepan. Mix the reserved flour with a little water and thicken the sauce. Stir in the sour cream and pour back over the casserole. Reheat to the bubbling point and sprinkle with parsley. Serves 6.

Serve with hot fluffy rice, a salad of cold cooked vegetables (peas, sweet corn, carrots, beans, and torn-up lettuce mixed with mayonnaise thinned out considerably with French dressing), and warm French bread.

VEAL SWEETBREAD CASSEROLE

2 pairs sweetbreads
1 teaspoon salt (scant)
3 tablespoons lemon juice (scant)
1 oz. flour
3 tablespoons butter or margarine
2 small onions minced
2 slices bacon diced
4 oz. coarsely chopped mushrooms

2 small carrots diced in ¼-inch pieces
½ teaspoon dried thyme or 1½ teaspoons
  fresh, chopped
½ small bay leaf
1 tablespoon tomato purée
¼ pt sherry
¼ pt boiling water
¼ pt condensed **cream** of mushroom soup

IF you like sweetbreads there are few greater delicacies, and this recipe brings out all their flavour.

1. Soak the sweetbreads 1 hour in cold water just as soon as you get them home. Cover with boiling water, add the salt and lemon juice, and simmer 12–15 minutes. Plunge them at once into very cold water and when they are cold remove all gristle and membrane. After this you can refrigerate them and prepare the casserole at your convenience.

2. Slice each sweetbread in half lengthwise, roll in flour, and brown delicately in sizzling butter. Lift out and set aside.

3. In the fat remaining in the frying-pan sauté lightly the onions and bacon. Add the mushrooms and cook 2–3 minutes longer. Stir in the carrots, thyme, and bay leaf. Pour into a small casserole and lay the sweetbreads on top.

4. In the same pan mix the tomato purée, sherry, boiling water, and soup and pour over the sweetbreads. Bake 15–20 minutes in a 350° oven. If you like, sprinkle the top with 2 tablespoons of buttered crumbs before baking. Serves 4.

Serve with fluffy mashed potatoes and buttered baby green peas.

VEAL SCALLOPS ALMONDINE

2½ lbs. veal cutlets
4 tablespoons flour
1 teaspoon salt
6 tablespoons salad oil
2 tablespoons butter or margarine
2 large onions sliced thin

⅛ teaspoon thyme
½ bay leaf crushed
6 fluid oz. dry sherry
½ pt. chicken broth
1 teaspoon minced parsley
3 oz. toasted split almonds

1. Cut the veal into 12 portions, and pound very thin between sheets of waxed paper. Shake the pieces in a paper bag containing flour and salt.

2. Sauté in hot oil until brown on both sides. Arrange in a casserole.

3. Heat the butter in a frying-pan and sauté the onions until they have just begun to colour. Add to the casserole.

4. Add thyme, bay leaf, sherry, and chicken broth. Cover and bake in a 325° oven about 45 minutes, or until the veal is very tender.

5. Scatter almonds and parsley on top before serving. Or, if you prefer, drain off the liquid into a saucepan, thicken it somewhat with flour-and-water paste, stir in the almonds, and pour back over the meat; scatter parsley on top. Serves 6.

Serve with plain spaghetti mixed with plenty of grated cheese and French beans.

NOTES

POULTRY

CHICKEN

BAKED CHICKEN BREASTS DE LUXE

3 chicken breasts boned and halved
2 tablespoons butter or margarine
3 tablespoons brandy slightly warmed
  (optional)
1 tablespoon minced shallots or 2
  teaspoons minced onion
4 oz. toasted split almonds

1 tablespoon tomato purée
2 tablespoons flour
¼ pt. chicken broth
6 fluid oz. dry white wine
1 teaspoon dried tarragon or 1 tablespoon
  fresh, chopped
Salt and pepper

THIS is a truly de luxe dish, and not difficult to make. It is improved by being flambéed in brandy, but this is not indispensable.

1. It is surprisingly easy to bone chicken breasts yourself if you have a sharp knife, but the butcher can easily do it. Flatten the boned breasts with the flat side of a cleaver or a rolling pin, and brown them in 1 tablespoon of the butter, in a heavy frying-pan.

2. Pour over them the warmed brandy and ignite (or ignite the brandy and pour it over flaming). When the flames die down arrange the chicken breasts in a shallow casserole.

3. Add the remaining butter to the pan and lightly sauté the shallots. Add 3 oz. of the almonds and slowly stir in the tomato purée and flour.

4. Gradually stir in the chicken stock and wine, and when the sauce is smooth and velvety add the tarragon. Season to taste and pour over the chicken in the casserole.

5. Cover and bake in a 325° oven 35–40 minutes, or until the chicken is very tender. Scatter the remaining almonds on top. Serves 6.

Serve with fluffy mashed potatoes, buttered baby green peas, a plain green salad, and warm French bread.

REGENCY CHICKEN BREASTS

3 chicken breasts halved and preferably
   boned
4 tablespoons butter or margarine
3 tablespoons Cointreau liqueur
3 tablespoons brandy

Salt and pepper
½ lb. mushrooms sliced
1 tiny tin truffles chopped (optional)
¾ pt. thick cream whipped
2 tablespoons grated Parmesan cheese

HERE is a true gourmet dish, with its truffles, cream, and liqueurs.
1. Heat 2 tablespoons butter to sizzling in a heavy frying-pan and brown the chicken breasts on both sides. Arrange in a large shallow casserole and season to taste.
2. Flambé the chicken with the Cointreau and brandy mixed in a small saucepan and slightly warmed. When the flames die down cover the casserole and bake about 30 minutes in a 375° oven, or until chicken is tender.
3. Add the remaining 2 tablespoons butter to the frying-pan and lightly sauté the mushrooms. Stir in the truffles and whipped cream and heat almost to boiling point, stirring constantly.
4. Pour over the chicken breasts, sprinkle with cheese, and brown under the grill. Serves 6.

Serve with buttered noodles to which you have added generous amounts of poppy seeds and split toasted almonds, and a green salad with grated carrots, spring onions, and thin tomato wedges added. Warm French bread with toasted sesame seeds added to garlic butter is good with this.

CHICKEN BREASTS WITH BLACK CHERRIES

3 good-sized chicken breasts halved
3 tablespoons butter or margarine
½ pt. port wine
¼ pt. chicken broth

2 teaspoons meat glaze (e.g. Maggi)
1 teaspoon cornflour
6 oz. pitted black cherries

BLACK cherries make a party dish out of almost anything. Here they add greatly to both flavour and appearance.
1. Brown the breasts in sizzling butter in a large frying-pan and arrange them in a large casserole that will hold them in one layer, even though crowded. Cover and bake 20 minutes at 350°.
2. To the pan add the port, chicken broth, and meat glaze. Stir well and simmer 10 minutes.
3. Dissolve the cornflour in a little water, stir into the pan, and simmer until the sauce is clear, stirring constantly.
4. Add the cherries and pour over the chicken breasts.
5. Cover the casserole again and continue to bake 20 minutes longer. Serves 6.

Serve with creamed potatoes and asparagus with lemon-butter-crumb sauce.

CHICKEN BREASTS WITH KIRSCH

2 chicken breasts halved, boned, and
  skinned
  Salt
1½ tablespoons butter or margarine

3 tablespoons cognac
3 tablespoons kirsch
¼ pt. thick cream
2 egg yolks

1. Salt the chicken breasts lightly and sauté them to a golden brown in sizzling butter.
2. Arrange them in a shallow casserole, cover, and bake 20 minutes in a 375° oven.
3. Mix the cognac and kirsch in a small saucepan and warm a little. Remove the chicken from the oven, ignite the liqueurs, and pour over the chicken. Let flame until flames die down.
4. Whip the cream until it begins to thicken. Add the egg yolks and beat a moment more, until well blended. Heat the mixture in a saucepan, stirring constantly. When it is hot, but not boiling, pour over the chicken breasts gently and continue to bake 15–20 minutes, or until the meat is very tender. Serves 4.

BREAST OF CAPON WITH WILD RICE

Breast of 5–6 lb. roasting capon cut in
  two and skinned
8 oz. wild rice
1½ pts. boiling water
  Salt
3 tablespoons butter or margarine

¼ lb. mushrooms sliced
¾ pt. thick cream
3 tablespoons dry sherry
1 tablespoon brandy
¼ pt. Hollandaise sauce
  (tinned will do)

1. Wash the wild rice in several waters and cook in the boiling water and salt for 30–40 minutes, or until tender. Drain it and let it dry out 10 minutes or so over very low heat.
2. With a sharp knife slice the two halves of the capon breast in two and brown them in butter slowly until a golden brown. Salt lightly and remove to a plate for a few minutes.
3. In the fat remaining in the frying-pan cook the mushrooms 2–3 minutes over low heat. Reserve ¼ of the cream and stir the rest of the cream, the sherry, and the brandy into the mushrooms.
4. Blend well, replace the chicken breasts, and simmer over the lowest possible heat, covered, until the chicken is tender and the sauce thickened. Season to taste and keep warm on an asbestos mat.
5. In a well-greased shallow casserole spread out the rice. Lay the chicken breasts on top, and cover with the mushroom sauce.
6. Whip the remaining cream, blend it with the Hollandaise sauce, and spread smoothly over the casserole.
7. Brown well under the grill. Serves 4.

BALTIMORE CHICKEN WITH CRABMEAT

6 oz. cooked chicken diced (or 6-oz. tin)
6 oz. cooked crabmeat flaked coarsely (or 6½-oz. tin)
1 tin condensed cream of mushroom soup
1 tin condensed cream of chicken soup
¼ pt. top milk

1 tablespoon grated onion
½ teaspoon paprika
4 oz. mushrooms sliced and lightly sautéed (or tinned)
2 oz. buttered bread or cornflake crumbs

1. In a saucepan mix the two soups, the milk, onion, and paprika, and heat to just under boiling. Stir in the chicken, crabmeat, and mushrooms and blend well.

2. Pour into a medium casserole, top with buttered crumbs, and bake 15 minutes in a 325° oven, or until brown and bubbly. Serves 4.

Serve with fresh hot rice to take up the sauce. Buttered green peas and a dressed green salad complete the meal.

BRANDIED CHICKEN

2 tender young chickens, cut up
Salt and pepper
¼ lb. butter melted
6 tablespoons brandy
5 medium shallots minced
1 tablespoon chopped parsley

1 teaspoon fresh chopped tarragon or ¼ teaspoon dried
¼ pt. dry white wine
4 tablespoons Cointreau liqueur
¼ pt. thick cream

1. Season the chicken pieces well and brown them lightly all over in sizzling butter in a large frying-pan.

2. Warm 4 tablespoons of the brandy in a small saucepan, pour over the chicken, ignite, and let it burn off. (Or ignite the brandy in the saucepan and pour flaming over the chicken.) Arrange the chicken in a large casserole.

3. To the fat remaining in the pan add the shallots, parsley, and tarragon, cooking briefly.

4. Add the remaining 2 tablespoons brandy, the wine, and the Cointreau. Blend well and stir in the cream.

5. Pour over the chicken, cover the casserole, and bake 45 minutes in a 375° oven. Serves 6–7.

Serve with riced potatoes and asparagus spears with lemon-butter-crumb sauce, a green salad, and warm French bread.

CHICKEN ALMONDINE

1½–2 lbs. cooked chicken diced	1 clove
2 tablespoons butter or margarine	1 small bay leaf
1 tablespoon flour	3 oz. toasted split almonds
½ pt. top milk	3 egg yolks
Salt and pepper	3 tablespoons thick cream
1 tablespoon minced onion	3 tablespoons dry sherry
¼ pt. dry white wine	1 tablespoon Angostura bitters
½ pt. chicken broth	2 tablespoons bread or cornflake crumbs

1. Make a white sauce of 1 tablespoon of the butter, the flour, and the milk. Season to taste.
2. Lightly sauté the onion in ½ teaspoon of butter.
3. Stir in the white sauce, wine, chicken broth, clove, and bay leaf. Simmer about 5 minutes and stir in the chicken and almonds.
4. Mix the egg yolks with the cream, sherry and Angostura bitters. Blend well, stir into the chicken mixture, and pour into a medium casserole.
5. Melt the remaining butter, stir in the crumbs, and sprinkle on top of the casserole.
6. Bake 15 minutes in a 325° oven, uncovered, and brown under the grill. Serves 10.

Serve with plenty of hot fluffy rice to absorb the wonderful sauce, buttered baby carrots, and a green salad.

CHICKEN WITH AVOCADO

3-lb. young chicken cut up	Salt and pepper
1 large avocado peeled and sliced	½ teaspoon chili powder
4 tablespoons butter, margarine, or salad oil	Dash cinnamon
2 small onions chopped	1 tablespoon flour
1 chicken bouillon cube or 1 teaspoon chicken stock base	½ pt. orange juice (or ¼ pt. and ¼ pt. dry white wine)
	2 tablespoons grated orange rind

THE avocado here makes this a real party dish. The recipe can be doubled easily, still using just the one large avocado.
1. Brown the chicken in 3 tablespoons of butter in a large frying-pan and arrange in a large casserole.
2. In the fat remaining in the pan lightly sauté the onions.
3. Stir in the bouillon cube, mashed, seasoning to taste, chili powder, and cinnamon.
4. Spread over the chicken, cover the casserole, and bake 20 minutes in a 350° oven.
5. Heat the remaining fat in the same pan, stir in the flour and cook until smooth and lightly browned.
6. Blend in the orange juice or mixture of orange juice and wine. When smooth and some-what thickened pour over the chicken in the casserole, cover, and bake 25 minutes longer.
7. Check seasoning, cover entire top with avocado slices, salt very lightly, and bake 10 minutes longer, uncovered.
8. Sprinkle the top with the grated orange rind before serving. Serves 4.

Serve with riced potatoes and fresh corn on the cob (in season) or buttered sweet corn.

CHICKEN CACCIATORE À LA FRED HARVEY

2 young chickens (about 2½ lbs. each) cut in quarters
1 medium onion sliced
½ lb. fresh mushrooms sliced
2½ oz. flour
1 teaspoon salt
⅛ teaspoon pepper

2 oz. butter or margarine, or 3 tablespoons salad oil
1 clove garlic minced
12 pitted ripe olives
1 tin tomato purée or 1 6-oz. tin of tomatoes
¼ pt. dry red wine or sherry

Put the flour, salt, and pepper in a paper bag and shake the chicken quarters in it. Sauté in hot fat until well browned. Arrange the chicken pieces in a large casserole. Mix the remaining ingredients and pour over them. Cover and bake 30–40 minutes in a 375° oven. Serves 4.

Serve with buttered broccoli and a hearty green salad. If you want something to soak up the wonderful sauce serve with fresh hot rice or buttered noodles.

CHICKEN CASSEROLE WITH HERBS

4-lb. young chicken cut up (or two 2½-lb. ones)
2 tablespoons salad oil
2 tablespoons butter or margarine
6 tablespoons flour
1⅛ pt. milk scalded
2½ teaspoons salt

⅛ teaspoon pepper
¾ teaspoon dried thyme or 1 tablespoon fresh, chopped
¾ teaspoon dried tarragon or basil or 1 tablespoon fresh, chopped
3 tablespoons dry white wine

1. Cook the chicken in sizzling oil in a frying-pan until it is golden all over. Lay the pieces in a large shallow casserole.

2. Add the butter to the oil left in the pan and blend in the flour. Add a bit more butter if necessary to absorb the flour.

3. Stir in the milk, salt and pepper, and herbs, stirring until the sauce is smooth and thick.

4. Thin it out somewhat with the wine, pour over the chicken, and bake about 1 hour, or until the chicken is tender, in a 325° oven. Serves 6.

Serve with fresh hot rice, buttered green peas with a couple of fresh mushrooms chopped and sautéed stirred in, and French bread.

CHICKEN CASSEROLE WITH WALNUTS

1 lb. cooked chicken cut in large pieces
12 oz. cooked rice
4 oz. stuffed olives coarsely chopped
4 oz. coarsely broken walnuts
1 tin condensed cream of mushroom soup

½ pt. chicken broth or leftover chicken
  gravy thinned a bit
1 teaspoon parsley chopped
2 tablespoons grated Parmesan cheese

1. Mix the rice, olives, nuts, and chicken in a bowl.

2. In another bowl mix the soup, chicken broth, and parsley.

3. In a medium casserole spread half the chicken mixture, half the sauce, and repeat the layers.

4. Top with grated cheese and bake, uncovered, 30 minutes in a 350° oven. Serves 6.

Serve with riced potatoes and buttered runner beans.

CHICKEN CONTINENTAL

2½–3-lb. young chicken cut up
3 tablespoons lime juice (2 limes)
3 tablespoons lemon juice (1 lemon)
4 tablespoons dry white wine
1 clove garlic crushed

1 teaspoon salt
¼ teaspoon dried tarragon or ¾ teaspoon
  fresh, chopped
⅛ teaspoon fresh-ground pepper
2 oz. butter or margarine

1. Put the chicken pieces in a bowl and pour over them a mixture of the lime and lemon juice, the wine, garlic, salt, tarragon, and pepper. Let them stand at room temperature half an hour or put them in the refrigerator for 2–3 hours. Stir occasionally.

2. Remove the chicken from the marinade (save it) and arrange the pieces in a shallow casserole. Crowd them as much as you please, but keep them on one layer.

3. Dot the chicken with the butter and bake, uncovered, 30–40 minutes in a 425° oven. Using a baster, baste with the reserved marinade every 10 minutes. When you serve (from the casserole, of course) pour some of the sauce over each serving. Serves 4.

Serve with fluffy mashed potatoes and corn on the cob—in season—or buttered sweet corn with chopped green pepper and chopped pimento.

SPECIAL CHICKEN CURRY

1 lb. cooked chicken (or turkey) diced large
1 lb. diced cooked ham
¼ lb. butter or margarine, or 6 tablespoons salad oil
4 oz. mushrooms sliced
4 tablespoons green and sweet red peppers chopped
1 medium onion minced

¾ pt. chicken or turkey broth
3 tablespoons flour
2 teaspoons curry powder (or to taste)
¾ pt. top milk
Salt and pepper
3 oz. split toasted almonds
2 oz. desiccated coconut

1. Melt 2 oz. of the butter in a large casserole and cook the mushrooms, peppers, and onion a few minutes, until the onion is transparent.

2. Stir in the broth and simmer gently a few minutes.

3. Blend the remaining butter with the flour and curry powder and slowly stir it into the casserole, continuing to stir until the sauce is velvety smooth and thickened. Add the milk and season to taste.

4. Stir in the chicken and ham and simmer, uncovered, over the lowest possible heat until almost boiling, stirring occasionally to prevent sticking.

5. Add the almonds and coconut just before serving. Serves 10–12.

Serve with plenty of flaky hot rice, a large green salad, and the usual curry accompaniments: chutney, fresh coconut, chopped salted peanuts, preserved or candied ginger, puppadums and Bombay duck (obtainable from most delicatessens and Indian stores).

CHICKEN (OR TURKEY) DIVAN WITH NUTS

Cooked sliced chicken
enough to serve 6
Cooked broccoli for 6
(2 packets frozen)
3 oz. sliced toasted Brazil nuts or almonds
2½ tablespoons butter or margarine

2½ tablespoons flour
1¼ pts. milk
1½ teaspoons salt
3 egg yolks slightly beaten
¼ teaspoon Tabasco sauce
4 tablespoons grated Parmesan cheese

1. Make a white sauce of the butter, flour, and milk, and season to taste. Stir until it is smooth and thick. Add a little to the egg yolks and blend back into the white sauce. Cook a minute or two more, but do not let it boil. Stir in the Tabasco and cheese.
2. Arrange the cooked broccoli on the bottom of a large but fairly shallow casserole (if you use fresh broccoli cut off a good part of the stems, chop them, and cook them for another day).
3. Pour a thin layer of the sauce on the broccoli and cover with half of the nuts.
4. Arrange the chicken slices on top in a thick layer, overlapping them. Cover with the rest of the sauce.
5. Bake the casserole 20 minutes in a 375° oven.
6. Sprinkle with the remaining nuts and bake 5 minutes longer.
7. Put under the grill for a moment to brown. Serves 6.

Serve with a salad of cold cooked vegetables (green peas, sweet corn, beans, diced carrots), thinly sliced raw mushrooms, and thinly sliced avocado, tossed with a head of lettuce cut rather small. Warm French bread goes well with this meal.

CHICKEN AND LOBSTER CASSEROLE

Cooked chicken slices enough to serve 4
Salt and pepper
2 egg yolks
½ lb. cooked lobster diced (tinned will do)
1½ tablespoons butter or margarine
1½ tablespoons flour

¾ pt. chicken broth (or ¼ dry white wine)
¼ pt. thick cream
3 oz. sliced mushrooms (tinned will do)
6 oz. cooked peas
2 oz. grated Parmesan cheese
Paprika

1. Melt the butter in a saucepan, stir in the flour, and slowly blend in the chicken broth, stirring until it is smooth and thickened. Season to taste and remove from heat.
2. Beat the egg yolks and half of the cream together lightly and stir into the sauce. Add the mushrooms, peas, and lobster.
3. Whip the remaining half of the cream and fold into sauce.
4. Lay the chicken slices in a large flat casserole, overlapping them a little, and pour the lobster sauce over.
5. Sprinkle with cheese and paprika, and bake about 15 minutes in a 325° oven, or until golden brown. Serves 4.

Serve with wild rice and buttered runner beans.

CHICKEN AND NOODLE CASSEROLE WITH MUSHROOMS

¾ lb. cooked chicken diced
¾ lb. mushrooms sliced
½ lb. medium noodles cooked
½ green pepper diced
6 oz. stuffed olives chopped

½ lb. Cheddar or Swiss cheese grated coarsely
2 hard-boiled eggs chopped
¾ pt. white sauce, well seasoned
Chopped parsley

THIS is a flavourful dish, especially easy when you have leftover chicken.

Stir all the ingredients except the parsley together in a large casserole, cover, and bake 1 hour at 325°. Remove the cover after ½ hour. Sprinkle with parsley before serving. Serves 8.

Serve with a green salad and a dish of mixed vegetables: sweet corn, green peas, runner beans, diced carrots, and chopped asparagus.

CHICKEN ÉLÉGANTE

1 lb. cooked chicken diced
2 oz. butter or margarine
1¼ oz. flour
1 tin condensed cream of chicken soup
2 oz. blue cheese, crumbled
½ teaspoon dried marjoram or 1½ teaspoons fresh, chopped

3 oz. grated Parmesan cheese
1 packet frozen broccoli cooked and chopped
½ pt. sour cream
1 oz. buttered bread or cornflake crumbs
Paprika
Salt and pepper

1. Melt the butter in a large saucepan, stir in the flour and cook a minute or two. Gradually stir in the soup, blue cheese, marjoram, half of the Parmesan cheese, and the chicken and broccoli. Heat to just under boiling, remove from the heat, and stir in the sour cream. Season to taste.

2. Pour into a casserole and top with the remaining Parmesan cheese mixed with the buttered crumbs.

3. Sprinkle with paprika and bake in a 350° oven 20 minutes, or until browned and bubbly. Serves 6.

Serve with fried rice, fresh asparagus with lemon-butter-crumb sauce, and a green salad.

CHICKEN-ALMOND PIE

1 lb. cooked chicken cut in good-sized
  pieces
1 oz. butter or margarine
1¼ oz. flour
½ pt. thin cream or top milk
  Salt and pepper
½ pt. chicken broth

¼ teaspoon dill
1 teaspoon chopped parsley
¼ lb. mushrooms sliced and sautéed (or
  4-oz. tin)
3 oz. toasted split almonds
  Pastry for 1-crust 9-inch pie

1. Make a white sauce of the butter, flour, and cream, and season to taste.
2. Stir in the chicken broth, dill, and parsley, and cook, stirring, until the sauce is velvety and thick.
3. Stir in the chicken, mushrooms, and almonds.
4. Pour into a deep pie plate and top with pastry, slashed to permit steam to escape. Bake in a 400° oven 25–30 minutes, until golden brown. Serves 5–6.

Serve with well-buttered baked potatoes and buttered runner beans. Serve a bowl of sour cream and chives to go with the baked potatoes.

CHICKEN PILAFF

3½-lb. young chicken cut up
12 oz. raw rice
 4 tablespoons salad oil
 1 large chopped onion
 ½ pt. thin cream
 1 tablespoon lemon juice

2 teaspoons salt
¼ teaspoon pepper
½ teaspoon ground allspice
¾ pt. chicken broth heated
1 green pepper seeded and sliced thin

PILAFFS are everyday fare throughout the Middle East, and we are tending to use them more in this country. This recipe is a slight modification of the usual type.
1. Cover the rice with water (don't rinse if it is prepared rice), bring to a boil, turn off heat, and let stand 15–20 minutes. Drain.
2. Heat the oil in a large heavy casserole and brown the chicken pieces in it. Stir in the onion before the chicken is finished.
3. Remove the larger chicken pieces for a moment and stir into the casserole the cream, lemon juice, salt, pepper, and allspice. Stir rapidly to prevent the cream from curdling.
4. Stir in the rice and hot chicken broth.
5. Put back the chicken pieces and lay the green pepper rings on top.
6. Cover and bake about 35 minutes in a 325° oven, or simmer gently on top of the stove about 25–30 minutes.
7. Check 2 or 3 times while cooking. Pilaff should be on the dry side, but you may have to add a little water or broth. Serves 4–6.

Serve with young courgettes, sliced and slowly sautéed in butter or margarine with a bit of onion.

CHICKEN AND OYSTER PIE

1½ lbs. cooked chicken, diced coarsely
½ pt. raw oysters, fresh or frozen
2 hard-boiled eggs, sliced
3 oz. minced celery
¾ pt. chicken broth

4 tablespoons flour
Salt and pepper
8 oz. biscuit crust pastry
1 tablespoon softened butter or salad oil

Biscuit Crust Pastry

8 oz. flour
½ teaspoon salt
1 teaspoon castor sugar

4 oz. butter
1–2 egg yolks
Cold water

1. In a medium casserole make alternate layers (2 each) of chicken, oysters, and eggs, scattering some of the celery on each layer.

2. Heat the chicken broth, but first mix a little of it with the flour and use to thicken the broth. Season to taste and pour over the casserole.

3. Make the biscuit crust pastry. Mix the dry ingredients, then cut in the butter. Rub lightly until the mixture looks like fine breadcrumbs. Dilute the egg yolk or yolks with a tablespoon of water and use to make the mixture into a stiff dough, adding a little more water only if necessary. Pat it out on a lightly floured board to a thickness of ⅓ inch. Cut out small rounds and lay them close together as a topping for the casserole. Spread with the softened butter or brush with oil.

4. Bake in a 425° oven 25 minutes or until the pastry is golden and the pie bubbly. Serves 6.

Serve with mixed vegetables and sliced ripe tomatoes spread with chopped chives and parsley mixed with French dressing.

CHICKEN RAPHAEL

2 2½-lb. young chickens cut up
1½ teaspoons salt
⅛ teaspoon pepper
2 tablespoons flour
4 oz. butter or margarine
1 small onion chopped

6 oz. sliced mushrooms
¼ pt. dry white wine
1 tablespoon lemon juice
½ pt. thin cream
¼ teaspoon grated nutmeg (scant)
1 tablespoon minced parsley

1. Mix the salt, pepper, and flour in a paper bag and shake the pieces of chicken in it. Sauté lightly in a heavy frying-pan in hot butter and arrange in a medium casserole, just large enough to hold them spread out.

2. In the fat remaining in the pan cook the onion and mushrooms for 3–4 minutes and add them to the casserole.

3. Clean out the frying-pan with the wine and pour that over the casserole.

4. Cover and bake 20 minutes in a 375° oven.

5. Mix the lemon juice, cream, nutmeg, and parsley, and pour this over the chicken, stirring it in as best you can. Cover again and bake 20 minutes longer. Remove cover the last 5 minutes. Serves 4.

Serve with fluffy mashed potatoes and buttered green peas.

CHICKEN AND RICE ALMONDINE

1 lb. cooked chicken diced
12 oz. raw rice
1¼ pts. chicken broth (or half dry white
   wine)
1 teaspoon saffron
1 tin pitted black cherries
2 oz. split almonds or 4 oz. whole
   almonds

2 oz. sultanas
½ teaspoon dried rosemary or 1½ teaspoons
   fresh, chopped
½ teaspoon dill
¼ pt. salad oil
4 small white onions sliced
   Salt and pepper
1 tablespoon chopped parsley

1. Put the rice, the chicken broth, and the saffron (which you can omit if you don't care for yellow rice) in the top of a double boiler and cook it over boiling water, without stirring, 30–35 minutes, or until it is flaky and all the liquid is absorbed.
2. Stir in the cherries, raisins, almonds, and herbs.
3. Heat the oil in a heavy casserole and slightly brown the onions.
4. Stir the chicken in, continue cooking for a minute or two, and then add the rice mixture.
5. Correct the seasoning and bake, covered, in a 350° oven about 20 minutes.
6. Sprinkle with parsley before serving. Serves 6.

Serve with grated beetroot, warm French bread, and a green salad.

CHICKEN AND RICE CURRY

1 lb. cooked white meat of chicken
   (generous)
¼ lb. butter or margarine
2 tablespoons flour
1¼ pts. top milk
   Salt and pepper

2 teaspoons curry powder
3 tablespoons dry sherry
10 oz. cooked rice
1 tablespoon minced parsley
   Grated Parmesan cheese

1. Slice chicken and cut the slices into squares about 1 by 1 inch.
2. Melt half the butter in a saucepan, blend in the flour, and gradually stir in the milk. Season to taste.
3. Melt the rest of the butter in a medium casserole and lightly sauté the chicken pieces.
4. Stir in the white sauce, curry powder, and sherry. Cook a moment and blend in the rice and parsley.
5. Top with cheese and brown under the grill. Serves 4.

Note: If you have made this casserole early and kept it in the refrigerator, let it come to room temperature and then bake it 10 minutes in a 350° oven before you grill it.

Serve with butter beans and buttered baby carrots.

CHICKEN AND SHRIMP WITH RICE

5-lb. roasting chicken cut up
1½ lbs. shrimps cooked, cleaned, and
shelled
8 oz. raw rice
1 medium onion sliced
1 medium carrot sliced thin

1½ quarts salted water
Salt and pepper
½ teaspoon dried dill or 1½ teaspoons
fresh
12 small white onions or 1 small tin boiled
1 lemon sliced thin

MANY good dishes combine chicken, shrimps, and rice, especially Spanish dishes.
1. Simmer the chicken pieces in a large saucepan with the onion, carrot, and the water, for
25–30 minutes, covered. Remove the chicken and strain the broth.
2. Skin the chicken pieces and arrange them in a large casserole, with the shrimps, a little
salt and pepper, and the dill. Add the dry rice, whole onions, and lemon slices.
3. Boil the broth hard to reduce it to ¾ pt. and pour over the casserole.
4. Cover and bake 40 minutes in a 350° oven, or until chicken is tender and rice has absorbed
all the broth. Stir a little with a long-tined fork to release steam. Serves 6.

Serve with mixed vegetables and a green salad.

CHICKEN STROGANOFF

2½–3-lb. young chicken cut up
1 oz. flour
1 teaspoon salt
⅛ teaspoon pepper
3 tablespoons butter, margarine, or salad
oil
1 medium onion chopped
1 clove garlic mashed

3 tablespoons lemon juice
½ pt. chicken broth
½ lb. mushrooms sliced and sautéed or
2 4-oz. tins
8-oz. packet medium noodles broken up
½ pt. sour cream
¼ teaspoon paprika

1. Coat the chicken pieces with the flour, salt, and pepper mixed and brown in hot butter.
Drain on paper towels and pour off any fat remaining in the frying-pan.
2. Mix in the pan the onion, garlic, lemon juice, chicken broth, and mushrooms (and their
liquid, if tinned). Cook 3–4 minutes.
3. Stir in the chicken, pour into a medium casserole, cover, and bake 30 minutes in a 325°
oven.
4. Stir in the uncooked noodles and bake 15 minutes longer, covered.
5. Just before serving stir in the sour cream and paprika and blend well. (Blending is easier
if you remove a few pieces of chicken while you do it.) Serves 4–5.

Serve with fluffy hot rice, tinned sweet corn with green peppers, and a green salad.

CHICKEN WITH SPAGHETTI AND NUTS

1 lb. chicken slices cut rather small
1 lb. thin spaghetti cooked
3 oz. split almonds
1 tin condensed cream of chicken soup
1 tin condensed cream of mushroom soup

6 fluid oz. thin cream
2 oz. grated Cheddar or Swiss cheese
1 pimento sliced thin
Paprika

HEAT together the soups, cream, and cheese. Mix in the spaghetti, nuts, and pimento. Stir in the chicken lightly. Spread in a medium casserole, sprinkle with paprika, and bake 20 minutes in a slow oven, 325°. Serves 6.

Serve with buttered green peas and a mixed salad.

CHICKEN TARRAGON

2 2½-lb. young chickens cut up, or 3 whole
  chicken breasts halved
2½ oz. flour
1 tablespoon salt
½ teaspoon pepper

4 oz. butter or margarine, or 6
  tablespoons salad oil
1 medium onion minced
1 teaspoon crushed dried tarragon or
  1 tablespoon fresh
8 fluid oz. white wine

1. Dredge the chicken pieces by shaking them in a paper bag containing the flour, salt, and pepper.

2. Heat the fat in a heavy frying-pan and cook the onion 3–4 minutes, until it is soft but not brown. Skim out and put in a large casserole.

3. In the same pan brown the chicken well and arrange in the casserole.

4. Sprinkle the tarragon evenly on the chicken and pour in the wine. Cover and bake about 45 minutes, or until chicken is tender, in a 350° oven.

5. If you like a thickened sauce, drain off the liquid from the casserole into a small saucepan and thicken it to your taste with flour-and-water paste. Season, and stir in a little sour cream if you like. Pour back over the chicken. Serves 6.

Serve with a rice casserole (see Index) and buttered broccoli.

COQ AU VIN

2 3-lb. young chickens cut up
2 teaspoons salt
¼ teaspoon ground cloves or allspice
¼ teaspoon pepper
2–3 tablespoons tarragon vinegar
½ lb. salt pork diced small
12 small white onions peeled
3 tablespoons brandy warmed
1 bottle dry red table wine

1 tablespoon sugar
¼ teaspoon dried thyme or oregano or
    ¾ teaspoon fresh, chopped
1 tablespoon minced celery leaves
8–10 baby carrots cooked barely tender
24 button mushrooms lightly sautéed in
    butter or 6-oz. tin
Chopped parsley

1. Use the backs, necks, wing tips, and giblets to make chicken broth for another time, and use only the better parts here. Rub them with a mixture of the salt, cloves, and pepper. Sprinkle with vinegar and let stand 20–30 minutes.
2. Melt the salt pork in a large heavy frying-pan. Brown the onions lightly in this fat and skim out both pork bits and onions, spreading them in a large casserole.
3. Brown the chicken pieces in the remaining fat and arrange them in the casserole.
4. Ignite the warmed brandy and pour it flaming over the chicken.
5. When the flames die down add the remaining ingredients to the casserole, except the mushrooms and parsley.
6. Cover the casserole and bake 1 hour in a 325° oven.
7. Add the mushrooms 15 minutes before the time is up.
8. Sprinkle with parsley before serving. Serves 8–10.

Serve with plenty of rice, buttered broccoli, and warm French bread. A green salad goes well, too.

CHICKEN TERIYAKI

3-lb. young chicken cut up
¼ pt. soy sauce
3 tablespoons dry white wine

2 tablespoons sugar
½ tablespoon ground ginger
1 small clove garlic crushed

THIS is a simple dish with outstanding flavour.
1. In a small bowl mix the soy sauce, wine, sugar, ginger, and garlic.
2. Put the chicken in a large bowl and pour the marinade over it. Let it marinate from 1 to 3 hours.
3. Remove the chicken pieces from the marinade and lay them in a large casserole.
4. Bake, uncovered, 1 hour in a 325° oven. Baste with the marinade every 15 minutes. Serves 4.

Serve with riced potatoes, glazed onions, and buttered asparagus.

CHINESE CHICKEN CASSEROLE

3-lb. chicken cut up
1 tablespoon salad oil
½ teaspoon salt
2 teaspoons ginger
1 tablespoon whisky
½ pt. boiling water
½ lb. mushrooms sliced

1 tin bamboo shoots
  (1 lb. 4 oz.)
4 spring onions cut in 1-inch pieces
1 tablespoon cornflour
2 teaspoons soy sauce
1 teaspoon sugar
3 tablespoons water

LIKE most Chinese dishes, this one is full of flavour and quite out of the ordinary.
1. Heat the oil in a large frying-pan and brown the chicken pieces well. (You may have to add a little more oil.) Sprinkle with salt and ginger and arrange in a casserole.
2. Sprinkle the whisky over them. Add the boiling water, cover the casserole, and bake 40 minutes in a 325° oven.
3. Drain the liquid from the casserole into a saucepan and to it add the bamboo shoots, mushrooms, and spring onions. Bring to a boil.
4. Blend the cornflour, soy sauce, sugar, and 3 tablespoons of water and stir this into the hot mixture. Cook until slightly thickened, stirring constantly, and pour over the chicken. Continue baking about 10 minutes. Serves 6.

Serve with plenty of fresh hot rice, creamed spinach, and a green salad.

CREAM OF CHICKEN MARENGO

4½-lb. chicken cut up
¼ lb. fresh mushrooms
3 tablespoons dry white wine
1 large onion quartered
2 cloves garlic cut up
2 oz. parsley sprigs
2½ oz. flour

1½ teaspoons salt
¼ teaspoon fresh-ground pepper
¼ teaspoon dried tarragon or ¾ teaspoon
  fresh
½ teaspoon dried rosemary or 1½
  teaspoons fresh
3 tablespoons butter or margarine

THIS delectable dish owes its texture and its ease of making to a blender.
1. Put in the blender the stems of the mushrooms, wine, onion, garlic, parsley, flour, salt, pepper, tarragon, and rosemary. Cover and blend on high speed 40 seconds. Stop two or three times to scrape the sides down if necessary.
2. Melt the butter in a large frying-pan and brown the chicken pieces on all sides. Arrange in a casserole with the mushroom caps.
3. Pour over the sauce from the blender. Cover and bake about 45 minutes in a 350° oven, stirring occasionally. Serves 5–6.

Serve with fluffy mashed potatoes, braised celery with split almonds, and buttered asparagus tips.

CREAMY CHICKEN HASH À LA LOUIS DIAT

1 lb. cooked chicken coarsely cut up
8 fluid oz. thin cream
2 teaspoons flour
½ teaspoon grated lemon rind
⅛ teaspoon mace (optional)

¼ teaspoon salt
⅛ teaspoon fresh-ground pepper
1 teaspoon grated onion
3 tablespoons grated Parmesan cheese

PUT in a frying-pan the chicken, cream and flour mixed, lemon rind, seasonings, and onion. Cook over low heat, stirring constantly, until thickened. Pour into a shallow casserole, sprinkle with Parmesan cheese, and brown 5 inches from the grill heat. Serves 4.

Serve with buttered noodles, green pepper squares cooked tender in butter, and a green salad.

GOURMET CHICKEN SAUTÉ

3–4 lb. young chicken cut up
  Salt and pepper
3 tablespoons butter or margarine
3 tablespoons brandy warmed

3 tablespoons Madeira wine
1 dozen small whole mushrooms or
  ½ dozen large, quartered
8 fluid oz. sweet or sour cream

THIS delicious casserole is surprisingly easy to make.

1. Season the chicken pieces with salt and pepper and brown them in sizzling butter in a heavy frying-pan. Lay them in a large casserole and bake in a 350° oven 45–50 minutes. Baste frequently with the butter left in the pan, adding a little more if necessary.

2. After the chicken has baked 20 minutes or so remove it from the oven, light the warmed brandy, and pour it flaming over the chicken. Return to the oven when the flames die down.

3. Ten minutes later pour the Madeira over the chicken, add the mushrooms, and continue to cook ten minutes longer.

4. Drain off the liquid into a saucepan at this point, stir in the cream, and when it is well blended and almost boiling pour back over the chicken. Continue to bake until chicken is very tender. Serves 5–6.

Serve with plenty of fluffy rice to absorb the wonderful sauce. Buttered little green peas, a green salad, and warm French bread will complete a fine meal.

INDIA CHICKEN WITH SESAME SEEDS

2 2½–3 lb. young chickens cut up
2½ oz. flour
2 teaspoons salt
¼ teaspoon fresh-ground pepper
1 teaspoon paprika
3 tablespoons butter, margarine, or salad oil

2 tablespoons brown sugar
½ teaspoon ground ginger
8 fluid oz. red wine (or ½ wine
  and ½ water)
2 tablespoons soy sauce
3 oz. toasted sesame seeds

THIS tangy chicken casserole will appeal to those who like savoury foods.

1. Shake the chicken pieces in a paper bag containing the flour, salt, pepper, and paprika.

2. Brown lightly in hot butter in a large heavy frying-pan and arrange in a large casserole.

3. To the fat remaining in the pan add the brown sugar, ginger, wine, and soy sauce. Clean out all the brown particles in the pan and pour over the chicken in the casserole.

4. Toast the sesame seeds to a golden colour in the oven or in another pan (stir them constantly) and sprinkle over the chicken pieces.

5. Cover the casserole and bake 45 minutes to an hour in a 350° oven. Serves 6–8.

Serve with fresh hot rice, purée of spinach, and a large green salad.

GEORGIA CHICKEN

2 3½-lb. young chickens cut up
8 oz. butter or margarine
6 oz. fine bread or cornflake crumbs
3 oz. grated Parmesan cheese

1 oz. chopped parsley
1 clove garlic crushed
1 tablespoon salt
⅛ teaspoon fresh-ground pepper

THIS oven-fried chicken is one of the easiest ways imaginable to prepare chicken, and one of the best.

1. Melt the butter in a small frying-pan.

2. Combine the crumbs, cheese, parsley, garlic, salt, and pepper.

3. Wipe the pieces of chicken with a damp cloth, dip in the melted butter, roll in the crumb mixture, and arrange in a shallow casserole.

4. Pour the remaining butter over the chicken, cover, and bake in a 350° oven for 1 hour, or until tender. Uncover the last half hour. Serves 8.

Serve with Dutch potato salad (warm) or, in hot weather, with cold potato salad. Mixed vegetables (cooked peas, beans, sweet corn, diced carrots, and asparagus tips) and a green salad go well with this dish.

HAWAIIAN CHICKEN

3–3½-lb. young chicken cut up
1¼ oz. flour
1 teaspoon paprika
1 teaspoon salt
⅛ teaspoon pepper

2 oz. butter or margarine, or 3 tablespoons
   salad oil
1 tablespoon grated orange rind
¼ pt. orange juice
9-oz. tin crushed pineapple
1 large orange sliced

1. Shake the chicken pieces in a paper bag containing the flour, paprika, salt, and pepper, sauté them until golden on all sides in hot butter. Arrange in a large casserole.
2. Sprinkle the chicken pieces with the grated orange rind and pour in the orange juice.
3. Spread the crushed pineapple (not drained) on the chicken. Cover and bake 45 minutes to 1 hour in a 350° oven, or until chicken is very tender.
4. Five minutes before serving poke the orange slices (cut in two) into all the crevices. Continue to bake 5 minutes, uncovered. Serves 5–6.
Serve with herb-flavoured rice and steamed cauliflower covered with melted Cheddar cheese.

PARISIAN CHICKEN

2½-lb. young chicken quartered
   Salt and pepper
3 tablespoons butter, margarine, or salad
   oil
3 shallots or ½ small onion sliced thin

3 tablespoons cognac warmed
3 tablespoons dry vermouth
6 fluid oz. thick cream
4 large mushroom caps scored and
   sautéed lightly in butter

VERMOUTH adds flavour to many dishes. This French dish uses it with chicken, to excellent effect.
1. Season the chicken pieces and brown them well in hot butter. (It is easier to brown the wing quarters if you cut off the wing tips and run short skewers through to hold the rest of the wing flat.) Arrange in a rather shallow casserole.
2. In the fat remaining in the frying-pan sauté the shallots a moment and add to the chicken.
3. Light the warmed cognac and pour flaming over the chicken.
4. When the flames die down add to the casserole the vermouth and cream mixed. Cover and bake 30–40 minutes at 300°, or until chicken is tender.
5. Lay a mushroom cap on each piece before serving. (Scoring the caps, or cutting into them a pattern of parallel lines adds to their decorative effect.) Serves 4.

Serve with wild rice and broccoli Hollandaise.

HERB-FLAVOURED CHICKEN CASSEROLE

2 3-lb. young chickens cut up
1 teaspoon rosemary
1 teaspoon oregano
1 teaspoon chopped marjoram

2 tablespoons butter
4 tablespoons lemon juice
6 fluid oz. dry white wine

1. Remove all skin from the chicken pieces and lay them out on waxed paper. Mix the herbs and sprinkle over the chicken.

2. Brown the chicken in butter in a heavy frying-pan and arrange in a large casserole.

3. Combine the lemon juice and wine and pour over.

4. Cover and bake about 40 minutes in a 375° oven.
   If you cook this chicken on top of the stove you may have to add a little more wine to keep it from getting dry. Serves 6–8.

Serve with buttered noodles garnished with poppy seeds and split almonds, and butter beans.

POLYNESIAN CHICKEN-PEACH CASSEROLE

3½-lb. young chicken cut up
3 tablespoons butter, margarine, or salad
  oil
1 large white onion quartered
1 green pepper cut in 1-inch strips

1 large tin sliced peaches (1 lb. 13 oz.)
1 tablespoon cornflour
1 tablespoon soy sauce
3 tablespoons vinegar
2 medium tomatoes cut in wedges

1. Brown the chicken pieces in sizzling butter. Cover the frying-pan, reduce the heat to very low, and simmer about 20 minutes, or until the chicken is somewhat tender. Arrange in a large casserole.

2. Separate the onion quarters into their layers, and sauté onion and green pepper in the fat remaining in the frying-pan until the onion is transparent.

3. Drain the peaches well, but reserve the syrup. Mix ½ pt. of the syrup with the cornflour, soy sauce, and vinegar, and add to the pan. Cook until the sauce is clear and somewhat thickened, stirring frequently.

4. Stir in peaches and tomatoes and pour over the chicken in the casserole.

5. Cover the casserole and bake 20 minutes in a 375° oven. Remove the cover the last 5 minutes. Serves 6.

Serve with wild rice to which sliced sautéed mushrooms are added, and buttered green peas.

POULET CINTRA

3-lb. young chicken cut up or 2 chicken breasts halved
2 tablespoons butter, margarine, or salad oil
1 clove garlic
1 shallot minced or 1 slice of onion
Salt and pepper

4 fluid oz. port wine
4 fluid oz. dry white wine
1 liqueur glass brandy
1 liqueur glass cherry brandy or kirsch
8 fluid oz. cream
2 egg yolks slightly beaten
2 tablespoons chopped parsley

EVEN though the alcohol is burned off, the various liquors nevertheless impart a subtle and wonderful flavour to this delightful French dish. It is of course better when chicken breasts are used.

1. Heat the butter in a heavy frying-pan or directly in a large heavy casserole.

2. Add the garlic clove and shallot. Brown a moment, and then remove the garlic. Brown the chicken pieces well. Arrange compactly in the casserole and sprinkle with salt and pepper.

3. Put both wines and both brandies in a small saucepan and warm them slightly. Light and pour flaming over the chicken.

4. When the flames die down cover the casserole tightly and bake in a slow oven, 325°, about 40 minutes, or until tender.

5. Pour whatever liquid remains into a small saucepan, bring it almost to a boil, and stir in the cream mixed with the egg yolks, stirring over low heat until thick. Pour over the casserole, sprinkle with parsley, and serve. Serves 4.

Serve with wild rice and buttered asparagus.

RACHEL'S CHICKEN DELIGHT

5-lb. fowl cut up
  Salt
2–3 slices onion
1 carrot cut in several pieces
1 small bay leaf
2 sprigs parsley
3 tablespoons butter or margarine
3 tablespoons flour

4 fluid oz. thick cream
4 fluid oz. top milk
3 tablespoons dry sherry
  Fresh-ground black pepper
$\frac{1}{2}$ lb. salted almonds (whole)
1 large tin button mushrooms, drained
  Buttered bread or cornflake crumbs

THIS is a sinfully rich dish, but makes a wonderful treat for a very special occasion.
1. Put the chicken in a large pot, with 1 teaspoon salt, onion, carrot, bay leaf, and parsley. Cover with water, bring to a boil, and simmer until the meat almost falls off the bones—$1\frac{1}{2}$–2 hours.
2. Lift out the chicken pieces, skin them, and tear off the meat in quite large chunks. Strain the liquid and discard the vegetables.
3. Melt the butter in a large saucepan, blend in the flour, cook 3–4 minutes over low heat, and blend in the cream, milk, sherry, and 1 cup of the chicken broth. (Save the rest for another day.)
4. Season the cream sauce very mildly and stir in the chicken, almonds, and mushrooms.
5. Pack the mixture into a shallow casserole, top quite thickly with buttered crumbs, and bake 30–40 minutes in a very slow oven, 250°, or until it is golden brown and bubbly. Serves 8.

Serve with buttered French or runner beans and buttered sweet corn.

SESAME CHICKEN

3-lb. young chicken cut up
2 oz. toasted sesame seeds
$2\frac{1}{2}$ oz. flour
1 egg slightly beaten

$\frac{1}{4}$ pt. milk
2 oz. butter melted
1 teaspoon salt
$\frac{1}{4}$ teaspoon fresh-ground pepper

1. For practically all sesame seed recipes the seeds should be toasted before using. Toast them over slightly higher than medium heat in a heavy pan, stirring constantly, until they begin to brown. Or spread them in a cake tin or pie plate and toast them 12–15 minutes in a hot oven, 400°.
2. Blend the toasted sesame seeds with the flour.
3. In separate soup plates put the egg blended with the milk, the flour-sesame seed mixture, and the melted butter. Dip the pieces of chicken first in the egg-milk plate, then in the flour plate, and then roll in melted butter.
4. Sprinkle with salt and pepper and lay in a well-buttered shallow casserole and bake, uncovered, about 1 hour in a 350° oven, or until tender. Serves 4.

Serve with a rice casserole (see Index) or wild rice with mushrooms added, and buttered asparagus.

CHICKEN-SPAGHETTI CASSEROLE

1½ lbs. cooked chicken (or turkey) diced
   rather small
1 lb. spaghetti cooked and drained
3 tablespoons salad oil
1 medium onion chopped
1 small green pepper chopped
1 cup sliced mushrooms

2 tins tomato sauce (8-oz.)
1 teaspoon salt
⅛ teaspoon pepper
½ teaspoon dried oregano or 1½
   teaspoons fresh, chopped
½ lb. Mozzarella cheese coarsely grated or
   sliced thin

1. Heat the oil in a frying-pan and sauté the onion and green pepper until the onion begins to colour.

2. Stir in the mushrooms, tomato sauce, salt, pepper, and oregano.

3. Cover and simmer over the lowest possible heat for 25–30 minutes, stirring frequently. Check seasoning.

4. In a good-sized casserole arrange layers of spaghetti, chicken, and cheese—at least 2 layers of each, ending with cheese.

5. Bake about 30 minutes in a 375° oven. Serves 8.

Serve with a mixed vegetable salad and warm French bread.

GLAZED BREAST OF CHICKEN WITH GRAPES

4 large chicken breasts, skinned and boned
2 oz. flour
½ teaspoon salt
¼ teaspoon nutmeg

6 oz. melted butter or margarine
½ lb. green grapes, washed, drained and
   seeded
2 tablespoons orange marmalade

1. With a very sharp knife cut the meat of the chicken breasts into lengthwise strips, about ½ inch wide. Shake the flour, salt, and nutmeg in a flour shaker. Sprinkle over the chicken to make a light dusting. Shake off any excess.

2. Melt the butter or margarine in a large heavy frying-pan, heat it to 300°, and lightly brown the chicken strips. When they are lightly browned, push them aside, and stir in the seeded grapes. Stir until they are lightly heated through.

3. Add the orange marmalade and stir the chicken, grapes, and marmalade until they are well mixed and warmed through. Arrange on a warmed platter. Serve with wild rice, or a mixture of wild and white rice. (Uncle Ben's mixture is best for this.) Serves 6 to 8.

Serve with buttered carrots, baby peas, and a green salad.

TURKEY

CURRIED TURKEY (OR CHICKEN)

1½ lbs. cooked turkey diced large
2 tablespoons margarine or oil
1 medium onion minced
2 tablespoons diced green pepper
2 tablespoons flour
¾ pt. turkey or chicken broth

6 oz. sliced mushrooms lightly sautéed,
   or 6-oz. tin
1 large tart apple cored and diced
3 tablespoons chopped pimento
1 tablespoon minced parsley
   Salt and pepper
1½ teaspoons curry powder or to taste

1. Heat the fat in a large casserole and sauté the onion and green pepper until soft. Stir in the flour, cook a moment, and blend in the turkey or chicken broth and the mushrooms, with their liquid if you use tinned mushrooms. Simmer the mixture 15–20 minutes.

2. In a large bowl mix the turkey, apple, pimento, parsley, and salt and pepper.

3. Stir the curry powder into the sauce—as much as you like—and check seasoning.

4. Stir in the turkey mixture, heat slowly, and simmer 10–15 minutes over the lowest possible heat. Serves 6–8.

Note: Remember that curry always improves with time. Make this in the morning or the day before, bring to room temperature, and merely reheat at serving time.

Serve with plenty of fresh hot rice and the usual curry accompaniments: chutney, fresh coconut grated or broken in chunks, chopped salted peanuts, preserved or candied ginger, puppadums and Bombay duck (obtainable from most delicatessens and Indian stores). A large green salad is almost a must.

LEMON-TURKEY CASSEROLE WITH RICE

1½ lbs. coarsely diced turkey
8 oz. cooked rice
  Salt and pepper
½ teaspoon whole celery seed
8-oz. bottle tomato sauce
½ pt. chicken broth

4 slices lemon
5 thin slices onion (or more)
4 tablespoons dry white wine
2 tablespoons butter
1 teaspoon paprika

THIS casserole is out of the ordinary in both flavour and texture.

1. Spread the rice in a good-sized but shallow casserole and arrange the turkey evenly over it.
2. Sprinkle with salt, pepper, and celery seed.
3. Mix the tomato sauce and chicken broth well and pour over the turkey
4. Cut the lemon and onion slices in two and cover the top with them, adding more if needed.
5. Cover the casserole and bake 1¼ hours in a 350° oven. Check halfway through, and add a little broth if it seems quite dry.
6. When done, uncover the casserole, pour the wine over, dot with butter cut in bits, sprinkle with paprika, and grill until browned and sizzling. Serves 6.

Serve with slices of aubergine dipped first in slightly beaten egg and then in bread or cornflake crumbs and sautéed until golden brown on both sides and tender. A green salad is in order, too.

TURKEY ALMONDINE

1 lb. cooked turkey diced coarsely
1½ tablespoons butter or margarine
1½ tablespoons flour
¾ pt. milk
1¼ teaspoons salt
2 tablespoons dry white wine

6 oz. cooked peas
2 oz. toasted split almonds
2 egg yolks
2 tablespoons bread or cornflake crumbs
1 tablespoon butter
2 tablespoons Parmesan cheese

1. Make a white sauce by melting the butter, stirring in the flour, and blending in the milk. Season to taste.
2. Stir in the wine, and keep stirring until the sauce is smooth.
3. Stir in the turkey, the peas, and half of the almonds.
4. Beat the egg yolks a little with a fork, add a little of the sauce, and rapidly stir it back into the turkey mixture.
5. Pour the mixture into a small casserole. Scatter the remaining almonds on top, then the crumbs, the butter, and finally the Parmesan cheese.
6. If you make the casserole just before serving, so that it is already hot, merely brown it well under the grill. However, if you make it early in the day and refrigerate it, bring it to room temperature (1 hour) and bake 10 minutes in a 375° oven before grilling it. Serves 4.

Serve with riced potatoes and broccoli with lemon-butter-crumb sauce.

TURKEY SHEPHERD'S PIE

1 lb. cooked turkey diced medium small
3 oz. chopped celery
1 small onion chopped
2 oz. sliced and lightly sautéed
  mushrooms or 4-oz. tin
1 tablespoon minced parsley
1½ tablespoons dry sherry
2 tablespoons butter, margarine, or salad
  oil

1¼ lbs. hot mashed potatoes or 4-serving
  portion instant potatoes made with
  1 cup water and 1 egg
1 tin condensed cream of mushroom
  soup
1 egg (if raw potatoes are used)
2 tablespoons buttered crumbs
  Paprika

1. Sauté the celery, onion, and mushrooms in hot fat in a frying-pan until the onion is transparent. Stir in the turkey.
2. Mix the soup with the parsley and sherry and blend it smoothly with the turkey mixture. Spread in a shallow casserole.
3. Beat the hot mashed potatoes well with the egg and spread over the turkey mixture.
4. Top with crumbs and sprinkle with paprika. Bake 25 minutes in a 350° oven, or until golden. Serves 4.

Serve with buttered runner beans and cole slaw.

TURKEY-SPAGHETTI CASSEROLE

¾–1 lb. cooked turkey diced rather small
6 oz. spaghetti
2 oz. pimento diced fine
2 oz. green pepper chopped
½ medium onion minced

1 tin condensed cream of mushroom soup
¼ pt. turkey broth, water, dry white wine,
  or a combination of these
3 oz. grated cheese
  Salt and pepper

1. Cook the spaghetti in boiling salted water until it is barely tender—about 7 minutes—and drain well.
2. Mix the turkey, pimento, green pepper, and onion and spread in a medium casserole.
3. Heat the soup and stir in the turkey broth.
4. Stir in the cooked spaghetti. Pour this over the turkey in the casserole and blend the two mixtures. Season to taste.
5. Top with the grated cheese and bake, uncovered, about 45 minutes in a 350° oven, or until bubbling and browned. Serves 5–6.

Serve with buttered baby Brussels sprouts and a green salad with grated carrot, cucumber slices, and tomato wedges added.

TURKEY WITH WILD RICE

1 lb. cooked turkey diced medium small
8 oz. raw wild rice
¼ lb. mushrooms sliced and sautéed
   lightly
12 fluid oz. heavy cream

1 pt. turkey stock or gravy thinned with
   chicken broth
2 tablespoons chopped chives
   Salt and pepper
3 oz. grated Parmesan cheese
1 tablespoon butter

1. Wash the rice in several waters and let it soak in cold water for an hour or two.
2. Drain the rice well and mix with the turkey, mushrooms, cream, ⅔ pt. of the turkey stock, chives, and seasoning to taste.
3. Put in a buttered casserole, cover, and bake 1 hour in a 350° oven.
4. Add the remaining turkey stock and bake 25–35 minutes longer, or until the liquid is absorbed and the rice is tender and fluffy when stirred with a fork.
5. Sprinkle the top with cheese, dot with bits of butter, and grill to a golden brown. Serves 6.

Serve with sliced tomatoes topped with chopped chives and parsley mixed with French dressing, and diced cucumbers in sour cream, together with a green salad.

DUCK

DUCKLING ALMONDINE

2 4-lb. ducklings cut up
2 oz. flour
1 teaspoon salt
⅛ teaspoon pepper
¼ lb. spring onions sliced

2 oz. margarine or butter, or 3
   tablespoons salad oil
4 oz. split toasted almonds
¾ pt. dry white wine
   Minced parsley

1. Put the flour, salt, and pepper in a paper bag and dredge the duckling pieces in it.
2. Sauté to a golden brown in hot fat and arrange in a large casserole, crowding the pieces.
3. Scatter the spring onions and almonds over the duck, pour on the wine, cover tightly, and bake in a moderate oven, 375°, about 1 hour, or until the duck is very tender. Remove the cover the last 15 minutes.
4. Sprinkle with parsley before serving. Serves 6–8.

Serve with small parsley-butter boiled potatoes (or potato balls) and buttered tiny green peas.

DUCK AND PINEAPPLE CANTON

5-lb. duck cut in pieces
3 tablespoons soy sauce
1 tablespoon sugar
½ teaspoon ginger or ground ginger root
1 clove garlic cut in 2 pieces
4 tablespoons salad oil

½ pt. pineapple juice
¾ pt. water
1 tablespoon cornflour
12 oz. pineapple chunks (frozen or tinned)
    well drained
Salt and pepper

1. Mix the soy sauce, sugar, ginger, and garlic in a bowl and dip the pieces of duck in the mixture, draining each one as you remove it and laying the pieces on paper towelling.
2. Heat the oil in a heavy frying-pan and brown the duck pieces well all over. Arrange in a large casserole.
3. Mix the pineapple juice with all but 3 tablespoons of the water and clean out the pan with it. Pour over the duck, cover, and bake about an hour in a 300° oven.
4. Drain the liquid from the casserole into a saucepan and stir into it the cornflour and the remaining 3 tablespoons water mixed to a paste. Simmer about 10 minutes, stirring constantly.
5. When the sauce is thickened and clear stir in the pineapple. Pour back over the duck in the casserole and bake about 10 minutes longer, uncovered. Serves 4–5.

Serve with plenty of hot fluffy rice, glazed onions, and a green salad.

SPANISH DUCK

5-lb. duck cut up
3 tablespoons salad oil
1 tablespoon paprika
1 medium onion chopped
1¼ oz. flour

¾ pt. chicken broth
4 fluid oz. dry sherry
1 medium tomato sliced
2 oz. chopped stuffed olives

1. Thoroughly mix the oil and paprika, heat in a heavy frying-pan, and brown the pieces of duck on all sides. Arrange in a large casserole.
2. In the fat remaining in the pan sauté the onion until it begins to be transparent.
3. Blend in the flour and gradually add the chicken broth and sherry, stirring constantly until smooth and thickened.
4. Add the sliced tomato and chopped olives to the sauce and pour over the duck in the casserole.
5. Cover and bake in a slow oven, 325°, about an hour, or until the duck is tender. Serves 4.

Serve with small parsley-butter potatoes and purée of spinach.

SWEET AND SOUR DUCKLING

6-lb. duckling cut up
1½ teaspoons salt
1 teaspoon pepper
2 teaspoons paprika
¾ pt. water

4 oz. sugar
1 tablespoon cornflour
4 fluid oz. vinegar
1 teaspoon soy sauce
12-oz. tin pineapple chunks

THIS is an exceptionally flavoursome dish, as most sweet-sour dishes are.

1. Cut off as much fat as possible and season the duck pieces well with salt, pepper, and paprika. Arrange them in a large casserole, closely packed together.

2. Cover the casserole and bake 1 hour in a 350° oven, turning the pieces 2 or 3 times. Uncover the last 15 minutes.

3. Simmer the giblets in the water until tender, cutting the gizzard into several pieces so that it will cook in the same time as the other giblets.

4. Strain the broth from the giblets into a small saucepan, and add the liquid that has accumulated in the casserole from the duck.

5. Combine the sugar, cornflour, vinegar, and soy sauce and stir into the saucepan. Cook until thickened and smooth, stirring constantly.

6. Add the pineapple and pour over the duck. Bake fifteen minutes longer, uncovered. Serves 4.

Serve with fresh hot rice and buttered peas.

DUCKLING CASSEROLE

5–6-lb. duckling cut up
2 oz. butter or margarine, or 3
   tablespoons salad oil
2 small onions sliced
2 carrots sliced thin
8 fluid oz. dry white wine
1¼ pts. chicken broth

1 teaspoon minced parsley
½ teaspoon dried oregano or 1½
   teaspoons fresh, chopped
¼ small bay leaf crumbled
   Salt and pepper
1 tablespoon cornflour
3 tablespoons water

1. Brown the duckling pieces in hot fat in a heavy casserole. When half browned add the onions and carrots.

2. Stir in the wine, chicken broth, herbs, and salt and pepper to taste.

3. Cover and bake in a slow oven, 300°, 1½ hours.

4. Pour the liquid from the casserole into a saucepan and boil hard until it is reduced to ¾ pt.

5. Reduce the heat and stir in the cornflour mixed to a paste with the water, continuing to stir until the sauce is thickened and smooth.

6. Pour the sauce back over the duck and bake 5 minutes longer, uncovered. Serves 4–6.

Serve with hot fluffy rice and buttered French beans or peas.

DUCKLING NIPPONESE

4–5-lb. duckling cut up
1 egg slightly beaten
1 teaspoon soy sauce
2 oz. desiccated coconut

1¼ oz. flour
1½ teaspoons salt
⅛ teaspoon fresh-ground pepper
3 tablespoons cognac slightly warmed

Nipponese Sauce

11-oz. tin mandarin orange segments
7 oz. maple syrup
1 tablespoon cornflour (generous)
2 tablespoons lemon juice
1 tablespoon grated orange rind

3 tablespoons frozen orange juice,
  undiluted
1 tablespoon grated lemon rind
2 firm bananas sliced
2 tablespoons butter

1. Cut off as much fat from the duckling pieces as you possibly can. Prick the skin well with a sharp-tined fork and arrange the pieces on a rack in a large casserole or baking pan. Bake 30 minutes in a hot oven, 400°.

2. Pour off all the fat and arrange the pieces in the casserole, without using the rack.

3. Brush the pieces well with the egg and soy sauce blended.

4. Combine the coconut, flour, salt, and pepper and sprinkle evenly over the duckling. Return to the oven and bake another 25–30 minutes, or until golden brown.

5. Remove the casserole from the oven, ignite the warmed cognac, and flambé the duckling.

6. When the flames die down, spread the sauce over and let stand in the oven, heat off, 5 minutes or so. Serves 4.

Sauce: Combine the juice of the mandarin oranges, the maple syrup, cornflour, lemon and orange juices and rinds, and bring to a boil, stirring constantly until somewhat thickened. Stir in the orange segments, bananas, and butter and simmer about 5 minutes. The sauce can be held in a double boiler a long time, and hence can be made long ahead of time. This recipe is a generous one, and there is actually enough sauce for two ducks.

Serve with a rice casserole (see Index) *and a large green salad.*

NOTES

FISH

FISH FILLETS AU GRATIN

1 lb. any white or light fish fillets
1 tin condensed cream of celery or cream
  of mushroom soup
2 oz. grated Cheddar cheese

Salt and pepper to taste
2 tablespoons bread or cornflake crumbs
1 tablespoon grated Parmesan cheese
Paprika

1. Spread the fillets in a well-greased flat casserole.

2. In a small saucepan mix the soup, Cheddar, and salt and pepper to taste. Heat until the cheese is melted, and pour over the fish.

3. Mix the crumbs with the Parmesan cheese and sprinkle on top. Shake a little paprika over it.

4. Bake 35–45 minutes in a 375° oven, until the fish flakes readily and the surface is bubbly and golden. The exact time will depend upon the thickness of the fish. Serves 4.

Serve with a rice casserole (see Index) *and buttered baby Brussels sprouts.*

FISH FILLET ROLLS WITH SESAME SEEDS

1½ lbs. fillet of flounder
1 teaspoon salt
⅛ teaspoon pepper
¾ pt. milk
1½ tablespoons butter

1½ tablespoons flour
2 oz. toasted sesame seeds*
¼ lb. grated Cheddar cheese
3 tablespoons lemon juice
Paprika

1. Roll up the fillets, fasten with toothpicks, and lay in a rather shallow greased casserole. Sprinkle them with salt and pepper and pour the milk over them.

2. Bake in a 350° oven, covered, 30–40 minutes, or until the fish flakes readily.

3. Melt the butter in a saucepan, stir in flour and sesame seeds, and let cook a moment.

4. When the fish is cooked, pour off the milk and add it slowly to the flour mixture, stirring constantly over low heat until smooth and thickened.

5. Stir in the cheese and the lemon juice, and keep stirring until the cheese is melted.

6. Pour the sauce over the fish, sprinkle with paprika, and brown well under the grill. Serves 6.

Note: If you wish, remove the toothpicks from the fish rolls after you pour off the milk.

Serve with riced potatoes and any cooked greens: spinach, broccoli, curly kale, etc.

* See p. 107 for how to toast sesame seeds.

AMERICAN FISH CASSEROLE

1 lb. cut-up white fish, any kind
1¼ pts. milk
  Small onion sliced
1 sprig parsley
1 blade mace (optional)
2 oz. butter or margarine

2 oz. flour
2 egg yolks slightly beaten
  Salt and pepper to taste
2 tablespoons lemon juice
⅔ cup buttered cracker crumbs

1. Cook the fish 20–25 minutes in a double boiler with the milk, onion, parsley, and mace. Drain, reserving the liquid.

2. Break up the fish coarsely with a fork and spread it in a shallow casserole.

3. In a small saucepan melt the butter, blend in the flour, and slowly stir in the milk in which the fish was cooked. Season to taste.

4. Add a bit of the sauce to the egg yolks and stir back into the sauce. Add the lemon juice and pour over the fish in the casserole.

5. Top the casserole with the cracker crumbs and bake about 25 minutes in a 350° oven. Serves 4–5.

Serve with fresh hot rice and buttered baby carrots.

BAKED HALIBUT

1½-lb. halibut steak
  Salt and pepper
2 oz. butter or margarine softened

3 oz. mushrooms sliced
8 fluid oz. thin cream
1 tablespoon Angostura bitters

HALIBUT is one of our most tasty fishes, and the flavour here is enhanced by the bitters.

1. Wipe the steak, place in a greased shallow casserole, sprinkle with salt and pepper, and spread the butter on it.

2. Bake 15 minutes in a moderate oven, 375°.

3. Cover with the mushrooms and cream and bake 15 minutes longer.

4. Dribble the bitters into the sauce around the fish, stir it in as best you can, and bake 10 minutes longer, basting the fish twice with the pan juices. Serves 4–5.

Serve with a rice casserole (see Index) *and butter or French beans.*

GRILLED HALIBUT

4 portions halibut cut 1 inch thick
6 tablespoons butter
8 fluid oz. vermouth

Salt and pepper
1 tablespoon fine bread or cornflake crumbs
1 tablespoon grated Parmesan cheese

VERMOUTH adds wonderfully to the flavour of many foods. Here it performs its magic for halibut.

1. Lay the pieces of halibut in a flat casserole. Pour over them the butter and vermouth heated together in a small saucepan. Salt and pepper lightly.

2. Place the casserole about 6 inches under the grill (preheated, of course) and baste frequently while it cooks. It should take about 20 minutes to cook the halibut tender.

3. When it is about ready, remove the casserole from the grill and sprinkle the fish with the crumbs and cheese mixed.

4. Return to the grill for a minute or two, or until the topping browns. Serves 4.

Serve with fluffy mashed potatoes and either corn on the cob or buttered sweet corn.

DEVILLED HALIBUT

$1\frac{1}{2}$ lbs. halibut steak (one piece)
2 oz. chopped green pepper
1 small onion minced
1 tablespoon prepared mustard
1 teaspoon Worcestershire sauce
$\frac{1}{8}$ teaspoon Tabasco sauce

$3\frac{1}{2}$ tablespoons lemon juice
4 oz. butter or margarine melted
6 oz. fine bread or cornflake crumbs
2 tablespoons grated Parmesan cheese
Salt and pepper

THIS is an outstanding casserole, worth every minute of the time it takes to prepare.

1. Mix the green pepper, onion, mustard, Worcestershire sauce, Tabasco, and lemon juice.

2. Mix the butter and crumbs and combine both mixtures, blending well.

3. Spread half of this mixture on top of the steak, patting it down well.

4. Quickly turn it crumb-side-down in a shallow greased casserole. Season the top side and spread with the rest of the crumb mixture.

5. Bake the casserole 25–30 minutes in a 350° oven, or until the fish flakes easily with a fork.

6. Spread the cheese on top and brown 3–4 minutes under the grill, watching carefully to see that it doesn't burn. Serves 4.

Serve with creamed chopped spinach and little parsley-buttered potatoes.

SESAME HALIBUT STEAK

2 large halibut steaks 1¼ inches thick
  (about 2½ lbs.)
  Salt and pepper
2 tablespoons butter or margarine softened
6 oz. soft bread crumbs

3 tablespoons toasted sesame seeds*
½ teaspoon dried thyme or 1½ teaspoons
  fresh, chopped
2 oz. melted butter
  Paprika

IN this recipe sesame seeds enhance the flavour of one of our best-liked fish.

1. Arrange the steaks in a shallow casserole that will hold them comfortably. Salt and pepper them lightly and spread the softened butter on them.

2. Mix the crumbs, ¾ teaspoon salt, ⅛ teaspoon fresh-ground pepper, toasted sesame seeds, thyme, and melted butter together and spread half on each steak.

3. Sprinkle lightly with paprika and bake 25–30 minutes in a moderate oven, 350°. The fish should then flake readily. Serves 6.

Serve with buttered asparagus and riced potatoes.

BAKED SALMON STEAKS

3 lbs. salmon steaks cut 1 inch thick
¼ lb. mushrooms minced
1 medium onion minced
2 tablespoons minced parsley

2 oz. butter or margarine
4 fluid oz. dry sherry
1 oz. fine bread or cornflake crumbs

THIS is a French Canadian way of preparing their wonderful fresh salmon from the St. John's River.

1. Lay the steaks in a well-greased shallow casserole.

2. Mix the mushrooms, onion, and parsley and spread over the fish.

3. Cut the butter into bits and dot over the top.

4. Pour the sherry in and bake in a moderate oven, 350°, 15 minutes.

5. Spread the steaks with the crumbs and continue baking another 10 or 15 minutes, or until fish flakes readily. Baste 2 or 3 times during the baking. Serves 6.

Serve with parsley-butter potatoes and buttered green beans.

* See Index for how to toast sesame seeds.

BAKED SALMON STEAKS ALMONDINE

4 salmon steaks 1 inch thick
¾ pt. water
3 tablespoons vinegar
1 small onion sliced
  Salt and pepper

1 lemon sliced thin
2 oz. toasted split almonds
2 oz. sultanas
2 egg yolks
1 tablespoon chopped parsley

1. Lay the steaks in a greased shallow casserole. Add the water and vinegar mixed, and the onion.

2. Season with salt and pepper, cover, and bake 30 minutes in a 350° oven.

3. Drain off the liquid from the casserole and measure ½ pt. into a small saucepan.

4. Add the lemon, almonds, and raisins to the casserole, cover again, and cook 5 minutes more.

5. Beat the egg yolks well and stir in the ½-pt. of liquid from the salmon. Cook over low heat until it begins to thicken, stirring constantly. Season to taste, pour over the casserole, sprinkle with parsley, and serve.
    Serves 4, though sometimes salmon steaks are large enough to make two servings each.

Serve with purée of spinach and riced potatoes.

BAKED TINNED SALMON

1-lb. tin salmon
1 tablespoon butter or margarine
1 small onion chopped fine
½ medium green pepper chopped

1 tin condensed cream of mushroom soup
3 tablespoons milk
2 oz. coarse bread crumbs or tiny dice
1 tablespoon grated Parmesan cheese

EVEN tinned salmon can make an appealing casserole.

1. Heat the butter in a small frying-pan and lightly sauté the onion and green pepper.

2. Add the soup and milk, blend well, and heat almost to boiling point.

3. Drain the tin of salmon and remove skin and bones. Break it into good-sized chunks and lay in a small greased casserole.

4. Pour the soup mixture over, cover with crumbs, and sprinkle with cheese.

5. Bake in a hot oven, 400°, 20 minutes. Serves 4.

Serve with a casserole of rice (see Index) *and buttered baby Brussels sprouts.*

SALMON TETRAZZINI

1-lb. tin salmon	3 tablespoons dry sherry
2 oz. butter or margarine	4 fluid oz. thin cream
2 oz. flour	$\frac{1}{2}$ lb. mushrooms sliced
$\frac{3}{4}$ pt. hot chicken broth	$\frac{1}{2}$ lb. spaghetti cooked
$\frac{1}{2}$ teaspoon salt	2 tablespoons butter or margarine
$\frac{1}{8}$ teaspoon pepper	2 oz. grated Parmesan cheese
$\frac{1}{8}$ teaspoon nutmeg	2 oz. bread or cornflake crumbs

THE name Tetrazzini has by now become a method, and can be used with chicken, turkey, various fish, and various meats. Whatever the main ingredient is, the dish is a wonderful concoction.

1. Make the white sauce first. Melt the 2 oz. butter, blend in the flour, and gradually add the hot chicken broth, stirring until the sauce is smooth and velvety. Season with salt and pepper, nutmeg, and sherry.

2. Drain the salmon and stir its liquid into the sauce also. Let it simmer 8–10 minutes, stirring occasionally. Add the cream and keep hot on an asbestos mat.

3. Sauté the mushrooms lightly in the 2 tablespoons butter and add them to the sauce.

4. Stir half of the sauce into the cooked spaghetti and spread it on a large flat casserole or deep oversize pie plate.

5. Flake the salmon coarsely and mix with the rest of the sauce. Carefully pour this over the spaghetti.

6. Sprinkle the top with the cheese and crumbs mixed and bake 15–20 minutes in a 350° oven, until well browned. If everything is hot when you put the casserole together you can merely brown the top well under the grill. Serves 4.

Serve with a mixed vegetable salad and warm French bread.

BAKED FLOUNDER FLORENTINE

1½–2 lbs. fillet of flounder (or plaice)
2 tablespoons butter or margarine
2 tablespoons minced onion
1 clove garlic minced
1 8-oz. packet frozen chopped spinach
¼ teaspoon salt
⅛ teaspoon fresh-ground pepper
⅛ teaspoon nutmeg

3 tablespoons lemon juice
1 teaspoon Worcestershire sauce
2 oz. melted butter or margarine
6 oz. sliced mushrooms
2 tablespoons flour
8 fluid oz. sour cream
3 tablespoons Parmesan cheese

1. Melt the 2 tablespoons butter in a heavy frying-pan and lightly sauté the onion and garlic. Lay in the block of frozen spinach, lower the heat to a bare simmer, cover, and cook until the spinach is thawed, turning the block 2 or 3 times. Press out excess moisture with a spatula and drain off.

2. Stir salt, pepper, and nutmeg into the spinach.

3. Wipe the fillets with paper towels or a damp cloth. Lay them out on a board or counter, and spread the spinach on them. Roll them up, fasten with toothpicks, and lay, seam side down, in a shallow greased casserole.

4. Mix the lemon juice, Worcestershire sauce, and melted butter and drizzle over the fish rolls.

5. Bake, covered, 20 minutes in a 400° oven, or until the fish flakes readily.

6. Remove casserole from the oven, drain off the liquid into a saucepan, and cook the mushrooms in it 5 or 6 minutes. Stir in the flour, blend in the sour cream, and pour back over the casserole.

7. Sprinkle with cheese and brown under the grill. Serves 5–6.

Serve with fluffy mashed potatoes and a green salad.

FILLET OF SOLE WITH GRAPES

2½ lbs. fillet of sole (or plaice)　　2 tablespoons butter or margarine
¾ pt. milk　　　　　　　　　　　　2 tablespoons flour (scant)
¼ lb. mushrooms sliced　　　　　　Salt and pepper
2 oz. butter or margarine　　　　2 oz. buttered bread or cornflake crumbs
¾ lb. green grapes, seeded　　　　2 tablespoons grated Parmesan cheese

THE grapes here add an unexpected and delightful flavour.

1. Put the milk in a large heavy frying-pan, heat to just below boiling, and poach the fillets in it 5 minutes, reducing the heat immediately so that the milk just simmers.

2. Sauté the mushrooms in the 2 oz. of butter about 3 minutes.

3. Combine mushrooms with grapes and spread in a large shallow casserole.

4. With a slotted spatula lift the fish fillets carefully from the milk and lay them on top of the grape-mushroom mixture.

5. Make a white sauce with the 2 tablespoons of butter, the flour, and the milk in which the fillets were cooked. Season to taste and spread over the fish.

6. Top with the crumbs and cheese mixed together and bake in a hot oven, 400°, about 25 minutes, or until golden. Serves 6.

Serve with little parsley-butter potatoes and buttered green peas.

SOLE AU GRATIN ON MUSHROOMS

8 fillets of sole (or plaice)
2 lbs. mushrooms chopped fine
3 tablespoons wine vinegar
1 tablespoon Cointreau liqueur
4 tablespoons brandy
6 fluid oz. salad oil
1 tablespoon minced parsley
1 medium onion sliced
  Few celery leaves
8 fluid oz. dry white wine

2 tablespoons butter or margarine
2 tablespoons flour
  Salt and pepper
2 egg yolks slightly beaten
1 tablespoon grated onion
1 tablespoon minced chives
1 teaspoon dried tarragon or 1 tablespoon
  fresh, chopped
$\frac{1}{4}$ lb. Swiss cheese coarsely grated
2 tablespoons grated Parmesan cheese

THIS is a real gourmet dish, obviously designed for a dinner party, and good for that because it can be prepared, up to the last step, early in the day.

1. Mix the vinegar, Cointreau, 1 tablespoon of the brandy, the oil, parsley, grated onion, chives, and tarragon, and stir in the chopped mushrooms to marinate.

2. In a large heavy frying-pan put the sliced onion, celery leaves, wine, the rest of the brandy, and a little water. Bring to a boil and lay in the fillets. If there is not enough liquid to barely cover them add a little more water. Lower the heat and just simmer the fillets 15 minutes.

3. Cook the mushrooms in their marinade in a saucepan, 2 minutes on high heat and 7 minutes on low. Drain through a fine sieve and spread mushrooms in a large shallow greased casserole.

4. With a slotted spatula lift out the fish fillets and lay on the mushrooms.
    Up to this point the dish can be prepared hours ahead of time. If you do this, however, be sure to bring the casserole to room temperature (1 hour), and bake it 10 minutes in a 350° oven before you grill it.

5. Make a white sauce with the butter, flour, and the stock the fish was cooked in, plus a little of the liquid drained from the mushrooms if needed. Discard remainder. Season to taste and stir in the Swiss cheese.

6. When the cheese is all melted, stir a little of the sauce into the egg yolks and quickly stir back into the sauce.

7. Pour over the fish, top with Parmesan cheese, and put under the grill until golden brown. Serves 8.

Serve with buttered noodles to which poppy seeds and split almonds have been added, buttered baby green peas, and a green salad, with warm French bread.

FILLET OF SOLE ALMONDINE

4 fillets of sole (or plaice)
  Salt and pepper
3 tablespoons milk
3 tablespoons thin cream

½ teaspoon dried rosemary or 1½
  teaspoons fresh, chopped
2 oz. blanched, split, and toasted
  almonds

1. Spread the fillets in a shallow greased casserole and season with salt and pepper.
2. Pour the milk and cream over, sprinkle with rosemary, and bake 20 minutes in a hot oven, 400°.
3. Sprinkle the almonds over the top and bake 10 minutes longer, or until the liquid is practically all absorbed.
4. If fish has not browned put under the grill a minute or two. Serves 4.

Serve with potatoes au gratin and buttered runner beans.

FILLET OF SOLE CASSEROLE

2 lbs. fillet of sole (or plaice)
  Salt and pepper
3 tablespoons dry white wine
2 tablespoons lemon juice
1¼ oz. flour
4 tablespoons butter or margarine
1 medium minced onion
3 oz. chopped mushrooms

2 tablespoons chopped carrot
2 tablespoons chopped parsley
¼ teaspoon dried thyme or ¾ teaspoon
  fresh, chopped
4 small tomatoes peeled and sliced
2 oz. bread or cornflake crumbs
2 tablespoons grated Parmesan cheese

1. Lay the fillets in a shallow greased casserole or oversize pie plate. Salt and pepper them lightly and pour in the wine and lemon juice mixed.
2. Cover and bake 10 minutes in a moderate oven, 350°—not long enough to completely cook the fish.
3. Put the flour in a shallow soup plate. Carefully lift out the fillets with a slotted spatula and dredge them with flour on both sides.
4. Melt 2 tablespoons of the butter in a heavy frying-pan and when it is sizzling quickly brown the fillets on both sides.
5. Add the vegetables, except tomatoes, and herbs to the liquid in the casserole in which the fish was cooked. Gently lay the fillets on top as they are browned.
6. Cover with a closely fitted layer of tomato slices. Season with salt and pepper.
7. Melt the remaining 2 tablespoons of butter, and mix with the crumbs and cheese. Scatter on top of the tomatoes and bake an additional 20 minutes. Serves 5–6.

Serve with fluffy mashed potatoes and buttered asparagus.

BAKED SEA BASS

Whole bass weighing 3–5 lbs. dressed
Salt and pepper
2 tablespoons salad oil
4 oz. melted butter or margarine

1 medium tin whole tomatoes drained
1 small bay leaf
$\frac{1}{4}$ pt. dry white wine

THIS fish will be easier to serve if you have the backbone removed, but keep the two halves together if you do.

1. Season the fish inside and out with salt and pepper and lay in a greased shallow casserole. Bake 10 minutes in a 350° oven.
2. Remove the casserole from the oven. Mix the oil and butter and sprinkle over the fish.
3. Add to the casserole the tomatoes, broken into 2 or 3 pieces each, the bay leaf, and the wine. Season the tomatoes.
4. Return the casserole to the oven and bake until the fish flakes readily but is still moist. The total time should be about 10 minutes per pound. Serves 4–6, according to size.

Serve with fluffy mashed potatoes and chopped spinach mixed with a little sour cream and a touch of nutmeg.

STUFFED FILLET OF SOLE ROLLS WITH MUSHROOM SAUCE

6 fillets of sole (or plaice)
7$\frac{3}{4}$-oz. tin of salmon, drained, boned, and
  flaked
2 tablespoons minced parsley
2 tablespoons chopped chives

$\frac{1}{2}$ teaspoon dried tarragon or 1$\frac{1}{2}$
  teaspoons fresh, chopped
$\frac{1}{2}$ teaspoon paprika
1 tablespoon lemon juice
1 tablespoon melted butter

Mushroom Sauce

1 shallot minced or 1 teaspoon minced
  onion
1 tablespoon butter or margarine

1 tin condensed cream of mushroom
  soup
3 tablespoons thin cream

1. Mix together the salmon, parsley, chives, tarragon, paprika, and lemon juice. Spread on the fillets, covering them to within $\frac{1}{4}$ inch of the edges. Beginning with the tail end, roll up and fasten with toothpicks.
2. Lay the rolls in a small shallow buttered casserole or pie plate, brush with melted butter, cover, and bake in a 350° oven 20 minutes, or until the fish flakes readily.
3. Drain the casserole and spread some of the mushroom sauce over the rolls. They can be served at this point, or you can sprinkle sauce-topped rolls with about 2 tablespoons buttered crumbs and grill 2–3 minutes, until golden. Serve with a bowl of mushroom sauce. Serves 6.

Mushroom Sauce: Cook the shallot or onion 2–3 minutes in butter in a small saucepan, stir in soup and cream, and heat to boiling point.

Serve with buttered new potatoes and buttered baby carrots.

CHINESE TUNA CASSEROLE

1 tin tuna broken into small chunks
1 tin condensed cream of mushroom soup
4 tablespoons milk, chicken broth, or water
3-oz. tin chow mein noodles

6 oz. thin-sliced celery
4 oz. whole salted cashew nuts
2 oz. minced onion
Salt and pepper to taste

TUNA fish is becoming popular in this country—for salads, for sandwiches, and for main dishes. The remaining recipes in this section suggest some intriguing ways to use it in casseroles, beginning with this unusual Chinese recipe.

In a saucepan put the soup, the milk or broth, half of the noodles, the celery, cashews, onion, and salt and pepper. Heat and stir in the tuna. Pour into a quart casserole and bake 20 minutes in a 350° oven. Sprinkle the remaining noodles on top and bake 5 minutes more. Serves 4.

CURRIED TUNA AND EGGS

7-oz. tin tuna drained and flaked
2 hard-boiled eggs quartered
4 tablespoons butter or margarine
$\frac{1}{4}$ clove garlic crushed
$\frac{1}{2}$ teaspoon curry powder
2 oz. chopped almonds
2 tablespoons flour

$\frac{3}{4}$ pt. milk
$\frac{1}{4}$ teaspoon Worcestershire sauce
$\frac{1}{2}$ teaspoon salt
1 tablespoon lemon juice
2 tablespoons buttered bread or cornflake
    crumbs

1. Melt 1 tablespoon of the butter in a saucepan. Stir in the garlic, curry powder, and almonds and cook until slightly browned.

2. Melt the remaining 3 tablespoons butter in the top of a double boiler over simmering water, stir in the flour, and cook until bubbly. Blend in the milk and stir until smooth.

3. Add to this white sauce the Worcestershire sauce, salt, lemon juice, tuna, eggs, and finally the curry-almond mixture. Stir gently until well mixed and pour into a smallish casserole.

4. Top with buttered crumbs and bake in a moderate oven, 350°, 25–30 minutes, or until nicely browned. Serves 4–5.

Serve with fresh hot rice, as all curry is served, and buttered young marrow. A green salad is always a good idea with curry.

TUNA-BROCCOLI CASSEROLE

7-oz. tin tuna fish drained and flaked
2 lbs. fresh broccoli or 2 packets frozen
2 tablespoons butter or margarine
2 tablespoons flour
½ pt. thin cream

½ pt. chicken broth
Salt and pepper to taste
1 tablespoon chopped parsley
2 hard-boiled eggs sliced
2 oz. grated Parmesan cheese

1. If the broccoli is fresh, trim off almost all of the stem part. (It can be cooked separately, chopped, buttered, and served as a separate vegetable another day.) Whether fresh or frozen, cook in boiling salted water until barely tender and arrange in a single layer in a shallow greased casserole.
2. Melt butter, blend in flour, and stir in the cream and broth to make a smooth sauce. Season to taste.
3. Stir in gently the parsley, tuna fish, and eggs. Pour carefully over the broccoli and top with the cheese.
4. Bake 15–20 minutes in a moderate oven, 350°, and then put under the grill a minute or two to brown well. Serves 4–5.

Serve with spaghetti cooked barely tender and mixed well with butter and grated cheese. A large mixed salad and warm French bread go well, too.

TUNA-CHEESE CASSEROLE

7-oz. tin tuna fish drained and coarsely
flaked
4 oz. grated Swiss cheese
10 slices white bread, buttered, crusts
removed
4 eggs well beaten

¾ pt. milk
1 teaspoon salt
¼ teaspoon paprika
½ teaspoon Worcestershire sauce
Dash cayenne pepper

1. Cut 8 slices of the buttered bread into ½-inch cubes.
2. In a greased medium casserole make alternate layers of bread cubes, cheese, and tuna (3 layers of bread and cheese and 2 of tuna).
3. Blend the eggs, milk, salt, paprika, Worcestershire sauce, and cayenne and pour carefully over the casserole.
4. Cut the remaining 2 slices of buttered bread into triangles and stand them around the edge of the casserole, the broadest sides pushed into the dish a little way.
5. Bake an hour in a 350° oven, or until well browned and firm in the centre. Serves 6.

Serve with a plate of sliced ripe tomatoes, topped with chopped chives and parsley mixed with French dressing, and cucumbers and carrots.

TUNA-EGG CASSEROLE

7-oz. tin tuna fish drained and coarsely
  broken up
4 hard-boiled eggs quartered
1½ tablespoons butter or margarine
1½ tablespoons flour
¾ teaspoon salt

½ pt. evaporated milk
¼ pt. water
⅛ teaspoon Tabasco sauce
2 tablespoons minced green pepper
2 tablespoons minced pimento
3 oz. buttered crumbs

1. Melt the butter in a saucepan, blend in flour and salt, and gradually stir in the milk and water. Cook until it thickens, stirring constantly.
2. Add the Tabasco, tuna, green pepper, and pimento.
3. Arrange the quartered eggs on the bottom of a medium greased casserole and carefully pour the tuna mixture over them.
4. Top with a thick layer of crumbs.
5. Bake 20–25 minutes in a moderate oven, 375°. Serves 5–6.

Serve with herb-flavoured rice and buttered French beans.

TUNA-MACARONI CASSEROLE

7-oz. tin tuna fish drained, rinsed, and
  broken into chunks
12 oz. elbow macaroni cooked and drained
2 tablespoons butter, margarine, or salad
  oil
2 tablespoons chopped onion

1 tin condensed cream of celery soup
½ pt. milk
1 teaspoon salt
  Dash pepper
¼ teaspoon whole celery seed
4 oz. coarsely chopped Cheddar cheese

1. Sauté the onion lightly in hot fat. Gradually stir in the soup and the milk.
2. Fold in the tuna, season to taste, and add the celery seed and half of the cheese.
3. Mix the macaroni and the tuna mixture, put in a greased casserole, and top with the remaining cheese.
4. Bake 10–15 minutes in a moderate oven, 350°, or until the cheese is melted and the casserole bubbly. Serves 5–6.

Serve with green peppers cut in 1-inch squares and slowly sautéed tender in butter or margarine, and cole slaw.

NOTES

SHELLFISH

DEVILLED SEAFOOD

1 lb. diced cooked shrimps, crabmeat, lobster, and fish, in any combination
4 tablespoons butter or margarine
2 tablespoons flour
1 pt. milk scalded
  Salt and pepper
1 teaspoon grated onion
2 tablespoons minced parsley

¼ teaspoon dried oregano or ¾ teaspoon fresh, chopped
½ teaspoon dry mustard
1 teaspoon Worcestershire sauce
2 tablespoons ketchup
3 hard-boiled eggs chopped
1 oz. bread or cornflake crumbs

1. Melt 2 tablespoons butter over medium heat and stir in flour and milk. Season to taste and stir until smooth and thickened.
2. Add the onion, parsley, oregano, mustard, Worcestershire sauce, and ketchup. Blend well.
3. Gently fold in the chopped eggs and seafood.
4. Pour into a small greased casserole, top with crumbs, dot with remaining butter, and bake 15–20 minutes in a hot oven, 475°. Serves 4.

Serve with hot fluffy rice and shredded green cabbage cooked until barely tender.

SEAFOOD SOUFFLÉ

½ lb. crabmeat picked over and coarsely flaked (fresh, frozen, or tinned)
1 lb. shrimps cooked, shelled, deveined, and broken up
2 hard-boiled eggs chopped
3 tablespoons sweet pickle relish

2 tablespoons minced parsley
2 tablespoons lemon juice
  Salt and pepper
1 tin lobster bisque
4 fluid oz. thin cream
4 eggs separated

1. In a greased medium casserole or straight-sided soufflé dish mix the crabmeat, shrimps, chopped eggs, relish, parsley, lemon juice, and salt and pepper to taste.
2. In a small saucepan heat the lobster bisque slowly and blend in the cream.
3. Remove from the heat and stir in the well-beaten yolks and the crab-shrimp mixture.
4. Beat the egg whites until stiff but not dry and gently fold into the seafood mixture.
5. Bake 40–50 minutes in a moderate oven, 350°, or until a knife inserted in the middle comes out clean. If you prefer a soufflé somewhat on the soft side bake it only until the knife comes out with a little egg on it. Serve at once. Serves 4–5.

Serve with buttered French beans and buttered baby carrots.

MUSSEL AND SWEET-CORN CASSEROLE

10-oz. jar or tin of mussels, undrained
6 oz. whole-kernel sweet corn, tinned, fresh, or frozen
2 eggs well beaten
½ pt. milk
4 oz. coarse oatmeal

3 tablespoons melted butter or margarine
2 tablespoons minced onion
1 tablespoon minced green pepper
½ teaspoon Worcestershire sauce
Salt and pepper
2 oz. grated Cheddar cheese

HERE is a delicious combination of flavours, calling for the simplest possible preparation.
1. Combine the eggs, milk, and oatmeal and let them stand about 10 minutes.
2. Stir in all remaining ingredients except the cheese, seasoning to taste. Pour into a medium casserole and bake 50 minutes in a 350° oven, or until the centre feels firm.
3. Spread the cheese on top and bake 5 minutes longer, or until the cheese is melted. Serves 4.

Serve with buttered mixed vegetables and a green salad.

SEAFOOD CASSEROLE

20 cooked small shrimps, shelled and deveined
½ lb. crabmeat, fresh, frozen, or tinned, picked over and coarsely flaked
½ lb. cooked lobster meat
½ lb. cooked scallops sliced thin crosswise
1 teaspoon chopped shallots or spring onions
3 tablespoons butter or margarine
10 mushroom caps sliced thin
1 tablespoon flour

4 fluid oz. dry white wine
½ pt. water
12 anchovy fillets, washed, dried, and cut up
Juice of 1 lemon
1 teaspoon chopped chives
1 teaspoon Worcestershire sauce
1 tablespoon chili sauce (optional)
3 tablespoons thick cream
Salt and pepper
2 tablespoons buttered crumbs
2 tablespoons grated Parmesan cheese

A LOT of ingredients, perhaps, but the result is truly worth it!
1. Sauté the shallots in 1 tablespoon of the butter in a heavy frying-pan until golden.
2. Add the mushrooms and cook 3–4 minutes.
3. Sprinkle with flour and stir until flour is absorbed.
4. Blend in the wine and cook until very thick.
5. Add the water and simmer gently about 5 minutes, stirring occasionally, until the sauce is smooth and thick.
6. Stir in the seafood gently and simmer over very low heat 5 minutes or so, stirring frequently.
7. Add the anchovies, the remaining 2 tablespoons butter bit by bit, lemon juice, chives, Worcestershire sauce, chili sauce, and cream.
8. Season to taste, pour into a 2-quart casserole, top with crumbs, sprinkle with cheese, and brown under the grill. Serves 8.

Note: If you prepare this casserole early in the day and refrigerate it, bring it to room temperature (1 hour) and bake it 20 minutes in a moderate oven, 375°, before grilling it.

Serve with plenty of fluffy hot rice, mixed vegetables, and a large green salad. Warm French bread goes well, too.

SEAFOOD QUICHE

½ lb. crabmeat or lobster lumps
½ lb. cooked shrimps, shelled, deveined,
   and broken up if large
¼ lb. scallops cooked (quartered if large)
   Pastry for 9-inch pie shell
1 egg white
2 tablespoons butter or margarine
2 tablespoons minced shallots or scallions
   (spring onions)

2 tablespoons cognac
1 teaspoon chopped chives
½ teaspoon dried tarragon or 1½ teaspoons
   fresh, chopped
4 eggs well beaten
¾ pt. thin cream
4 drops Tabasco
   Salt and pepper
2 tablespoons grated Parmesan cheese

THIS is a real gourmet treat, an outstanding 'company' dish.

1. Line a deep pie plate with the pastry, rolled out to ⅛-inch thickness, and crimp the edges. Brush with the egg white.

2. In a frying-pan melt the butter and cook the shallots 2–3 minutes.

3. Stir in the crabmeat, shrimps, and scallops and simmer long enough to heat well.

4. Remove the frying-pan from the heat and add the cognac, chives, and tarragon.

5. To the well-beaten eggs add the cream, Tabasco, and salt and pepper to taste. Stir in the seafood mixture and pour into the pie shell.

6. Sprinkle the top with Parmesan cheese and bake 15 minutes at 450°. Reduce heat to 350° and bake 20–25 minutes longer, or until the centre is firm to the touch, or until a knife inserted in the centre comes out clean. Serve at once. Serves 6.

Serve with diced cucumbers, sliced ripe tomatoes spread with chopped chives and chopped parsley mixed with French dressing, a green salad with a sliced avocado stirred in, and warm French bread.

MUSSELS AND SPAGHETTI

2 10-oz. tins or jars mussels
1 lb. thin spaghetti broken up and cooked
2 tablespoons butter or margarine
1 large onion chopped
1 small garlic clove crushed

6 oz. sliced mushrooms (tinned will do)
  Salt and pepper
3 8-oz. bottles tomato sauce
4 oz. grated Parmesan cheese
2 oz. buttered bread or cornflake crumbs

1. Heat the butter in a heavy frying-pan and lightly sauté the onion, garlic, and mushrooms.
2. Stir in the mussels, salt and pepper to taste, and tomato sauce.
3. In a good-sized casserole arrange layers of spaghetti and mussel sauce, sprinkling a little cheese on each layer.
4. Top the casserole with remaining cheese and crumbs mixed and bake 30 minutes in a moderate oven, 375°, or until browned and bubbly. Serves 6 generously.

Serve with buttered green beans, a green salad, and warm French bread.

COLONIAL MUSSELS-AND-CHICKEN PIE

2 dozen mussels chopped (tinned will do—
  2 tins)
½ lb. diced cooked chicken
12 tiny white onions (tinned will do)
2 tablespoons butter, margarine, or salad
  oil
2 hard-boiled eggs diced

½ lb. diced cooked potatoes
3 oz. chopped celery
3 tablespoons dry sherry
  Salt and pepper
1 tablespoon flour
¼ pt. cream
  Pastry for 1-crust pie

THIS is an old American recipe for a 'solid' meat pie—one without gravy, in the English or Scottish style.
1. Sauté the onions in hot butter in a heavy frying-pan until they are somewhat soft. If you use tinned onions, merely heat them.
2. Stir in the mussels, chicken, eggs, potatoes, celery, and sherry. Season to taste and simmer about 5 minutes over very low heat.
3. Make a paste of the flour and cream and blend in well. Simmer another 5 minutes and pour into a small casserole that will be filled to within ¼ inch or so of the top.
4. Roll out the pastry to about ⅛ inch thickness and lay on top of the pie. Slash several times to permit steam to escape. Bake 15 minutes in a 400° oven and an additional 20 minutes with the heat reduced to 350°. Serves 6.

Serve with sliced young courgettes (unpeeled) gently sautéed in butter in a covered frying-pan 10–15 minutes.

CRABMEAT ALMONDINE

½ lb. fresh, frozen or tinned crabmeat
1½ oz. butter
1½ oz. flour
½ pt. evaporated milk
4 tablespoons water
4 oz. chopped celery
2 oz. chopped green pepper

1 pimento chopped
2 hard-boiled eggs chopped
2 oz. split and toasted almonds
1 teaspoon salt
2 oz. shredded or grated Cheddar cheese
Buttered crumbs
Paprika

As always, the almonds here add flavour to an already pleasing combination of ingredients.

1. Pick over the crabmeat carefully and flake it coarsely.

2. Melt butter in saucepan, blend in flour, and gradually stir in the milk and water mixed. Simmer until smooth and thickened, stirring constantly.

3. Add to the sauce the crabmeat, celery, green pepper, pimento, eggs, and almonds. Season and pour into a small greased casserole.

4. Top with a mixture of cheese and crumbs, dust with paprika, and bake 30–35 minutes in a 350° oven. Serves 4.

Serve with herb-flavoured rice and buttered green peas.

CRABMEAT AU GRATIN

½ lb. crabmeat picked over and flaked
   (tinned, fresh, or frozen)
1½ tablespoons butter
1½ tablespoons flour
⅛ teaspoon pepper
½ teaspoon salt

¼ teaspoon paprika
¾ pt. thin cream
2 oz. grated Cheddar cheese
1 tablespoon Worcestershire sauce
2 tablespoons dry sherry
2 oz. bread or cornflake crumbs

1. Melt the butter in a saucepan, stir in the flour, pepper, salt, and paprika, and gradually blend in the cream, stirring constantly until the sauce is smooth and velvety.

2. Add to the sauce the cheese, Worcestershire sauce, and crabmeat, stirring until the cheese is melted.

3. Add the sherry and pour into a buttered casserole.

4. Top with crumbs and bake 15–20 minutes in a hot oven, 400°, or until golden brown. Serves 4.

Serve with buttered noodles and buttered baby carrots.

CRAB AND SWEET CORN CASSEROLE

½ lb. crabmeat picked over and flaked
(tinned, fresh, or frozen)
10-oz. tin sweet corn
3 hard-boiled eggs, minced
1 tablespoon chopped parsley
2 teaspoons lemon juice
1 tablespoon butter or margarine
1 tablespoon minced onion
1 tablespoon flour

1 teaspoon dry mustard
½ pt. milk
¼ teaspoon salt
½ teaspoon Worcestershire sauce
1 tablespoon melted butter or margarine
2 oz. bread crumbs or cornflake
crumbs
1 oz. grated Parmesan cheese

THIS is an interesting combination of flavours, with just enough lemon juice, mustard, etc., to keep it from being bland.
1. Mix the crabmeat lightly with the sweet corn, eggs, parsley, and lemon juice.
2. Put the 1 tablespoon butter in a saucepan and cook the onion until it is transparent.
3. Stir in the flour, mustard, and milk, stirring until the sauce is smooth and thickened. Add salt and Worcestershire sauce.
4. Combine the crabmeat mixture and sauce and pour into a medium casserole.
5. Top with a mixture of the melted butter, crumbs, and cheese.
6. Bake 20–25 minutes in a 375° oven, or until golden brown and bubbly. Serves 6.

Serve with creamed chopped spinach and cole slaw.

AMERICAN CRABMEAT CASSEROLE

6-oz. tin crabmeat flaked
6 oz. broad noodles broken up and
cooked
1 tablespoon butter or margarine
14-oz. tin white asparagus tips drained
4-oz. tin sliced mushrooms drained

1 small green pepper chopped
½ teaspoon salt
¼ teaspoon fresh-ground pepper
½ pt. seasoned white sauce
4 oz. grated Cheddar cheese

1. Drain the noodles well, stir in the butter, and pour into a medium casserole, well buttered.
2. Arrange in layers over the noodles first the crabmeat, and then the asparagus tips, mushrooms, and green pepper. Salt and pepper lightly.
3. Make the white sauce with 1 tablespoon butter or margarine, 1 tablespoon flour, and ½ pt. milk. Season to taste and pour over the casserole.
4. Top with grated cheese and bake in a moderate oven, 350°, about 35 minutes, or until golden brown and bubbly. Serves 4.

Serve with buttered green peas and a green salad.

CRABMEAT CRÊPES

Crêpes

3 eggs
½ pt. milk
½ teaspoon salt

3 oz. flour
3 tablespoons melted butter

Filling

¾ lb. flaked crabmeat
¾ pt. rich white sauce
3 tablespoons dry sherry
¼ teaspoon grated lemon peel

¼ teaspoon grated nutmeg
1 teaspoon curry powder
Salt and pepper
2 tablespoons minced parsley

Topping

6 oz. Hollandaise sauce (tinned will do)
¼ pt. sour cream

2 oz. toasted sliced almonds

STUFFED pancakes can be one of the most delicate dishes imaginable. Stuffings vary greatly, but none is better than crabmeat.

Crêpes: Mix the ingredients in order and beat until just blended. Make the crêpes one at a time. Pour 2 tablespoons of the batter into a hot buttered omelette pan not over 6 or 7 inches in diameter, and rotate it quickly to cover the bottom. Cook until brown on both sides. Keep warm in the oven if you are going to serve right away, but they can be made well in advance and reheated without loss of flavour.

Filling: Make the white sauce with 3 tablespoons butter or margarine, 3 tablespoons flour, and ¾ pt. top milk or half-and-half. Season to taste. Stir in the remaining ingredients.

Put 2 tablespoons of this filling on each crêpe, roll it up, and lay in a buttered shallow casserole, seam side down.

Topping: Blend Hollandaise sauce and sour cream and spread over the top of the crêpes. Scatter almonds on top and bake in a hot oven, 475°, 10–15 minutes, until heated through. Serves 6.

Note: If you make this casserole early in the day, bring it to room temperature (1 hour) before baking, and add the topping then. Instead of the almonds you can use 2 tablespoons grated Parmesan cheese, for a different flavour.

Serve with buttered asparagus and a green salad.

CRAB-STUFFED MUSHROOMS

1 lb. crabmeat, fresh, frozen, or tinned
12 very large mushroom caps
2 oz. + 2 tablespoons butter or
  margarine
2 tablespoons chopped shallots or
  1 tablespoon chopped onion
2 tablespoons dry sherry

½ pt. white sauce
1 teaspoon dry mustard
1 teaspoon dried marjoram or
  1 tablespoon fresh, chopped
  Salt and pepper
6 oz. Hollandaise sauce (tinned will do)
4 fluid oz. thick cream whipped

1. Soak the mushroom caps in cold water 2 hours to keep them from shrinking. Dry, and sauté 7–8 minutes in the 2 oz. butter.
2. Heat the 2 tablespoons butter in a saucepan and sauté the shallots (or onions) just until they are transparent.
3. Add the crabmeat, carefully picked over and flaked, and sauté over very low heat 5 minutes. Add the sherry.
4. Make the white sauce with 1 tablespoon butter, 1 tablespoon flour, and ½ pt. milk. Stir in the mustard and marjoram, season to taste, and mix well with the crabmeat mixture.
5. Use this mixture to fill the mushroom caps and lay them in a shallow greased casserole, close together.
6. Mix the Hollandaise sauce and the whipped cream and spread over the mushrooms.
7. Put under the grill, at least 5 inches from the heat, until they are bubbly and brown. Serves 6.

If serving for lunch serve with chipped potatoes, a green salad, and hot sesame seed rolls. For Sunday-night supper serve with a rice casserole (see Index), sliced ripe tomatoes, and a green salad.

CRABMEAT CASSEROLE WITH EGGS

6-oz. tin crabmeat flaked
2 hard-boiled eggs sliced
1 tablespoon butter or margarine
1 tablespoon flour
½ pt. milk
  Salt and pepper

3 oz. chopped celery
3 oz. chopped green pepper
1 teaspoon Worcestershire sauce
  Grated Parmesan cheese
  Dash paprika

1. Make a white sauce of the butter, flour, and milk, seasoning to taste.
2. Blend in the crabmeat, celery, and green pepper.
3. Remove the saucepan from the heat and gently stir in the eggs and Worcestershire sauce.
4. Spread in a small shallow casserole, sprinkle with grated cheese and paprika, and brown under the grill 3–4 minutes, until golden and bubbly. Serves 4.

Serve with buttered green peas to which you have added 2 or 3 coarsely chopped mushrooms lightly sautéed in butter, French fried potatoes, and a green salad.

CRAB GOURMET

1 lb. tinned crabmeat or frozen crabmeat
  thawed, picked over, and flaked
3 oz. toasted walnuts broken up coarsely
2 hard-boiled eggs chopped
$\frac{1}{4}$ pt. mayonnaise
2 teaspoons lemon juice
1 teaspoon Worcestershire sauce

$\frac{1}{4}$ teaspoon dry mustard
$\frac{1}{4}$ teaspoon salt
  Dash cayenne pepper
3 oz soft bread crumbs
2 oz. melted butter or margarine
  Chopped parsley

THIS delectable dish is true gourmet fare.
1. Mix the crabmeat lightly with the walnuts and eggs.
2. Mix the mayonnaise with lemon juice, Worcestershire sauce, mustard, salt, and cayenne. Stir into the crab mixture.
3. Pour gently into a small shallow casserole.
4. Top with the fresh bread crumbs mixed with melted butter and parsley, and bake in a hot oven, 400°, about 20 minutes, or until the top is well browned. Serves 4.

Serve with asparagus Hollandaise and a green salad to which is added grated carrot, sliced cucumber (unpeeled), and thin tomato wedges.

CRAB IMPERIAL

3 6-oz. packets frozen king crab or 1$\frac{1}{2}$ lbs.
  tinned or fresh crab
1 tablespoon butter or margarine
2 tablespoons minced green pepper
1 tablespoon flour
$\frac{1}{2}$ teaspoon dry mustard

$\frac{1}{2}$ teaspoon salt
$\frac{1}{8}$ teaspoon paprika
$\frac{1}{4}$ pt. creamy milk
$\frac{1}{4}$ pt. mayonnaise
1 tablespoon dry sherry
2 tablespoons minced pimento

CRAB Imperial is a noted dish, and, as with many other famous dishes, there are many ways of making it. This recipe is a delectable one.
1. Melt butter in saucepan and lightly cook the green pepper, just for 2–3 minutes.
2. Blend in flour, mustard, salt, and paprika. Cook for a moment and stir in the milk.
3. Remove from the heat and stir in the mayonnaise.
4. Pick over the crabmeat carefully, keeping it in quite large chunks. Stir gently into the white sauce with the sherry and pimento.
5. Spread out in a shallow casserole or in 6 crab shells or ramekins and bake in a 375° oven, 25 minutes for the single casserole, 15 minutes for the individual ones. Serves 6.

Serve with a rice casserole (see Index) and a green salad with frozen (or tinned) cooked hearts of artichokes added, together with wedges of ripe tomatoes.

CRAB QUICHE

$\frac{3}{4}$ lb. crabmeat, fresh, frozen, or tinned
4 eggs lightly beaten
  9-inch pie shell, unbaked
$\frac{3}{4}$ pt. thin cream
$\frac{3}{4}$ teaspoon salt
$\frac{1}{4}$ teaspoon nutmeg

Dash of pepper
1 tablespoon chopped celery
1 tablespoon chopped parsley
1 tablespoon chopped onion
2 tablespoons dry sherry

1. Beat the eggs and use a little to brush the pie shell. Chill it while you prepare the filling.

2. Pick over the crabmeat carefully to remove bits of shell, cartilage, etc. Break it into rather coarse chunks.

3. Mix the eggs, cream, and seasoning.

4. Mix the celery, parsley, onion, and sherry with the crabmeat and spread this in the chilled pie shell. Pour the egg mixture over.

5. Bake 35–40 minutes in a hot oven, 425°, reducing the heat to 375° the last 15 minutes. When the quiche is done a knife inserted in the centre should come out clean. Serves 6.

Serve with sliced ripe tomatoes and a green salad for luncheon. For supper add asparagus with lemon-butter-crumb sauce.

CRABMEAT ORIENTAL

6-oz. packet frozen crabmeat or 6½-oz. tin
1 packet chow mein noodles
1 tin condensed cream of celery soup
$\frac{1}{4}$ pt. thin cream
3 oz. sliced mushrooms lightly sautéed

2 oz. whole cashew nuts or whole salted
  almonds
1 tablespoon minced onion
  Salt and pepper

1. Pick over the crabmeat carefully, to remove bits of shell and cartilage. Flake coarsely.

2. Set aside half of the noodles, and combine the remainder with all the other ingredients, mixing gently.

3. Place in a small greased casserole and bake 30 minutes in a moderate oven, 350°.

4. After 15 minutes top the casserole with the remaining noodles. Serves 4.

Serve with buttered French beans and cole slaw.

Baked ham with ginger pears

CRAB SARDI

1½ lbs. crabmeat, fresh, frozen, or tinned
¼ pt. warmed dry sherry
1 pt. sauce (see below)

2 packets frozen asparagus (jumbo size),
  or 24 stalks fresh, cooked barely tender
2 oz. grated Parmesan cheese

Sauce

 4 fluid oz. dry sherry
12 fluid oz. white sauce made with chicken
   broth instead of milk (Velouté sauce)
 4 tablespoons thin cream

4 fluid oz. Hollandaise sauce (tinned or
  bottled will do)
4 fluid oz. cream whipped

THIS is a mouth-watering dish, though sinfully rich.
1. Pick over the crabmeat carefully, to get out bits of shell and cartilage.
2. Pour over the warmed sherry and let stand 10 minutes.
3. Spread out in a buttered shallow casserole, with the sherry.
4. Lay the asparagus stalks over the crabmeat, cover with the sauce, top with Parmesan cheese, and brown under the grill. Serves 4–5.

Sauce: Reduce the sherry to half its volume by boiling rapidly in a small saucepan. Make the Velouté sauce with 2 tablespoons butter, 2 tablespoons flour, and the chicken broth. Season to taste. Add the thin cream and reduced sherry to it and cool somewhat. Fold in the Hollandaise and whipped cream blended together.

Serve with petits pois, potato puffs, green salad, and sesame seed rolls.

CRABMEAT WITH SPAGHETTI

1½ lbs. crabmeat picked over and flaked
  coarsely
10 oz. thin spaghetti broken up and cooked
 1 tin condensed cream of mushroom soup
 1 large tin evaporated milk
 4 oz. grated Cheddar cheese
 2 oz. minced green pepper

1 tablespoon minced onion
½ teaspoon salt
¼ teaspoon dried thyme or ¾ teaspoon fresh
1 teaspoon chopped parsley
1 tablespoon butter or margarine
2 oz. soft bread crumbs

1. Stir together the drained spaghetti, crabmeat, soup, milk, cheese, green pepper, onion, salt, and herbs. Pour into a greased 2-quart casserole.
2. Melt the butter, stir in the crumbs, and spread on top of the casserole.
3. Bake 45 minutes in a moderate oven, 350°, or until golden and bubbly. Serves 8.

Serve with sliced ripe tomatoes, mixed vegetables, and a green salad.

Blanquette of veal

DEVILLED CRAB

1 lb. crabmeat, preferably fresh or frozen
2 tablespoons chopped onion
1 tablespoon chopped green pepper
1 tablespoon butter or margarine
½ teaspoon salt
 Dash cayenne
¾ pt. white sauce

1 teaspoon prepared mustard
2 egg yolks
3 tablespoons thin cream
1 tablespoon chopped chives
1 tablespoon chopped parsley
½ teaspoon Worcestershire sauce
 Buttered crumbs

1. Pick over the crabmeat to remove bits of shell and cartilage, but leave in fairly good-sized chunks.
2. Cook the onion and green pepper in butter until the onion is transparent. Add salt and cayenne.
3. Make the white sauce with 1½ tablespoons butter or margarine, 1½ tablespoons flour, and ¾ pt. milk. Season to taste and stir in the mustard.
4. Add the egg yolks beaten with the cream, the chives, parsley, and Worcestershire sauce, then the onions and green pepper, and finally the crabmeat.
5. Spread in a shallow casserole and top with crumbs.
6. Bake in a moderate oven, 350°, 35 minutes, or until golden brown and bubbly. Serves 4.

Serve with thin spaghetti tossed with grated cheese and butter and a green salad with grated carrot, sliced cucumbers (unpeeled), and tomato wedges added. Warm French bread goes well, too.

DEVILLED CRAB WITH ALMONDS

½ lb. crabmeat (fresh, frozen, or tinned)
 picked over and coarsely flaked
1½ oz. butter or margarine
1 tablespoon chopped onion
5 oz. thinly sliced celery
1½ oz. flour
¾ pt. milk
¾ teaspoon salt
⅛ teaspoon fresh-ground pepper

 Dash cayenne pepper
½ teaspoon prepared mustard
¼ teaspoon Worcestershire sauce
2 hard-boiled eggs diced
3 tablespoons chopped parsley
3 tablespoons diced pimento
2 oz. blanched and sliced almonds
1 oz. buttered crumbs

1. Melt the butter in a heavy frying-pan, stir in the onion and celery, cover, and cook over very low heat about 5 minutes.
2. Stir in the flour, milk, salt and pepper, cayenne, mustard, and Worcestershire sauce, stirring until the sauce is smooth and thick.
3. Gently mix into the sauce the crabmeat, eggs, parsley, pimento, and almonds.
4. Spread out in a shallow buttered casserole, top with crumbs, and bake 15 minutes in a 375° oven. Serves 4.

Serve with herb-flavoured rice and tinned sweet corn.

CHINESE LOBSTER OR CRABMEAT CASSEROLE

2 lbs. lobster or crabmeat (fresh, frozen, or tinned)
2 oz. butter or margarine
1 egg lightly beaten
3 tablespoons minced onion
1 tablespoon soy sauce
1 tablespoon cornflour

4 tablespoons water
8 oz. hot cooked rice
1 6-oz. tin bean sprouts drained
1 tablespoon chopped candied or preserved ginger
1 tablespoon grated orange rind
Salt

1. Heat the butter in a medium casserole in a 300° oven. When it is melted stir in the lobster or crab, picked over and broken into good-sized lumps. Return to the oven.
2. Blend the egg, onion, soy sauce, and the cornflour mixed with the water. Stir into the lobster and continue to bake about 10 minutes, stirring 2 or 3 times.
3. Remove the casserole from the oven and push the lobster mixture into the middle. Mix the rice and bean sprouts and arrange around the lobster.
4. Top the rice with ginger and orange rind, cover, and bake 20 minutes. Serves 4.

Serve with buttered baby Brussels sprouts and a green salad.

LOBSTER PIE

2 2-lb. boiled lobsters or 2 lbs. lobster meat diced
2 tablespoons butter or margarine
2 tablespoons flour
¾ pt. top milk or half-and-half
4 fluid oz. Madeira or dry sherry

2 egg yolks
4 tablespoons thin cream
Salt and pepper
8 oz. biscuit crust pastry or pastry for 1-crust pie

1. Melt the butter in a saucepan and blend in the flour. Gradually blend in the milk and cook, stirring, until the sauce is smooth and thickened.
2. Add the wine and the egg yolks beaten with the cream. Season to taste and remove from the heat.
3. Remove lobster meat from shells if boiled lobsters are used. Arrange the lobster meat in a medium casserole and pour the sauce over it.
4. Pat the biscuit crust pastry to ½-inch thickness on a lightly floured board and cut out small rounds. Lay them gently, close together, on top of the casserole.
5. Brush with melted butter and bake 20–25 minutes in a hot oven, 425°, or until golden brown. If you prefer, make the topping of short-crust pastry, slashing it well to permit steam to escape. Serves 6.

Serve with fluffy mashed potatoes and runner beans.

LOBSTER QUICHE

1 lb. lobster meat in good-sized chunks
3 tablespoons butter or margarine
  Salt and pepper
3 tablespoons dry sherry or Madeira
  Pastry for 9-inch pie
4 eggs

1 tablespoon flour
½ teaspoon salt
  Dash cayenne
¾ pt. thin cream
2 tablespoons grated Parmesan cheese
1 tablespoon melted butter or margarine

1. Melt the 3 tablespoons butter in a heavy frying-pan and sauté the lobster meat lightly in it 2–3 minutes.
2. Season with a very little salt and pepper, stir in the sherry or Madeira, cover, and simmer over very low heat 3–4 minutes.
3. Roll out the pastry to ⅛-inch thickness, line a shallow casserole or pie plate with it, and pour in the lobster, with juice.
4. Beat together the eggs, flour, salt, and cayenne. Stir in the cream and pour over the lobster in the pie shell.
5. Sprinkle with the Parmesan cheese and sprinkle the melted butter over. Bake in a moderate oven, 375°, about 40 minutes, or until the custard is firm to the touch and the crust brown. Serves 6.

Serve with steamed cauliflower flowerets with lemon-butter-crumb sauce and a green salad with slices of ripe tomato.

DEVILLED OYSTERS

1 quart shelled and bearded oysters with
  their juice
2 tablespoons salad oil
2 oz. minced onion
4 oz. water biscuit crumbs
2 tablespoons Worcestershire sauce
2 tablespoons ketchup

4 dashes Tabasco sauce
  Juice of ½ lemon
2 tablespoons minced parsley
2 tablespoons fine bread or cornflake
  crumbs
1 tablespoon butter

THIS tangy dish will please those who like their food hot.
1. Heat the oysters in their own liquor until the edges curl.
2. Heat the oil in a frying-pan and sauté the onion lightly.
3. Stir in the biscuit crumbs, Worcestershire sauce, ketchup, Tabasco, lemon juice, and parsley.
4. Stir the oysters and their juice into this mixture and turn into a greased shallow casserole.
5. Top with crumbs, dot with bits of butter, and bake 15 minutes in a hot oven, 425°, or until sizzling. Serves 4–5.

Serve with cole slaw, buttered green peas, and a green salad.

OYSTERS BAKED IN WINE SAUCE

3 dozen oysters shelled and bearded
12 fluid oz. dry white wine
2 tablespoons butter
2 tablespoons flour

6 fluid oz. thick cream
Salt and pepper
Dash of cayenne
3 tablespoons buttered crumbs

HERE is a wonderful way to prepare cooked oysters, and simple, too.
1. Heat the wine in a large heavy frying-pan. When it is just under boiling lay in the oysters and poach them 1 minute. Lift them out with a slotted spoon or spatula and arrange in a large shallow casserole.
2. Strain the wine through a fine sieve.
3. Melt the butter in a saucepan, stir in the flour, and cook briefly. Gradually blend in the wine in which the oysters were poached, stirring until the sauce is smooth and thick.
4. Stir in the cream, season to taste with salt, pepper, and cayenne, and pour the sauce over the oysters.
5. Top with crumbs and bake in a hot oven, 450°, 10 minutes, or until golden brown. Serves 5–6.

Serve with buttered baby beetroots and buttered baby carrots.

OYSTERS FLORENTINE

1 quart shelled oysters with their liquor
4 tablespoons butter or margarine
10 oz. chopped spinach (1 packet frozen,
   thawed and well drained)
2 oz. chopped onion
⅛ teaspoon nutmeg
   Salt and pepper
2 tablespoons chopped parsley

2 tablespoons flour
½ pt. fish stock
3 tablespoons cream
½ teaspoon garlic salt
1 tablespoon lemon juice
2 oz. buttered bread or cornflake crumbs
2 tablespoons grated Parmesan cheese

HERE is a pleasant combination of flavours, especially useful because it can be completely prepared early in the morning and refrigerated until an hour before baking.
1. Melt 2 tablespoons of the butter in a frying-pan and simmer in it the spinach and onion. Season to taste and add the nutmeg and parsley.
2. In a saucepan melt the remaining 2 tablespoons of butter and make a white sauce with the flour, fish stock, liquor drained from the oysters, and cream. Stir until smooth and thick. Season with garlic salt and lemon juice.
3. Spread the spinach on the bottom of a large flat greased casserole. Lay oysters on top in one layer and cover with the sauce.
4. Top with the crumbs and cheese mixed. Bake in a hot oven, 400°, 15–20 minutes, or until bubbly and golden. Serves 5–6.

Serve with fluffy mashed potatoes, sliced ripe tomatoes, and a plain green salad.

BAKED OYSTERS WITH POTATO TOPPING

1 pt. shelled and bearded oysters with
   their liquor
1¼ lbs. hot mashed potatoes
2 oz. butter or margarine melted
4-oz. tin sliced mushrooms
1 tablespoon chopped onion
1 tablespoon cornflour

2 tablespoons minced green pepper
   Thin cream
½ teaspoon salt
⅛ teaspoon pepper
2 oz. chopped pimento
2 tablespoons dry sherry
1 egg beaten

1. Simmer the oysters in their own liquor 5 minutes. Drain, saving the liquid.
2. In a saucepan heat the butter and lightly sauté the mushrooms, onion, and green pepper 5 minutes.
3. Add enough cream to the oyster liquid to make ½ pt. Mix a little of this with the cornflour. Add the rest to the saucepan and when it is hot stir in the cornflour mixture, continuing to stir until thick and smooth. Season to taste.
4. Add the oysters, pimento, and sherry to the sauce and pour into a medium casserole or 9-inch pie plate.
5. Beat the egg into the mashed potatoes and make a border around the top of the casserole.
6. Grill 5 minutes, or until golden brown, about 4 inches from the heat. Serves 4.

Serve with thin-sliced courgettes gently sautéed in butter, covered, about 15 minutes.

OYSTER SOUFFLÉ

1 pt. shelled and bearded oysters with their
   liquor
   Milk
1 oz. butter or margarine
1 oz. flour

   Dash grated nutmeg
1 teaspoon salt
   Fresh-ground pepper
4 eggs separated
2 tablespoons brandy

1. Simmer the oysters in their liquor 5 minutes. Drain them, reserving the liquid. Add enough milk to the liquid to make ¼ pt.
2. Chop the oysters quite fine.
3. Melt the butter in a saucepan, stir in the flour, nutmeg, salt, and pepper. Gradually blend in the milk mixture, stirring until the sauce is smooth and thick.
4. Blend a little of it into the beaten egg yolks and quickly stir back into the sauce.
5. Stir in the oysters and brandy. Cool somewhat and blend in the egg whites beaten until stiff.
6. Pour into a deep quart casserole or soufflé dish, well greased, and bake in a moderate oven, 350°, 30 minutes, or until firm in the centre. Serve at once. Serves 4.

OYSTERS TETRAZZINI

3 dozen oysters, shelled and bearded
  with their liquor
½ lb. fine noodles cooked
4 oz. butter or margarine melted
3 oz. soft bread crumbs
1 oz. grated Parmesan cheese
2 oz. flour

2½ teaspoons salt
¼ teaspoon fresh-ground pepper
2 teaspoons Worcestershire sauce
1¼ pts. milk
3 tablespoons dry sherry
½ teaspoon paprika

1. Drain the oysters, reserving about ¼ pt. of their liquor.

2. Drain the noodles well and arrange them in a shallow greased casserole or deep pie plate.

3. Mix 3 tablespoons of the melted butter with the fresh bread crumbs and cheese.

4. Use the rest of the butter to make a white sauce, blending in the flour, 2 teaspoons salt and ⅛ teaspoon pepper, Worcestershire sauce, and finally the milk and the oyster liquor. Cook until it is smooth and thick, stirring constantly. Add the sherry.

5. Spread the oysters on top of the noodles, sprinkle with ½ teaspoon of salt and ⅛ teaspoon pepper. Carefully pour over the sauce.

6. Top with the crumb mixture and sprinkle with paprika. Bake 30–35 minutes in a 400° oven, or until bubbly and golden. Serves 6.

SCALLOPS DUXELLES

2 lbs. scallops
5 tablespoons butter
2 tablespoons minced onion
¾ lb. minced mushrooms
½ pt. dry white wine
1 tablespoon lemon juice
2 teaspoons chopped parsley
½ teaspoon salt
¼ teaspoon pepper
¼ teaspoon nutmeg

¼ pt. water
¼ teaspoon dried thyme or ¾ teaspoon
  fresh, chopped
1 sprig parsley
1 small bay leaf
2 tablespoons flour
½ pt. thin cream
6 tablespoons grated
  Parmesan cheese
Pinch cayenne

1. Melt 3 tablespoons of the butter in a heavy frying-pan and sauté the onion until it is barely soft.

2. Add the mushrooms and continue to cook until the liquid evaporates.

3. Stir in half the wine, the lemon juice, chopped parsley, salt, pepper, and nutmeg. Cook until the wine evaporates, and set aside.

4. In a saucepan heat the rest of the wine, the water, thyme, sprig of parsley, and bay leaf. Bring to a boil and add the scallops. Poach them gently 5–6 minutes, or until they turn white and are tender. Strain them, reserving the broth.

5. In a frying-pan melt the remaining 2 tablespoons butter, blend in the flour, and stir in the cream and ½ pt. of the scallop broth. Keep stirring until the sauce is thick and smooth. Correct the seasoning.

6. Combine ¼ pt. of the sauce with the mushroom mixture and spread on the bottom of a medium casserole. Arrange the scallops on top.

7. Add to the rest of the sauce 4 tablespoons of the cheese and the cayenne and pour over the scallops. Sprinkle with the remaining cheese and bake 10 minutes in a hot oven, 425°, or brown under the grill. Serves 6.

Serve with parsley-butter potatoes and buttered baby beetroots.

SCALLOPS MÉNAGÈRE

1 lb. scallops
8 large mushrooms sliced and lightly
  sautéed
$\frac{1}{4}$ pt. dry white wine
$\frac{1}{2}$ pt. water
1-inch piece of celery
  Small sprig parsley
2 peppercorns bruised
  Pinch of thyme
1 teaspoon chopped onion

$\frac{1}{4}$ teaspoon salt
  Bones of any white fish
1$\frac{1}{2}$ tablespoons butter or margarine
1$\frac{1}{2}$ tablespoons flour
$\frac{3}{4}$ pt. milk
  Salt and pepper
  Pinch nutmeg
2 tablespoons bread or cornflake crumbs
4 tablespoons grated Parmesan cheese
2 tablespoons melted butter

1. Make a *court bouillon* by boiling in a saucepan about 15 minutes the wine, water, celery, parsley, peppercorns, thyme, onion, $\frac{1}{4}$ teaspoon salt, and fish bones. Drain the bouillon, discard the bones and vegetables, and reheat the broth. Drop in the scallops, bring to a boil again, and simmer about 8 minutes. Drain and cut each one crosswise in three slices.
2. Make a white sauce with the 1$\frac{1}{2}$ tablespoons butter, the flour, and milk. Season to taste and add the nutmeg.
3. Stir the mushrooms and scallops into the sauce and pour into a medium casserole.
4. Top with crumbs and cheese mixed and sprinkle the melted butter over.
5. Put under the grill, about 5 inches from the heat, and brown well. Serves 4.

Serve with riced potatoes and runner beans.

BAKED SCALLOPS

1 quart scallops
1 green pepper chopped very fine
5 oz. fine bread or cornflake crumbs
$\frac{1}{2}$ teaspoon dry mustard
  Salt and pepper

1 teaspoon Worcestershire sauce
  Dash Tabasco
2 oz. melted butter or margarine
2 oz. solid butter or margarine

1. Mix together the green pepper, crumbs, mustard, a little salt and pepper, Worcestershire sauce, and Tabasco. Spread in a soup plate.
2. Put the melted butter in another soup plate, warmed.
3. Have ready a medium casserole, preferably rather wide and shallow. Roll the scallops first in the melted butter, then in the crumb mixture, and lay in the casserole.
4. Dot with butter and bake in a moderate oven, 350°, about 30 minutes.
5. Garnish with parsley and serve with lemon wedges. Serves 6.

Serve with buttered noodles, to which poppy seeds and split toasted almonds are added, and mixed sweet corn and beans.

CHINESE SHRIMP CASSEROLE

¾ lb. cooked and cleaned small shrimps
3 oz. chopped celery
6 oz. chopped onion
¼ pt. water
4-oz. tin sliced mushrooms
2 tablespoons butter or margarine

6 oz. chopped green pepper
6-oz. cashew nuts chopped
4-oz. tin pimento drained and chopped
1 pt. medium white sauce
Salt and pepper
2 3-oz. tins Chinese noodles

1. Simmer the celery and onion in the water in a covered saucepan until the onion is soft, 5–7 minutes. Drain.
2. Sauté the mushrooms lightly in the butter. Stir in the celery-onion mixture, green pepper, cashews, pimento, and shrimps.
3. Make the white sauce with 3½ tablespoons butter or margarine, 3½ tablespoons flour, 1 pt. milk, and salt and pepper to taste.
4. Combine the white sauce and the shrimp mixture and mix well.
5. Spread 1 tin of the noodles on the bottom of a casserole.
6. Pour the shrimp mixture over, and top with the other tin of noodles.
7. Bake 30 minutes in a moderate oven, 350°. Serves 8–10.

Serve with French beans and a green salad with additions of grated carrot, sliced unpeeled cucumbers, and thin wedges of tomato.

CHINESE SHRIMP WITH BAMBOO SHOOTS AND HAM

1 lb. small shrimps shelled and deveined
1 egg white
2 tablespoons dry sherry
1 teaspoon cornflour
3 tablespoons salad oil
1 teaspoon sugar

½ teaspoon salt
2 tablespoons diced cooked ham
2 tablespoons chopped
  bamboo shoots
3 oz. partly cooked green peas
Chicken stock, white wine, or water

1. Whip the egg white lightly with a fork and combine with half of the sherry and the cornflour.
2. Heat the oil to sizzling in a heavy frying-pan.
3. Roll the shrimps in the egg-white mixture and cook in the oil, lowering the heat as soon as the shrimps are added. Stir frequently until tender, or until they are all pink.
4. Stir in the sugar, salt, remaining sherry, ham, bamboo shoots, and peas.
5. Put in a casserole and add a little liquid—chicken stock, white wine, or water—not more than ¼ pt.
6. Cover and bake in a hot oven, 400°, 10 minutes. Serves 4.

Serve with buttered narrow noodles and buttered Brussels sprouts.

QUICK SHRIMP CURRY

2 lbs. shrimps shelled and deveined	8½-oz. tin pineapple chunks
2 tablespoons salad oil	¾ pt. thin cream
1 medium onion chopped	4 oz. chutney
2 tablespoons flour	Salt and pepper
2 teaspoons curry powder, or to taste	3 oz. salted peanuts

LIKE all curries, this one improves on standing, and it is a good idea to make it in the morning and merely reheat at serving time. If you do this do not add the peanuts until you are ready to serve.

1. Heat the oil in a heavy casserole on top of the stove and sauté the shrimps and onion until the onion becomes transparent and the shrimps begin to turn pink.
2. Blend the flour and curry powder into the shrimp mixture and gradually add the pineapple (with its juice) and cream. Bring just to a boil.
3. Stir in the chutney and season to taste. Turn down the heat and simmer, covered, 15–20 minutes.
4. Stir in the peanuts just before serving. Serves 4–6.

Serve with the usual curry condiments, as listed in the recipe for Special Chicken Curry (see p. 92). A large green salad is needed, too.

SHRIMP FIESTA PIE

¾ lb. cooked shrimps cut up	3 tablespoons milk
2 tablespoons butter, margarine, or salad oil	2 tablespoons chopped pimento
	1 teaspoon Worcestershire sauce
2 oz. chopped onion	12 oz. biscuit crust pastry
3 tablespoons chopped green pepper	2 oz. grated Cheddar cheese
2 tins condensed cream of mushroom soup	

1. Heat the butter in a saucepan and sauté the onion and green pepper until tender.
2. Stir in soup, milk, shrimps, pimento, and Worcestershire sauce and heat almost to boiling. Pour into a small casserole.
3. Roll out the biscuit crust pastry into a rectangle 7″ × 12″ × ¼″ and sprinkle the cheese evenly over it. Since this is to be rolled up, it will expedite the rolling if you roll out the pastry on a lightly floured piece of waxed paper.
4. Roll the pastry lengthwise, lifting the waxed paper as you roll.
5. With a sharp knife cut into 1-inch slices, laying them close together on top of the shrimp mixture as you cut. Bake 25 minutes in a 400° oven. Serves 6.

Serve with fluffy mashed potatoes and green peppers, cut in 1½-inch squares and gently sautéed in butter.

SHRIMP AND NOODLE CASSEROLE

1 lb. small shrimps cooked, shelled, and
  deveined
8 oz. narrow noodles cooked
1½ oz. butter or margarine
1½ oz. flour
¾ pt. milk

Salt and pepper
8 oz. grated Cheddar cheese
10 oz. whole-kernel sweet corn cooked
  (tinned or frozen)
4 oz. sliced mushrooms (or 6-oz. tin)
2 tablespoons buttered crumbs

1. Make a white sauce with the butter, flour, and milk, adding salt and pepper to taste.
2. Stir in the cheese, continuing to stir until it is melted.
3. Add the noodles, shrimps, sweet corn, and mushrooms to the sauce. Blend well and pour into a greased medium casserole.
4. Top with crumbs and bake about 30 minutes in a hot oven, 400°, or until browned and bubbly. Serves 5–6.

Serve with young courgettes sliced (unpeeled) and gently sautéed, covered, in butter or margarine.

SHRIMPS FLORENTINE

1½ lbs. cooked and deveined shrimps
1 lb. cooked chopped spinach
8 tablespoons butter or margarine
2½ tablespoons flour
1¼ pts. milk scalded
  Salt and pepper
¼ pt. thick cream

Few drops lemon juice
⅛ teaspoon nutmeg
2 tablespoons shallots or spring onions
  minced
¼ pt. dry white wine
1½ tablespoons grated Parmesan cheese

1. Melt 2½ tablespoons of the butter in the top of a double boiler over direct heat.
2. Blend in the flour and cook a minute or two, but don't let it colour. Beat in the hot milk vigorously. Season to taste and let cook over low heat about 2 minutes.
3. Thin out with cream until the sauce just coats the spoon.
4. Stir in lemon juice to taste and keep hot over hot water.
5. Melt 2 tablespoons of the butter in a heavy frying-pan and heat the spinach until the liquid is all evaporated, stirring frequently.
6. Stir in ¼ pt. of the cream sauce and season to taste with salt, pepper, and nutmeg. Spread evenly in a large greased casserole.
7. Heat 2 tablespoons of the butter to sizzling in a heavy frying-pan and add the shrimps and shallots. Season lightly with salt and pepper and sauté over medium heat 2–3 minutes, stirring often. Add the wine and increase the heat to evaporate most of the liquid.
8. Stir in half the remaining white sauce and spread over the spinach.
9. Pour over the rest of the sauce, top with cheese, and dot with the remaining butter.
10. Bake 15 minutes in a 400° oven, or until bubbly and golden. Serves 8.

Serve with chipped potatoes and a green salad.

SHRIMP AND RICE ALMONDINE

2½ lbs. shrimps cooked, shelled, and
  deveined
3 oz. raw rice cooked
1 tablespoon lemon juice
3 tablespoons salad oil
2 tablespoons butter or margarine
2 oz. minced green pepper
2 oz. minced onion

1 teaspoon salt
⅛ teaspoon pepper
  Dash cayenne
1 tin condensed tomato soup
½ pt. thick cream
¼ pt. dry sherry
5 oz. split blanched almonds

IF you like shrimps this is a delicious dish, and one that can be prepared completely early in the day, ready to bake when needed.
1. Spread the cooked rice in a good-sized greased casserole. Arrange the shrimps on top and sprinkle with lemon juice and salad oil.
2. Heat the butter in a saucepan and cook the green pepper and onion over low heat about 5 minutes, or until soft but not brown.
3. Stir in salt and pepper, cayenne, soup, cream, sherry, and half the almonds. Pour over the shrimps in the casserole and stir gently to mix.
4. Bake 35 minutes, uncovered, in a moderate oven, 350°.
5. Sprinkle the remaining almonds on top and continue to bake 20 minutes longer, or until bubbly and golden. Serves 6–8.

Serve with buttered green peas and a large green salad. Warm French bread goes well, too.

ORIENTAL SHRIMP CASSEROLE

1 lb. cooked small shrimps (or large ones
  cut up)
2 tablespoons butter or margarine
8 oz. diagonally sliced celery
6 oz. chopped onions
6 oz. sliced mushrooms (or 8-oz. tin)
3 oz. split toasted blanched almonds

2 3-oz. tins Chinese noodles
10-oz. tin condensed cream of mushroom or
  cream of chicken soup
¼ pt. top milk
2 teaspoons soy sauce
  Paprika

1. Sauté the shrimps lightly in butter 2–3 minutes.
2. Add the celery, onion, mushrooms, almonds, and half the noodles. Pour into a medium casserole and cover with the remaining noodles.
3. Mix the soup, milk, and soy sauce and pour over the noodles.
4. Sprinkle with paprika and bake in a moderate oven, 350°, 40 minutes. Serves 6.

Note: This recipe can also be made with leftover roast pork cut in ¾-inch dice.

Serve with chopped spinach mixed with a little sour cream and a green salad.

NOTES

ONE-DISH MEALS

BEEF AND CABBAGE WITH RICE

1 lb. lean chuck ground
1 small cabbage shredded fine
4 oz. cooked rice
1 medium onion chopped
3 tablespoons butter or margarine
2 hard-boiled eggs chopped
1 tablespoon flour
2 small cloves garlic crushed

2 tablespoons ketchup
8-oz. tin tomatoes
½ pt. water
3- or 4-oz. tin chopped mushrooms with liquid
1 tablespoon chopped parsley
Salt and pepper

1. Sauté the onion in 2 tablespoons butter until soft. Add the beef and cook 3–4 minutes, stirring.
2. Add the rice and eggs and heat well. Pour into a fairly shallow but wide casserole.
3. Spread the cabbage on top of the meat mixture.
4. Melt the remaining tablespoon of butter in a saucepan and blend in the flour. Cook 2–3 minutes and then stir in the garlic, ketchup, tomatoes, water, mushrooms, parsley, and salt and pepper to taste. Simmer about 5 minutes and pour on top of the cabbage.
5. Cover the casserole and bake about 30 minutes in a moderate oven, 350°. Uncover for the last 10 minutes. Serves 6–8.

BEEF CACCIATORE

3 lbs. lean beef cut in 1-inch cubes
  Olive oil or salad oil
2 medium onions chopped
  Flour
2 medium cloves garlic crushed
2 teaspoons salt
½ teaspoon oregano

½ teaspoon crushed red pepper or dash cayenne
6-oz. tin condensed consommé
¼ pt. red wine
1 lb. tin whole tomatoes
2 green peppers cut in strips
12 oz. noodles cooked

1. Heat the oil in a heavy frying-pan and lightly brown onions. Remove them to a bowl for the moment.
2. Dredge the beef with flour and brown it well on all sides in the same oil.
3. Transfer to a large casserole and add to it the onions, garlic, salt, oregano, red pepper or cayenne, and consommé.
4. Cover and simmer over very low heat or bake in a 300° oven 2 hours, or until the beef is *almost* tender. Look at it occasionally and add a little consommé if it seems dry.
5. Add the wine and tomatoes, cover, and simmer or bake 10 minutes more.
6. Stir in the green peppers and cook, uncovered, 15 minutes more.
7. Stir in the cooked noodles. Serves 8.

BEEF, SWEET CORN AND NOODLES

1 lb. lean beef ground
12-oz. tin whole-kernel sweet corn
8-oz. packet wide noodles
3 tablespoons salad oil
1 medium onion chopped
1 medium green pepper chopped
1 clove garlic crushed

1 teaspoon minced parsley
1 teaspoon salt
¼ teaspoon fresh-ground pepper
1-lb. tin tomatoes
6 oz. pitted ripe olives
4 oz. Cheddar cheese cut in small pieces

1. Heat the oil in a large frying-pan and sauté the onion, green pepper, and garlic until they are somewhat soft, and then add the meat. Continue cooking until the beef is browned.
2. Stir in the parsley, salt and pepper, tomatoes, sweet corn, olives, and the uncooked noodles, broken up into fairly small pieces.
3. Pour all this into a casserole and bake, covered, about an hour in a 350° oven. Stir the mixture a couple of times while baking.
4. About 10 minutes before you are ready to serve stir in the cheese and continue cooking about 10 minutes, uncovered. Serves 6.

BEEF, RICE AND AUBERGINE

1 lb. lean beef ground
1 medium aubergine cut in 1-inch cubes
  (unpeeled)
8-oz. cooked rice
5 tablespoons salad oil
2 oz. minced onion

1 oz. chopped green pepper
1 tablespoon chopped parsley
1 teaspoon salt
¼ teaspoon pepper
2 oz. bread or cornflake crumbs
2 tablespoons grated Parmesan cheese

1. Cook the aubergine cubes in boiling salted water until tender, about 10 minutes. Drain well and mash.
2. Brown the beef in 3 tablespoons of the oil.
3. Add onion and green pepper and cook over low heat until onions are transparent.
4. Stir together the aubergine, meat mixture, parsley, salt, pepper, and rice. Turn into a medium casserole.
5. Stir the crumbs into the remaining 2 tablespoons oil and spread on top of the casserole.
6. Top with cheese and bake in a moderate oven, 375°, 20–25 minutes, or until brown and bubbling. Serves 4–5.

BRAISED SHORT RIBS OF BEEF

4 lbs. lean short ribs
   Flour, salt, and pepper
4 tablespoons beef fat or salad oil
1 bay leaf
2 small cloves of garlic
1 onion stuck with 4 cloves

1 teaspoon dried rosemary or 1 tablespoon
   fresh, chopped
4 small carrots scraped and split both ways
$\frac{1}{2}$ pt. red wine
6 oz. runner beans
4 medium potatoes cut in half (optional)

1. Dredge ribs with seasoned flour and lay them in a large heavy casserole. Add beef fat or oil and brown them well. (Or brown them in a frying-pan.)
2. Add bay leaf, garlic cloves, onion, rosemary, carrots, and enough water barely to cover.
3. Bring to a boil on top of the stove, cover, and move to a 300° oven.
4. Bake one hour and add the wine and beans. If you use potatoes add them also at this time. Bake another hour.
5. If you prefer a sauce with more body, drain off the liquid into a saucepan and thicken it somewhat, using either flour-and-water paste or flour and butter kneaded together. Check the seasoning and pour sauce back in the casserole. Serves 4.

BEEF AND VEGETABLE CASSEROLE I

1$\frac{1}{2}$ lbs. lean beef ground
   Salt and pepper
4 tablespoons salad oil
1 lb. fresh runner beans
   cut in 1-inch diagonals

3 large tomatoes peeled and sliced
2 medium onions sliced
3 green peppers seeded and sliced
3 oz. chopped parsley
$\frac{1}{2}$ teaspoon marjoram or oregano

1. Season the meat to taste with salt and pepper and shape into balls the size of a walnut.
2. Heat half the oil in a heavy frying-pan and brown the meat balls on all sides. Set aside
3. Combine beans, tomatoes, onions, peppers, and parsley in a large casserole, salt to taste, stir in the rest of the oil, cover, and bake in a slow oven, 250°, for an hour.
4. Stir in the meat balls and any fat left in the frying-pan, add the marjoram, re-cover, and continue to bake another hour. Serves 6.

Note: If you want to enlarge the casserole, add 3 slender courgettes sliced thin, 6 large mushrooms sliced, and 8 oz. thin diagonal celery slices. Two or 3 potatoes, cut as for French fries, can also be added. However, this would call for another $\frac{3}{4}$ lb. of meat and additional seasoning.

BEEF AND VEGETABLE CASSEROLE II

2 lbs. topside of beef cut In 1-Inch cubes
3 tablespoons butter or margarine
3 tablespoons brandy slightly warmed
12 small white onions or 1-lb. tin cooked
  onions
6 small carrots scraped, split lengthwise,
  and cut in 3 or 4 pieces each
6 small white turnips peeled and
  quartered

1 celery heart sliced thin
6 large mushrooms quartered
½ teaspoon tomato purée
1 teaspoon meat glaze
1 tablespoon flour
¾ pt. condensed consommé
3 teaspoons dry red wine
  Salt and pepper
1 small bay leaf

1. Heat 1 tablespoon of the butter in a heavy frying-pan and quickly brown the meat in it.
2. Light the brandy and pour it flaming over the meat. When the flames die down transfer the meat to a good-sized casserole.
3. Add the remaining butter to the pan and in it brown lightly the onions, carrots, turnips, and celery. [If you use tinned onions, add them later.] Add the mushrooms and cook another minute or two. Lift all these vegetables out with a slotted spoon and arrange them on top of the meat in the casserole.
4. Reduce the heat to a simmer and blend into the fat in the pan the tomato purée, meat glaze, and flour. Add the consommé slowly, bring up the heat a little, and stir until the mixture thickens.
5. Stir in the wine, season to taste, and add the bay leaf. Pour over the casserole.
6. Cover and bake 1–1¼ hours, or until the meat is tender. Serves 5–6.

SPANISH STEW

2 lbs. boneless chuck cut in 1½-inch cubes
2 tablespoons chopped parsley
1 large tin tomatoes
3 tablespoons salad oil
3 small onions chopped
1 clove garlic

2 teaspoons salt
3 green peppers cut in strips
½ teaspoon dried sweet basil or 1½ teaspoons
  fresh, chopped
4 medium potatoes cut In wedges
  Flour-and-water paste

1. In a heavy medium-sized casserole heat the oil and lightly sauté onions and garlic. Remove the garlic as soon as it begins to brown and sauté the meat with the onions.
2. Add salt, green peppers, parsley, basil, and tomatoes.
3. Cover the casserole and bake in a slow oven, 300°, an hour.
4. Stir in the potatoes and continue baking until the potatoes are tender—15–20 minutes.
5. Thicken the sauce slightly with flour-and-water paste. Serves 4–5.

JOHNNY MAZETTE

1 lb. lean ground beef
1 lb. lean ground pork
4 oz. butter, margarine, or salad oil
12 oz. chopped green pepper
6 oz. chopped celery
12 oz. chopped onion
   Salt and pepper
2 oz. chopped stuffed olives

4-oz. tin sliced mushrooms and liquid
1 tin condensed tomato soup
8-oz. bottle tomato sauce
8-oz. tin meatless tomato-mushroom
   sauce
1 lb. broad noodles cooked
8 oz. grated Parmesan cheese

1. In a large frying-pan or saucepan melt the butter and lightly sauté the pepper, celery, and onion.
2. Add both meats and continue to cook until the red disappears.
3. Season to taste and stir in the olives, mushrooms, soup, and both sauces.
4. Turn the well-drained noodles into a large greased casserole. Pour the meat mixture on top and gently stir into the noodles. When well mixed spread the cheese on top.
5. Bake about 35 minutes in a 350° oven. Serves 10–12.

DOROTHEA'S LASAGNE

I. 3 tablespoons salad oil
   2 lbs. ground beef
   1½ teaspoons mixed herbs (oregano,
     basil, thyme)
   1 clove garlic mashed

2 medium onions chopped
4-oz. tin button mushrooms
8-oz. bottle tomato sauce
¾ pts. water
   Salt to taste

II. 6 oz. cooked chopped spinach or
    1 packet frozen, cooked
   3 oz. bread or cornflake crumbs
   ¼ pt. salad oil
   2 oz. grated Parmesan cheese

4 eggs beaten
½ teaspoon mixed herbs (oregano,
   basil, thyme)
   Salt to taste

½ lb. lasagne noodles cooked until just
   tender

4-oz. tin button mushrooms
Grated Parmesan cheese

1. Mix the ingredients in group I and simmer 15–20 minutes.
2. Mix the ingredients in II.
3. Arrange in a large shallow casserole, well oiled, beginning with a layer of lasagne noodles laid side by side and close together on the bottom. Cover with a layer of mixture II, and then with a layer of mixture I.
4. Spread another layer of lasagne noodles, this time going crosswise over the casserole, and close together. Cover with the same layers as before.
5. Top with a layer of mixture II, the other tin of button mushrooms, drained, and a generous sprinkling of grated Parmesan.
6. Bake 45 minutes in a 350° oven.
7. Add more cheese and bake 5 minutes more. Serves 8.

PARTY SPAGHETTI WITH BEEF

1 lb. linguine (a form of spaghetti) cooked
2 lbs. lean beef ground
3 tablespoons salad oil
½ lb. mushrooms sliced thin or 2 4-oz. tins
2 medium onions chopped
1 oz. chopped parsley
2 8-oz. bottles tomato sauce
1 tin tomato purée

1 teaspoon dried oregano or 1 tablespoon
  fresh, chopped
1 teaspoon garlic powder
  Salt and pepper
8 oz. cream cheese softened
1 lb. cottage cheese
¼ pt. sour cream
3 oz. chopped chives
2 oz. buttered crumbs

HERE is a delightfully flavoured hearty casserole for a party, especially for a buffet supper.
1. Heat the oil in a heavy frying-pan and cook the meat until it begins to brown.
2. Stir in mushrooms (and their juice if tinned), onions, parsley, tomato sauce, tomato purée, oregano, and garlic powder. Season to taste and simmer 15 minutes.
3. Combine cream cheese, cottage cheese, sour cream, chives, and salt to taste. Blend well.
4. Pour half the linguine, well drained, in a large buttered casserole. Cover with all the cheese mixture. Add the rest of the linguine. Top with the meat mixture.
5. Cover with buttered crumbs and bake 30–40 minutes in a moderate oven, 350°, or until browned and bubbly. Serves 12.

NASI GORENG

½ lb. lean beef ground
2 tablespoons bread or cornflake crumbs
1 egg
8 oz. chopped onions
½ teaspoon salt
⅛ teaspoon pepper
4 oz. margarine or salad oil

6 oz. diced celery
½ lb. cooked crabmeat
½ lb. shelled and deveined shrimps
¾ pt. chicken broth
10 oz. cooked rice
1–2 teaspoons curry powder

THIS famous Javanese dish is fine for a buffet supper.
1. Mix the beef, crumbs, egg, 2 oz. of the onions, and salt and pepper and shape into small balls, the size of a walnut. Let stand 30–40 minutes.
2. Heat 2 tablespoons of the fat in a frying-pan and lightly sauté the remaining onions and the celery. Spread them out in a large casserole.
3. In the same pan melt 2 oz. of the fat and sauté the carefully picked-over crabmeat and shrimps 2–3 minutes, or until the shrimps begin to turn pink. Add them to the onion mixture.
4. Brown the meat balls in the same pan, stirring constantly to prevent sticking. Add these to the casserole.
5. Still in the same pan heat the chicken broth, rice, curry powder, and the balance of the fat. Bring to a boil and pour over the casserole. Stir the contents of the casserole gently but thoroughly, cover, and bake 20–25 minutes in a moderate oven, 350°. Serves 6.

SWISS STEAK CASSEROLE DINNER

3½-lb. slice of rump steak
2 oz. flour
1½ teaspoons salt
½ teaspoon fresh-ground pepper
3 tablespoons salad oil
2 tins condensed onion soup undiluted

8 or more scrubbed new potatoes,
  unpeeled
6 scraped carrots, quartered
1 packet frozen peas
1 packet frozen runner beans

1. Cut the meat into 8 serving portions. Mix the flour with the salt and pepper and cut or pound into the meat with the blunt side of a heavy butcher's knife, edge of a saucer, etc.
2. In a large casserole heat the oil and brown the meat well on both sides.
3. Add the soup, cover, and bake in a moderate oven, 350°, 40 minutes, or until the meat begins to be tender. Or bake in a slow oven, 275°, 2 hours, or until tender.
4. Stir in the potatoes and carrots and bake 25 minutes more. Add more salt if needed.
5. Break up the frozen vegetables in chunks and poke down in the casserole. Cover again and bake 20 minutes longer. Serves 8.

MEAT BALL SUPPER

1 lb. lean beef ground
1 egg
3 oz. soft bread crumbs
1 tablespoon chopped parsley

1 teaspoon salt
¼ teaspoon dried marjoram or ¾ teaspoon
  fresh, chopped
1 tablespoon salad oil

Sauce

2 tablespoons butter or margarine
1 medium onion chopped
1 pt. tomato juice
½ pt. condensed consommé

1 teaspoon sugar
½ teaspoon salt
8 oz. wide noodles broken up
8 oz. cooked green peas or runner beans

1. Mix the beef, egg, crumbs, parsley, salt, and marjoram lightly and shape into balls about the size of a walnut.
2. Heat the oil in a heavy frying-pan, brown the meat balls on all sides, and arrange in a medium casserole.
3. Melt the butter in a saucepan and sauté the onion until transparent but not brown.
4. Add the tomato juice, consommé, sugar, and salt. Pour over the meat balls.
5. Stir in the noodles, cover, and bake in a slow oven, 325°, 20–25 minutes, or until the noodles are tender and the liquid mostly absorbed.
6. Five minutes before serving stir in the peas or beans. Serves 6.

BURGER-RICE CASSEROLE

2 lbs. lean beef ground
1 tablespoon salad oil
1 large onion chopped
6 oz. chopped celery
1 clove garlic mashed
1 large tin or 4 12-oz. tins V-8 juice
1 tablespoon sugar
1 tablespoon chopped parsley

1 teaspoon dried sweet basil or
  1 tablespoon fresh, chopped
1 teaspoon dried oregano or
  1 tablespoon fresh, chopped
2 teaspoons salt
1 pinch fresh-ground pepper
1 small bay leaf crushed
12 oz. raw rice

1. Heat the oil in a heavy pan—an electric frying pan is fine—until it is sizzling.
2. Shape the meat into one large patty about 1 inch thick and sauté it about 5 minutes on each side, reducing the heat to medium. Break it up carefully into pieces about the size of a large olive, and lay them in a large casserole.
3. To the fat left in the skillet add the onion, celery, and garlic and sauté lightly, adding a little more oil if necessary. Spread over the meat in the casserole.
4. Now add to the pan the V-8 juice, the sugar, all the herbs, the salt, pepper, and bay leaf. Heat just to boiling.
5. Sprinkle the rice over the casserole and pour on the boiling liquid. Cover and bake about 45 minutes in a 350° oven, or until the rice is tender and the liquid absorbed.
6. Check about 15 minutes ahead of time and if there seems to be too much liquid for the rice, remove the cover of the casserole. Stir lightly with a long-tined fork before serving. Serves 8.

HAM CASSEROLE WITH VEGETABLES

1 lb. cooked ham diced small
6 oz. cooked green beans
1 tin condensed cream of mushroom soup
¼ pt. milk

6 oz. cooked whole-kernel sweet corn
½ lb. cooked little white onions or medium-
  sized tin
2 oz. buttered crumbs

Mix all ingredients except crumbs in a medium casserole. Top with the buttered crumbs and bake 20–25 minutes in a 375° oven, or until golden and bubbly. (If you prepare it early bring it to room temperature before baking, or allow an extra 10 minutes.) Serves 4.

HAM AND TURKEY SANDWICH CASSEROLE

1 7½-oz. tin devilled ham
8 slices cooked turkey
4 slices bread, crusts removed
   Butter or margarine
1½ oz. flour
¾ pt. milk

8 oz. grated Cheddar
½ teaspoon dry mustard
1 teaspoon salt
2 eggs well beaten
3 oz. toasted split almonds

THIS is an easy and delicious luncheon dish. Select a casserole for it just the size to fit the 4 slices of bread, or use a deep Pyrex pie plate and cut the bread to fit.
1. Toast the bread on one side and spread the other side generously with butter. Fit the slices so as to make a fairly solid layer in the casserole, buttered side up.
2. Spread the devilled ham lavishly on the bread and arrange the turkey slices on top.
3. Make a cheese sauce by melting 1½ oz. butter, blending in the flour, and gradually adding the milk. Stir constantly until thick and smooth. Add the cheese and mustard and stir until the cheese is melted. Season to taste. Stir in the eggs.
4. Pour the sauce over the sandwiches, sprinkle with almonds, and bake in a hot oven, 450°, 15–20 minutes, until bubbly and well browned.
   If you have had to cut the bread to fit a round casserole, cut across both ways with a sharp knife to divide the turkey neatly before taking to the table. Serves 4.

HAM AND EGG PIE

1 lb. cooked ham cut in ½-inch dice
2 hard-boiled eggs sliced
1 tablespoon vegetable oil
2 tomatoes peeled and chopped
1 clove garlic crushed
1 teaspoon sugar
½ teaspoon cinnamon

½ lb. garlic sausage sliced
12 oz. cooked peas, fresh or frozen
4 tinned artichoke hearts diced small
   Salt and pepper
   Boiling water
8 oz. biscuit crust pastry
1 tablespoon melted butter

1. Heat the oil in a medium casserole on top of the stove and brown the pieces of ham lightly in it. Skim out the ham and reserve.
2. In the fat remaining in the casserole cook the tomatoes and garlic. Stir in the sugar, cinnamon, sausage, eggs, peas, artichokes, and seasoning to taste. Add boiling water barely to cover and simmer gently 20 minutes.
3. Stir in the reserved ham.
4. Roll out the biscuit crust pastry rather thin. Cut out rounds and lay them carefully on top of the mixture in the casserole, as close together as possible.
5. Brush with the melted butter and bake 15–20 minutes at 400°, or until the pastry is a deep golden brown. Serves 4.

LAMB, RICE, AND AUBERGINE CASSEROLE

3 lbs. boned lamb shoulder cut in 1-inch dice
6 oz. raw rice cooked
2 smallish aubergines cut in 1-inch dice
¼ pt. salad oil
6 oz. minced onions
3 oz. minced green peppers

Boiling salted water
1 large tin tomatoes (18 oz.)
½ pt. dry red wine
4 oz. grated Parmesan cheese
2 teaspoons salt
½ teaspoon garlic salt

1. Brown the lamb well in the oil, adding the onions and green peppers as the lamb begins to brown.
2. Transfer to a good-sized casserole, cover, and bake 30 minutes in a slow oven, 325°.
3. Cook the aubergines 5 minutes in boiling salted water, stirring it a couple of times. Drain.
4. Stir the aubergines, cooked rice, tomatoes, wine, 2 oz. of the cheese, salt and garlic salt into the casserole with the lamb.
5. Top with the rest of the cheese and bake another hour uncovered, or until brown and bubbly. Serves 8.

LAMB SHANKS DINNER IN A CASSEROLE

6 lamb shanks
1 clove garlic
1 oz. flour
2 teaspoons salt
1 teaspoon paprika
2 tablespoons salad oil
¼ pt. lemon juice
¼ pt. dry white wine

¼ pt. chicken broth
2 tablespoons grated lemon rind
1 small bay leaf
4 peppercorns
12–16 small new potatoes
1 large packet runner beans thawed
   (2 packets if no other vegetable)

1. Trim the fat from the shanks and rub well all over with the garlic clove cut in two. Roll in a mixture of the flour, salt, and paprika spread on a piece of waxed paper.
2. Brown all over in sizzling oil in a heavy frying-pan and lay in a large casserole.
3. Stir the lemon juice into the pan, loosening all the browned particles. Add wine and chicken broth. Pour over the lamb.
4. Sprinkle the lemon rind over and add the bay leaf and peppercorns.
5. Cover and bake 1 hour in a moderate oven, 350°.
6. Add the potatoes and beans and bake 45 minutes longer, covered.
7. Ten minutes before serving, fish out the lamb shanks and cut the meat off, leaving it in quite large chunks. Return to casserole. (Whole shanks are difficult to manage on one's plate.) Serves 6.

CASSOULET

¾ lb. dried haricot beans
8 slices bacon
2 oz. diced salt pork
1½ lbs. pork loin cut in ¾-inch cubes
1 lb. lamb shoulder cut in ¾-inch cubes
1 garlic sausage sliced
1 carrot cut in ¼-inch slices
1 onion stuck with 2 cloves

3 cloves garlic cut in two
Salt and pepper
6 oz. butter, margarine, or salad oil
2 large onions chopped
2 tablespoons tomato purée
1¼ pts. beef bouillon
9 oz. crumbs

ONE of the most delightful dishes of the French provinces is the cassoulet, and of course there are endless versions of it. The true cassoulet, though, is essentially a combination of haricot beans, sausage, pork, mutton, and preserved goose, cooked for a long time and served with a golden crust. The recipe given here is typical of this peasant dish.

1. Soak the beans in water to cover overnight, or at least 4 hours, and drain.
2. Line a large casserole or a large bean pot with the bacon.
3. In a bowl mix the beans, carrot, whole onion, 1 clove garlic, and salt and pepper to taste.
4. Pour this mixture into the pot, cover with water, and bake in a slow oven, 275°, 2 hours.
5. While the beans are cooking, brown the meats in 2 oz. of the butter. Stir in the chopped onions, the 2 remaining garlic cloves, the tomato purée, and the bouillon. Simmer over very low heat 1½ hours, stirring occasionally.
6. Turn the meat mixture into the bean pot, stir well, and top with 3 oz. of the crumbs. Dot with 2 oz. of butter, increase the heat to 375°, and bake until the crumbs are brown, about 15 minutes.
7. Stir the crumbs into the cassoulet and repeat this twice more, with the remaining crumbs. Serve when brown the third time. Serves 6.

Note: A duck or a chicken can be cut up, browned, and added if desired.

SWEDISH LAMB WITH DILL

3 lbs. lamb from leg or shoulder, cut in
  1½-inch cubes
2 tablespoons salad oil
12 small white onions
2 tablespoons flour

1-lb. tin tomatoes
1 tablespoon fresh dill or 1 teaspoon dried
½ pt. chicken broth
Salt to taste
4 medium potatoes peeled and quartered

THE dill flavour here makes this an unusual and delightful meal.

1. Brown the meat well in hot oil.
2. Add the onions and brown lightly, stirring almost constantly. Arrange in a large casserole.
3. Sprinkle with flour and stir well.
4. Add tomatoes, dill, and chicken broth.
5. Season to taste, cover, and bake 1½ hours in a 325° oven.
6. Add potatoes 20 minutes before you are ready to serve. Serves 8.

LAMB CHOP CASSEROLE DINNER

8 rib lamb chops
2 tablespoons butter
1 teaspoon salt
¼ teaspoon fresh-ground pepper
4 tomatoes peeled and cut in thick slices

4 small white onions
4 apples cored, pared and sliced thick
4 potatoes peeled and sliced rather thick
½ pt. tomato juice

1. Brown the chops delicately in butter, sprinkle with salt and pepper, and set aside.
2. In a good-sized greased casserole arrange the vegetables and apples in the order listed above, salting each lightly. Lay the chops on top. Pour the tomato juice over.
3. Cover the casserole and bake in a slow oven, 325°, 45 minutes, or until the chops are tender. Uncover the last 10 minutes. Serves 4.

LAMB RAGOÛT

3 lbs. spring lamb cut in 1½-inch cubes
1 tablespoon salt
3 tablespoons salad oil
1 stalk of celery with top, sliced thin
2 medium onions quartered
3 tablespoons flour
   Consommé and dry red or white wine, half-and-half, or half water
1 small clove garlic crushed

½ bay leaf
½ lb. tomatoes skinned and chopped
4 oz. runner beans partly cooked and buttered
4 oz. carrots diced, partly cooked and buttered
4 oz. green peas, slightly cooked and buttered
8 oz. potato balls, lightly sautéed in butter

1. Salt the lamb, heat the oil in a large heavy frying-pan, and brown the lamb on all sides.
2. With a slotted spoon remove to a large casserole, cover, and put in 325° oven for 45 minutes. Stir occasionally.
3. To the fat in the pan add the celery and onions and brown lightly. Stir in the flour and continue to cook until lightly browned, stirring frequently.
4. Blend in the consommé and wine (or water)—enough almost to cover the meat in the casserole—and stir until smooth and thickened.
5. To the meat in the casserole add the sauce, garlic, bay leaf, tomatoes, and all the buttered vegetables. Mix thoroughly. Continue to bake another hour, or slightly longer if lamb is not fork tender by that time.

   If there is too much or too thin sauce at this time, drain it off into a saucepan and boil hard to reduce. Serves 6–8.

LAMB STEW WITH SPRING VEGETABLES

2 lbs. shoulder of lamb cut in 1½-inch cubes
6 tablespoons salad oil
  Salt and pepper
  Bouquet of thyme and parsley, 2 sprigs each
1 small bay leaf
  Hot water
½ teaspoon sugar
2 tablespoons flour
4 oz. tomato purée
1 clove garlic crushed
8–12 small new potatoes
1 dozen baby carrots
6 oz. green peas

1. Sear the lamb cubes well in hot oil, season with salt and pepper, and sprinkle with sugar to caramelize the meat a bit. Pour off most of the fat.
2. Sprinkle the meat with flour and cook 2–3 minutes.
3. Stir in the tomato purée, garlic, herb bouquet, and bay leaf. Cover with hot water and bring to a boil. Let it cook a few minutes, removing any scum that develops. Remove to a medium casserole, cover, and bake in a 350° oven an hour.
4. Carefully drain the liquid from the casserole into a small saucepan and boil hard to reduce it about a third. Strain it back into the casserole.
5. Stir in the vegetables, cover again, and continue to bake about 45 minutes, or until lamb is fork tender and the potatoes done. Serves 4–5.

LANCASHIRE HOTPOT

4 lamb chops
1 clove garlic crushed
4 small white onions
4 medium potatoes pared and cut in half
1 lb. frozen runner beans
2 teaspoons salt
⅛ teaspoon pepper
1 tin condensed cream of mushroom soup
½ pt. water
  Paprika
1 tablespoon chopped parsley

1. Cut off bits of fat from the chops, melt them in a heavy frying-pan, and brown the chops on both sides. Arrange in a casserole large enough to take them without overlapping.
2. Add garlic, onions, and potatoes to the casserole, and the beans, thawed just enough to break up. Season with salt and pepper.
3. Stir the water into the soup and pour over.
4. Cover and bake 1 hour in a 375° oven, or simmer gently on top of the stove 45–50 minutes.
5. Sprinkle with paprika and parsley before serving. Serves 4.

LUNCHEON MEAT WITH NEW POTATOES AND PINEAPPLE

12-oz. tin luncheon meat cut in 4 pieces
  lengthwise
4 medium new potatoes cooked and halved
4 pineapple slices, drained
½ pt. pineapple syrup

2 oz. brown sugar
1 tablespoon cornflour
¼ teaspoon salt
3 tablespoons dry sherry
2 tablespoons butter or margarine

1. In a greased shallow casserole arrange the pineapple. Lay the meat slices on top and the potatoes over that.
2. Heat the pineapple syrup to boiling. Stir in the brown sugar, cornflour, and salt, stirring until the syrup is clear and thickened.
3. Stir the sherry and butter into the hot syrup and pour over the casserole.
4. Bake at 375°, uncovered, about 40 minutes. Serves 4.

PORK AND MACARONI CASSEROLE WITH SWEET CORN

4 pork chops cut ¾-inch thick
4 oz. thin macaroni broken up and cooked
1 tin cream-style sweet corn (17 oz.)
  Salt and pepper
1 tablespoon salad oil
2 tablespoons minced onion

2 oz. chopped green pepper
2 tablespoons flour
1 tablespoon brown sugar
¼ pt. water
¼ pt. chili sauce or ketchup
1 tablespoon vinegar

1. Trim excess fat from the chops, season with salt and pepper, and brown well in sizzling oil in a heavy frying-pan. (If you prefer, melt the fat scraps and brown the chops in that fat.) Remove the chops to a plate until the other ingredients are prepared.
2. In the fat remaining in the pan lightly brown the onion and green pepper. Stir in the flour, brown sugar, water, chili sauce, and vinegar. Stir until the sauce is thick and smooth. Season to taste.
3. Mix the cooked macaroni and sweet corn with the sauce, season to taste, and pour into a medium casserole.
4. Arrange the chops on top and bake, covered, about 1 hour, or until the chops are very tender. Remove the cover during the last 15 minutes. (If you prepare the casserole in the morning and refrigerate it, bring it to room temperature before baking and allow 1½ hours for baking.) Serves 4.

Pork chops in cider

PORK AND RICE CASSEROLE

4 loin pork chops cut ¾-inch thick
  Seasoned salt
3 oz. rice
1 tin condensed consommé

4 medium onions quartered
2 large carrots sliced
  diagonally in 1-inch pieces

1. Trim excess fat from chops and melt in a heavy frying-pan
2. Skim out the fat pieces when they are brown and brown the chops well in the fat, on both sides. Remove to a medium casserole that will hold them in one layer. Salt them lightly.
3. In the fat remaining in the pan brown the raw rice, stirring constantly until it is coloured.
4. Stir in the consommé.
5. Arrange the onions and carrots around the chops in the casserole, salt lightly, and pour the rice-consommé mixture over.
6. Cover the casserole and bake 1 hour in a 350° oven. Serves 4.

VEAL CASSEROLE MEAL

3 lbs. boneless veal cut in 1½-inch cubes
6 slices bacon cut in thin strips
6 medium onions sliced
  Salt and pepper
6 medium potatoes peeled and cut in wedges

3 large tomatoes skinned and quartered
2 tablespoons tomato purée
½ pt. chicken broth
2 8-oz. packets runner beans
3 oz. grated Parmesan cheese

1. Cook bacon in a heavy frying-pan. When it begins to sizzle add the veal and onions, cooking until lightly browned. Arrange in a large casserole. Season to taste.
2. In the fat remaining in the pan brown the potato wedges lightly and add to the casserole. Salt them lightly.
3. Put in the pan the tomatoes, tomato purée, and chicken broth. When it boils stir in the frozen beans. When they are well broken up add to the casserole, with the liquid.
4. Cover the casserole and bake an hour at 350°.
5. Sprinkle the cheese on top and brown under the grill. Serves 6.

Coq au vin

VEAL PARTY CASSEROLE

5 lbs. boneless veal cut in 1½-inch cubes
4 tablespoons salad oil
2 onions chopped or sliced thin
20-oz. tin tomatoes
5-oz. tin tomato purée
8-oz. bottle tomato sauce
10-oz. tin chicken broth
¼ pt. dry sherry
½ pt. dry white or rosé wine
1½ teaspoons salt

1 teaspoon Tabasco
1 teaspoon thyme or oregano
2 small bay leaves
6 oz. slice celery
1 oz. flour
¼ pt. water
½ lb. mushrooms sliced or 2 4-oz. tins
2 1-lb. tins small white onions drained
1 8-oz. packet frozen peas thawed
1 8-oz. packet frozen runner beans thawed

1. Brown the veal in small batches in sizzling oil, transferring the pieces to a large casserole or 2 medium-to-large ones.
2. In the remaining fat cook the onions lightly. Stir in the tomatoes, tomato purée, tomato sauce, chicken broth, sherry, white wine, salt, Tabasco, thyme, bay leaves, and celery. Simmer 5 minutes.
3. Stir in the flour and water mixed to a paste, stirring constantly until thick and smooth. Pour this mixture over the veal.
4. Cover and bake at 325°, 1¼ hours.
5. Stir in the mushrooms and whole onions. Bake 10 minutes more, uncovered.
6. Stir in the peas and beans and bake 15 minutes longer. Serve on buttered wide noodles. Serves 12–14.

QUICK SUPPER CASSEROLE

1 lb. chopped cooked meat (any kind), coarsely flaked tuna, or sliced hard-boiled eggs
6 oz. soft bread crumbs
2 oz. grated cheese
2 tablespoons melted butter or margarine
2 tablespoons butter

6 oz. cooked peas, beans, or chopped asparagus
2 tablespoons minced onion
1½ tablespoons flour
¾ pt. milk
Salt and pepper
1 large tomato skinned and cut in ¼-inch slices

1. Mix together the bread crumbs, cheese, and melted butter. Spread half in a rather wide shallow casserole and arrange the peas on top.
2. In a saucepan melt the 2 tablespoons butter, sauté the onion lightly in it, blend in flour, and gradually add the milk. Stir until smooth and thick and season to taste.
3. Stir into the white sauce the meat, fish, or eggs, and pour over the peas.
4. Lay the tomato slices on top of the sauce and cover with the remaining crumbs mixture.
5. Bake 25 minutes in a moderate oven, 350°. Serves 4.

CHICKEN HOTPOT

1½ lbs. chicken legs
2½ pts. well-salted water
   Salt
 6 oz. green peas
 6 oz. French beans

2 carrots diced
1 onion sliced
1 small cauliflower broken into flowerets
1 small head lettuce shredded
2 tablespoons chopped parsley

1. Bring the chicken legs to a boil in the water, skimming the froth off as it forms. Put in a large casserole both the chicken legs and the broth. Add the peas, beans, carrots, and onion. Cover and bake 1½ hours in a slow oven, 325°.
2. Add the cauliflower and lettuce and bake 35–40 minutes longer.
3. Fish out the chicken legs, skin and bone them, and cut the meat into fair-sized chunks. Return to the soup, add the parsley, and cook 10 minutes more. Check and correct seasoning.
4. If you prefer this slightly thickened, stir in a flour-and-water paste. For a little extra flavour stir in ¼ pt. sour cream too.
   Reheat and serve in large soup plates. Serves 6.

CHINESE CHICKEN CASSEROLE

¾ lb. cooked chicken diced
2 tablespoons salad oil
3 oz. thinly sliced onion
3 oz. sliced mushrooms
6 oz. thinly sliced celery
½ pt. chicken broth

1 teaspoon cornflour
¼ teaspoon salt
2 tablespoons water
1 tablespoon soy sauce
1-lb. tin bean sprouts
3 oz. toasted blanched split almonds

1. Heat the oil in a large frying-pan and lightly sauté the onion, mushrooms, and celery 5 minutes or so. Put in a medium casserole.
2. Add the chicken and the broth, cover, and bake about 15 minutes in a 350° oven.
3. Blend together the cornflour, salt, water, and soy sauce and stir into the casserole. Bake another 10 minutes.
4. Stir in the bean sprouts and almonds, heat well (about 5 minutes) and serve on hot fluffy rice. Serves 5–6.

PAELLA

4½–5-lb. chicken cut up
¼ pt. olive oil (or salad oil)
5 cloves garlic bruised but not peeled
1 medium onion minced
6 oz. green beans cut up
6 oz. cauliflower flowerets
¾ lb. lobster coarsely diced
¾ lb. shrimps shelled and deveined

2 medium tomatoes chopped
1½ teaspoons paprika
1½ lbs. dry rice (preferably wild, but then
    1 lb.)
3 oz. chopped parsley
Salt
Boiling water

PAELLA is certainly one of the most popular Spanish dishes, made in a slightly different way in each province of Spain. This recipe is a relatively simple one, and the following one is a little more elaborate. Both are delicious.

1. Heat the oil in a large heavy frying-pan and brown the garlic in it. Remove the garlic and brown the chicken pieces well. Arrange in a large casserole.

2. Sauté the onion lightly in the pan for 5 minutes.

3. At 5-minute intervals add the following, in order: beans, cauliflower, lobster and shrimps together, tomatoes, paprika, rice, parsley.

4. When the parsley has been in 5 minutes turn the whole mixture into the casserole. Pour over boiling water barely to cover and bake, covered, 40 minutes in a slow oven, 300°. Or simmer over very low heat 20–30 minutes, stirring occasionally. Check seasoning. Serves 6–8.

Note: If you use prepared rice add it dry—do not rinse. But if you use wild rice wash it well in several waters.

PAELLA VALENCIANA

4 chicken breasts (8 halves)
8 chicken legs
4 tablespoons salad oil
3 Spanish sausages (or Portuguese or Italian) sliced ½-inch thick
1½ lbs. shelled and deveined shrimps
12 mussels
6 oz. chopped onion
1 clove garlic crushed
1½ pts. chicken broth

3½ teaspoons salt
½ teaspoon pepper
¾ teaspoon dried tarragon or 1½ teaspoons fresh, chopped
½ teaspoon paprika
1 teaspoon saffron crumbled
10 oz. raw rice
12-oz. tin tomatoes
1 13-oz. packet frozen peas
7-oz. tin artichoke hearts (or frozen, cooked)

1. In a large saucepan or stew-pot heat the oil and brown the chicken pieces well. Remove and set aside.

2. In the same oil sauté the onion and garlic until soft.

3. Add the chicken broth, salt and pepper, tarragon, paprika, and saffron.

4. Bring to a boil, add rice, and simmer over medium heat until about half of the liquid has been absorbed—about 20 minutes.

5. Stir in the tomatoes, sausage, shrimps, and chicken. Cover, turn down the heat to a simmer, and cook until rice is almost dry—20–25 minutes.

6. Put the mussels in a saucepan with a little water over high heat until the shells open— 2–3 minutes. Cool enough to handle and take out the mussels. Add to the pot.

7. Add the peas and artichoke hearts, stir lightly, and continue to cook until the mussels are hot.

Serve in the pot if it is a modern one with porcelain jacket; otherwise pour the paella into a large casserole. Serves 8.

PARTY CHICKEN-NOODLE CASSEROLE

5-lb. fowl cut up
¾ lb. medium noodles broken up
2 oz. minced onion
2 oz. green pepper minced
3-oz. tin sliced mushrooms
6 oz. pitted ripe olives
1 tin condensed cream of mushroom soup

6 oz. grated Cheddar cheese
2 oz. minced pimentos
1 tablespoon minced parsley
½ teaspoon celery salt
  Salt and pepper
2 oz. buttered bread or cornflake crumbs

THIS is a good hearty dish for a buffet supper. It can be enlarged by adding tinned boned chicken and increasing all remaining ingredients a little.

1. Put the chicken in a large saucepan with barely enough water to cover and the usual items to give it flavour: 2 teaspoons salt, ½ onion cut in pieces, stalk of celery cut up, 1 carrot cut up, 2 sprigs parsley, a bay leaf, etc. Cover and simmer until well done—1½–2 hours.

2. Remove the chicken pieces from the broth, cool them, skin, and cut up the meat in rather large chunks.

3. Strain the broth and chill it so that you can skim off the fat. Save the fat. (The chicken can be cooked the day before you need it.)

4. Measure the chicken broth you have and add enough tinned chicken broth, or boiling water and chicken stock base, or bouillon cubes, to make 2½ pts. of broth. Include the juice from the mushrooms.

5. Bring to a boil and cook the noodles in it about 7 minutes.

6. In 2 tablespoons of the skimmed-off chicken fat lightly sauté the onion, green pepper, and mushrooms. Stir in the chicken and olives.

7. Partially drain the cooked noodles, leaving them just a little soppy.

8. Stir in the soup, cheese, pimentos, parsley, celery salt, and salt and pepper to taste.

9. In a large casserole make alternate layers of the chicken mixture and the noodle mixture.

Top with a fairly thick layer of buttered crumbs and bake about 1 hour at 325°, or until bubbly and golden. Serves 10.

RICE CASSEROLE DINNER

10 oz. raw rice
5 or 6 chicken livers cut in 3–4 pieces
  each
5 slices boiled ham, shredded
1 small sweetbread cooked and diced
4 oz. butter or margarine
2 oz. minced onion
¼ lb. mushrooms sliced

4 fluid oz. dry white wine
4 fluid oz. marsala wine or sherry
1 truffle chopped (optional)
1 tablespoon meat glaze
¾ pt. condensed consommé
6 oz. cooked peas
  Salt and pepper
2 oz. grated Parmesan cheese

1. Heat half the butter in a large casserole or saucepan. Stir in the onion, chicken livers, ham, sweetbread, and mushrooms. Brown lightly, stirring often.
2. Stir in the two wines, the rice, and the truffle, cooking over very low heat until the wines have evaporated.
3. Stir the meat glaze into the consommé and add to the pan, with the peas. Season to taste.
4. Cover and simmer until the rice is tender, about 20 minutes. Check occasionally and add a little more water or consommé if needed, but the dish should be quite dry.
5. Stir in the remaining butter and the cheese before serving. Serves 6.

RICE AND SAUSAGE WITH VEGETABLES

1 lb. cooked rice
¾ lb. sweet Italian sausages cut in ¼-inch
  slices
2 oz. butter or margarine
1 medium onion minced
13-oz. packet frozen peas partly thawed

15-oz. tin artichoke hearts drained and
  quartered
3-oz. tin boiled chopped mushrooms,
  drained
1 tin condensed consommé
2 oz. grated Parmesan cheese

1. Heat the butter in a large heavy frying-pan and lightly brown the onion and sausage.
2. Stir in the artichokes, peas, mushrooms, and ¼ pt. of the consommé. Simmer 10 minutes or so.
3. Stir in the rice and remaining consommé and pour into a greased medium casserole.
4. Sprinkle with cheese and bake 15 or 20 minutes in a moderate oven, 375°, or until cheese is well browned. Serves 6.

HAWAIIAN RICE

10 oz. cooked rice
3 tablespoons butter or margarine
½ lb. diced cooked ham, chicken, or
  tongue

6 oz. diced pineapple, tinned, fresh, or
  frozen
2 oz. split almonds
  Salt and pepper
1 oz. chopped watercress, stems removed

HEAT the butter in a small casserole and lightly brown the ham. Add the pineapple, rice, nuts, and seasoning to taste. Cover and bake in a moderate oven, 350°, 15 minutes, or until piping hot. Sprinkle with watercress before serving. Serves 4.

SPAGHETTI CASSEROLE MEAL

4 oz. thin spaghetti broken up and cooked
½ lb. cooked turkey, chicken, or diced roast meat
½ lb. cooked ham diced
4 oz. diced Cheddar
1 tablespoon butter or margarine

1 tablespoon flour
½ pt. top milk
Salt and pepper
½ pt. thick cream
1 Spanish onion sliced thin
Paprika

1. Make a white sauce with the butter, flour, and milk, seasoning it to taste.
2. Stir into the sauce the meat and cheese, the well-drained spaghetti, and the cream. Pour into a medium casserole.
3. Top with layers of onion carefully arranged.
4. Sprinkle with paprika and bake 20 minutes in a slow oven, 325°. Serves 6.

TURKEY ALMONDINE

1 lb. cooked turkey (or chicken) cut up
1½ oz. butter or margarine
1½ oz. flour
1 teaspoon salt
¼ teaspoon fresh-ground pepper
¼ teaspoon prepared mustard

¾ pt. milk
4 oz. grated Cheddar
1 14-oz. packet frozen broccoli cooked
4 oz. medium noodles cooked
3 oz. split toasted almonds

1. In a saucepan over low heat make a white sauce by melting the butter, blending in the flour, salt, pepper, and mustard, and gradually adding the milk. Stir constantly until smooth and thick.
2. Add the cheese and stir until melted.
3. Cut off the broccoli stems and chop them small. Spread the stems in a shallow greased casserole, cover with noodles, and then with turkey.
4. Pour the cheese sauce over the casserole and scatter the broccoli flowerets on top, pressing them lightly into the sauce.
5. Sprinkle the almonds over all.
6. Bake in a moderate oven, 350°, 15 minutes, or until bubbling. Serves 4–5.

TURKEY CASSEROLE FOR A PARTY

2 lbs. cooked turkey cut in strips
4 oz. butter, margarine, or salad oil
½ lb. cooked ham cut in strips
½ lb. mushrooms sliced
1 lb. thin spaghetti cooked
2 oz. Parmesan cheese
2 tablespoons thick cream
2 tablespoons sherry

¾ pt. thick cream whipped
2 teaspoons paprika
1¼ pts. rich white sauce (2½ oz. butter,
  2½ oz. flour, 1¼ pts. top milk, and
  seasoning to taste)
3 egg yolks beaten a little
3 tablespoons dry sherry
3 tablespoons melted butter

1. Heat 2 oz. of the butter in a large frying-pan and sauté the ham and mushrooms until the mushrooms are tender, about 5 minutes. Stir often.
2. Drain the cooked spaghetti and toss it with the remaining 2 oz. of butter, half of the grated Parmesan cheese, the 2 tablespoons cream, and the 2 tablespoons sherry. Spread the spaghetti on the bottom of a large greased casserole.
3. Stir the whipped cream and paprika into the white sauce and heat almost to boiling.
4. Stir ¼ pt. or so of the sauce into the egg yolks and stir quickly back into the sauce.
5. Stir in the ham and mushroom mixture and the turkey. Heat well.
6. Stir in the sherry. Correct the seasoning and pour the mixture over the spaghetti, being careful not to disturb it.
7. Dribble the 3 tablespoons melted butter on top and sprinkle with the rest of the cheese.
8. Bake 25–30 minutes in a slow oven, 275°, and brown quickly under the grill. Serves 12.

Note: If you prepare the casserole early in the day, bring it to room temperature—2 hours—before baking.

TUNA CASSEROLE SUPPER

2 14-oz. tins tuna fish rinsed in cold water
1 tin condensed cream of mushroom soup
1-lb. tin of peas
4-oz. tin pimento diced small

1 small onion chopped
1 tablespoon Worcestershire sauce
4 oz. grated Cheddar
4 oz. fried onions

1. Mix the soup, peas (with their liquid), pimento, onion, and Worcestershire sauce.
2. Fold in the tuna, broken in medium lumps, and the cheese. Pour into a medium casserole.
3. Arrange the fried onions around the outside edge, leaving the centre uncovered.
4. Bake in a moderate oven, 375°, about 25 minutes, or until the onions are crisp and the tuna mixture bubbly. Serves 6.

QUICK TUNA LUNCHEON CASSEROLE

2 tins tuna (6½–7 oz.)
  drained and broken into chunks
1 small onion chopped
3 oz. diced green pepper
1 oz. butter or margarine
1 oz. flour
1 teaspoon salt
¼ teaspoon pepper

¼ teaspoon dried thyme or ½ teaspoon fresh
  chopped
3-oz. tin button mushrooms
½ pt. evaporated milk
1 tablespoon Worcestershire sauce
4-oz. tin whole kernel sweet corn or 4 oz.
  frozen or fresh
4-oz. potato crisps

1. In a saucepan sauté the onion and green pepper lightly in the butter. Blend in the flour, salt, pepper, and thyme. Add gradually the liquid drained from the mushrooms and the milk. Stir until the sauce is smooth and thick.

2. Add the Worcestershire sauce, sweet corn, mushrooms, and tuna to the sauce.

3. Turn into a medium casserole and top with potato crisps.

4. Bake 20 minutes in a moderate oven, 375°, or until bubbly. Serves 4–6.

NOTES

VEGETABLES

CASSEROLE OF FROZEN VEGETABLES

HERE is an easy way to cook frozen vegetables in the oven when you are already using it for another casserole.

Put in a casserole a frozen block of any vegetable, with 2 tablespoons butter or margarine, $\frac{1}{2}$ teaspoon salt, $\frac{1}{8}$ teaspoon pepper, and 2 tablespoons water except in the case of marrow. Cover and bake 35–60 minutes, depending upon the temperature you are using for the main casserole.

An alternative method is to wrap the frozen block of vegetables in thick foil, double-sealing the package by folds. Lay the block in an open casserole. You can put 2 or 3 such blocks in one casserole.

RATATOUILLE (Mixed Vegetables)

3 large onions chopped fine
3 large peppers seeded and coarsely chopped
6 small courgettes sliced thin (unpeeled)
1 medium aubergine diced (unpeeled)
Salad oil
6 large tomatoes peeled, seeded, and coarsely chopped
4 oz. chopped parsley
3 cloves garlic minced
Salt and pepper
Grated Parmesan cheese

1. Cover the bottom of a large heavy frying-pan with oil and sauté the onions until they begin to colour.
2. Add the green peppers and cook about 2 minutes more.
3. Stir in courgettes and aubergine and cook about 5 minutes, or until they begin to look transparent.
4. Turn these vegetables into a large casserole and stir in the tomatoes.
5. Cover and bake in a very slow oven, 250°, 1½ hours.
6. Stir in the parsley and garlic, season to taste, cover again, and bake 20 minutes longer.
7. Sprinkle with cheese before serving. Or chill the casserole well and serve cold. Serves 8.

VEGETABLES WITH RICE

1 oz. chopped green pepper
1 small onion chopped
2 oz. butter or margarine
6 oz. raw rice
8-oz. tin tomatoes undrained
8-oz. tin small onions and juice
14-oz. tin creamed sweet corn or 1 packet frozen, thawed
2 tablespoons ketchup
$\frac{1}{2}$ teaspoon salt
$\frac{1}{8}$ teaspoon pepper
$\frac{1}{2}$ pt. chicken broth

1. Cook green pepper and chopped onion in butter until tender.
2. Stir in rice and cook until rice is yellow, stirring constantly.
3. Add remaining ingredients and turn into medium casserole.
4. Bake 40 minutes at 350°, or until rice is tender and liquid all absorbed. Serves 6.

TIAN (Cold Vegetable Casserole)

1 lb. raw spinach chopped
1 lb. raw seakale chopped
3–4 small courgettes diced small
(unpeeled)
1 medium onion chopped fine
Salad oil (preferably olive oil)
2 cloves garlic crushed (small)

1 oz. fresh sweet basil chopped fine or
1 tablespoon dried
¾ teaspoon salt
¼ teaspoon fresh-ground pepper
4 eggs slightly beaten
2–3 oz. grated Parmesan cheese
Bread or cornflake crumbs

1. Heat enough oil in a large frying-pan to cover the bottom. Cook the spinach and seakale in it until barely wilted. Remove and drain well.
2. Add more oil to the pan and cook the courgettes, onion, and garlic until the onion begins to be transparent.
3. Mix all the vegetables and stir in the basil, salt, and pepper. Arrange in a lightly greased casserole.
4. Pour over the eggs and top with cheese and crumbs mixed.
5. Bake in a 350° oven 25–30 minutes, or until the eggs are set. Chill and serve cold. Serves 6.

MIXED VEGETABLE CASSEROLE

8 small new potatoes scraped
8 baby carrots scraped
1 small cauliflower broken into flowerets
6 oz. fresh peas (or frozen)

¾ pt. white sauce
4 oz. coarsely grated Cheddar
Chopped parsley

1. Cook the vegetables in a minimum of boiling salted water until tender but still crisp—just short of done: potatoes alone, carrots and cauliflower together, peas alone. Arrange in a casserole.
2. Make a smooth white sauce of 3 tablespoons butter or margarine, 3 tablespoons flour, ¾ pt. whole milk, and seasoning to taste. When thick, stir in cheese until melted.
3. Pour over vegetables in the casserole and bake 15 minutes in a moderate oven, 350°, or until bubbly.
4. Sprinkle parsley on top before serving. Serves 4.

VEGETABLE GHIVETCHI (Rumanian Casserole)

12 baby carrots scraped and sliced
2 potatoes diced
½ aubergine diced (unpeeled)
8-oz. tin small white onions
3 oz. each peas, haricots and runner beans
½ green pepper cut in strips
½ small cabbage shredded
 Small cauliflower broken into flowerets
1 small marrow diced

½ celery root diced
5 small tomatoes quartered
2 onions sliced thin
2 cloves garlic crushed
2 oz. butter or margarine
½ pt. chicken stock or consommé
¼ pt. salad oil (preferably olive oil)
1 tablespoon salt
 Fresh-ground pepper

THIS is as good a casserole as you are likely to find in a long search. For a 'company' dinner or for a special buffet party it is sure to make a hit. Best of all, it can be completely put together early in the day and refrigerated until 2 hours before needed.

1. Arrange all the vegetables except the sliced onions in a large casserole, in the order given.
2. Sauté the onions and garlic in butter until golden.
3. Add the stock and bring to a boil.
4. Stir in the oil, salt, and pepper, pour over the casserole, cover, and bake in a 325° oven 30–40 minutes, or until tender but still crisp. Serves 10–12.

RED BEANS IN WINE

1 lb. red beans
2 pts. water
2 teaspoons salt
2 oz. salt pork
 Boiling water
2 tablespoons butter or margarine

1 small onion chopped
1 clove garlic mashed
1 glass dry red wine
1 medium carrot diced
 Bouquet of parsley, bay leaf, and thyme
 Chopped parsley

1. Combine the beans, water, and salt and let stand overnight. Or boil 2 minutes and let soak an hour. Do not drain.
2. Cover the salt pork with boiling water, let stand an hour, drain, and then dice pork rather fine.
3. Melt the butter in a saucepan and sauté the onion and garlic until tender but not brown.
4. Add the wine and bring to a boil. Reduce the heat at once and simmer a few minutes.
5. Add the salt pork to the beans and bring to a boil.
6. Stir in the carrot, bouquet of herbs tied in a bit of cheesecloth, and the wine mixture.
7. Pour into a casserole, cover, and bake 2–3 hours in a slow oven, 300°. Uncover the last half hour.
8. Sprinkle with parsley before serving. Serves 6–8.

ASPARAGUS-CHEESE PUDDING

1½ lbs. fresh asparagus
3 slices white bread, crusts removed
4 oz. shredded Cheddar
2 eggs lightly beaten

¾ pt. milk scalded
1 teaspoon salt
½ teaspoon pepper
1 tablespoon melted butter or margarine

1. Clean the asparagus well and cut off 2-inch tips to be used later. Cut the crisp part of remaining stalks into 1-inch pieces.
2. Toast the bread and cut in 1-inch squares.
3. In a shallow casserole or a rectangular baking dish 10″ × 6″ × 2″ arrange alternate layers of bread squares, asparagus, and cheese.
4. Combine the eggs, milk, salt, pepper, and butter.
5. Pour over the casserole and bake in a 325° oven 45 minutes to an hour, or until the custard is set.
6. At the same time salt the reserved tips and wrap them in a square of aluminium foil. Fold the edges to seal and put them in the oven with the casserole. Unwrap and arrange on the top of the pudding before serving. Serves 8.

ASPARAGUS-BACON PIE

1½ lbs. cooked asparagus cut in 1-inch
    pieces, or frozen asparagus stems
6 slices crisply cooked bacon
3 eggs lightly beaten
1 tablespoon chopped spring onions
1 teaspoon sugar

1 teaspoon salt or to taste
¼ teaspoon pepper
    Pinch nutmeg
¾ pt. thin cream
4 oz. grated Parmesan cheese
    Pastry for 9-inch pie shell

1. Line a deep pie plate with the pastry.
2. Crumble the bacon and spread it on the bottom.
3. Arrange the asparagus over the bacon.
4. Mix the eggs, spring onions, sugar, salt, pepper, nutmeg, cream, and half the cheese. Pour gently over the asparagus.
5. Spread the remaining cheese on top and bake 10 minutes in a 400° oven.
6. Reduce the heat to 350° and continue to bake 25–30 minutes longer, or until a knife inserted in the centre comes out clean. Serves 6.

QUICK GREEN BEAN CASSEROLE

2 10-oz. packets frozen French beans
½ pt. boiling salted water
7-oz. packet frozen French-fried onion rings

2 tins condensed cream of mushroom soup
¼ pt. top milk

1. Cook the beans in the water, but not more than 3–4 minutes after they come to a boil, and that over very low heat. Drain well.

2. Alternate layers of beans and onions in a casserole.

3. Heat the soup and mix with the milk. Pour over the casserole and bake 25 minutes in a 350° oven. Serves 6–7.

BRUSSELS SPROUTS DE LUXE

2 lbs. Brussels sprouts, or 3 packets
  frozen, cooked barely tender
3 oz. chopped carrots
3 oz. chopped onion
3 oz. chopped celery

3 oz. cooked chestnuts broken up
¾ pt. condensed consommé
3 tablespoons butter or margarine
  Salt and pepper
2 thin slices lemon quartered

1. Arrange the sprouts in a greased casserole.

2. Put in a saucepan the carrots, onion, celery, chestnuts, and consommé. Bring to a boil, reduce the heat, and simmer about 10 minutes.

3. Add the butter, seasoning to taste, and lemon pieces.

4. Pour over the sprouts and bake in a moderate oven, 350°, 30 minutes. Cover the casserole for the first 20 minutes. Serves 6.

LIMA BEAN SOUFFLÉ

8 oz. cooked lima beans (tinned will do)
3 tablespoons butter or margarine
3 tablespoons flour
½ pt. rich milk

Salt and pepper to taste
4 eggs separated
1 tablespoon brandy

Spanish Sauce

4 oz. chopped onion
3 tablespoons salad oil
8 oz. peeled and seeded tomatoes chopped
4 oz. ripe or green olives coarsely
  chopped

½ teaspoon celery salt
2 teaspoons Worcestershire sauce
½ teaspoon garlic salt
1 tablespoon meat glaze
2 tablespoons brandy

1. Make a cream sauce with the butter, flour, and milk.
2. Season to taste and put in blender with the lima beans. Blend 30 seconds.
3. Add the egg yolks and brandy and blend 20 seconds more.
4. Beat the egg whites until stiff but not dry and fold into the lima bean mixture. Pour into a greased medium casserole or soufflé dish and bake in a slow oven, 325°, 35–40 minutes, or until a knife inserted in the centre comes out clean. Serve with Spanish Sauce. Serves 6.

Spanish Sauce: Sauté the onion lightly in oil. Add the tomatoes and simmer 10 minutes. Stir in the olives and remaining ingredients except the brandy, which should be added just before serving.

If desired, the sauce may be thickened a little with flour-and-water paste.

Note: Tinned lima beans are available at Harrods.

BROCCOLI CASSEROLE

1 large bunch fresh broccoli or 2 8-oz.
  packets frozen
  Boiling salted water
4 oz. grated Cheddar

1 tin condensed cream of mushroom
  soup
5-oz. tin evaporated milk
3½-oz. tin French-fried onion rings

1. If the broccoli is fresh, trim off all the thick part of the stems and slit the untrimmed part. Split large pieces. (Stems can be cut up, cooked in boiling salted water, drained, chopped quite fine, and mixed with salt, pepper, and butter to make another vegetable for another day.) Cook in boiling salted water until stems are barely tender. Drain.
2. If broccoli is frozen cook it barely 4 minutes after it comes to a boil, and drain.
3. Arrange the broccoli in a casserole and sprinkle with the cheese. Mix the soup and milk and pour over.
4. Bake 25 minutes in a moderate oven, 350°.
5. Top with onion rings and bake 8–10 minutes more, or until onions are crisp. Serves 6.

CAULIFLOWER WITH GREEN BEANS

1 medium cauliflower
4 oz. finely sliced runner beans
¾ pt. hot milk
1½ oz. butter or margarine

1½ oz. flour
  Salt and pepper
2 oz. cornflake crumbs

1. Trim the cauliflower and break into flowerets. Steam for 10 minutes, or until just tender.
2. Cook beans in milk, keeping them just simmering. The beans should be crisp, not soft. Drain, reserving the milk.
3. Melt the butter in a saucepan, blend in the flour, and gradually add the milk the beans were cooked in. Season to taste and stir in the beans.
4. Arrange the cauliflower in a medium casserole, pour the sauce over, top with crumbs, and bake about 20 minutes in a hot oven, 400°, or until brown. Serves 4.

ALSATIAN SAUERKRAUT

3 lbs. sauerkraut, well rinsed, or 2 large tins
½ teaspoon caraway seeds
12 peppercorns
2 carrots scraped and quartered lengthwise
8 small pork chops or 4 large, bone removed

1 lb. boneless smoked pork tenderloin or pork butt trimmed and sliced thick
½ pt. dry white wine
  Salt to taste
½ lb. knackwurst sliced

THIS is practically a classic way of preparing sauerkraut. To be at its best, however, it should be prepared a day ahead, as it improves greatly on standing.
1. In a large heavy casserole mix the well-drained kraut with the caraway seeds, peppercorns, and carrots. Cover with slices of pork tenderloin and the chops (cut in two if large).
2. Stir in the wine, sprinkle with salt, cover tightly, and simmer, on top of the stove, over the lowest possible heat. If it tends to boil put an asbestos mat underneath. Cook 2–3 hours, cool, and refrigerate.
3. Next day allow the casserole to come to room temperature (1–2 hours), stir in the knackwurst, and correct seasoning.
4. Reheat over very low heat just long enough to heat thoroughly—20–30 minutes. Serve with boiled new potatoes. Serves 8.

CHOUCROUTE GARNIE

3 lbs. sauerkraut well rinsed, or 2 large tins
1 tablespoon butter or margarine
¾ lb. bacon diced
1 large onion with 3 cloves stuck in
1 Polish sausage cut in 2-inch pieces
1 lb. smoked pork shoulder
3 tablespoons brandy
1 carrot sliced

6 peppercorns tied in cheesecloth
2 small bay leaves
¼ teaspoon dried thyme
 Salt to taste
¾ pt. dry white wine
¾ pt. water
12 medium potatoes peeled and boiled
12 frankfurters

CHOUCROUTE Garnie is almost as well-known as Alsatian sauerkraut—better known in many places. And it is equally delicious if you like sauerkraut.

1. Melt the butter in a stew pot or large heavy pan. Add the bacon and onion and cook until browned. Add the sausage and pork shoulder and brown. Remove the meat and set aside.

2. Squeeze the kraut as dry as possible and add it to the pan. Stir until slightly browned.

3. Add the brandy and stir.

4. Add the carrot, peppercorns, bay leaves, thyme, salt, wine, and water. Bring to a boil, stir in the meat, cover, and simmer over the lowest possible heat 3 hours. Use an asbestos mat, or 2 mats, under the pot if the kraut tends to boil.

5. At this point the dish can be cooled and refrigerated. Next day bring it to room temperature, stir in the potatoes and frankfurters, and simmer 30 minutes. Slice the pork shoulder before serving. Serves 6–8.

SWEET-SOUR RED CABBAGE

1 medium head red cabbage shredded fine
 Boiling salted water
2 oz. pork or bacon drippings
1 large apple peeled and chopped
¼ pt. water

2 tablespoons sugar
2 tablespoons vinegar
1 onion stuck with 6–8 cloves
1 tablespoon flour

1. Cover the cabbage with boiling salted water and simmer 10 minutes. Drain thoroughly. Put in a large casserole.

2. Stir into the cabbage the drippings, apple, water, sugar, and vinegar. Push the onion well down in the middle. Cover and bake 1½ hours in a slow oven, 300°. Or simmer over the lowest possible heat on top of the stove.

3. Just before serving sprinkle the flour over and stir it in. Remove the onion. Serves 6.

CAULIFLOWER À LA MOUSSELINE

1 large head cauliflower
2 eggs separated
2 tablespoons cream
½ teaspoon salt

½ teaspoon sugar
¼ teaspoon paprika
2½ tablespoons lemon juice
2 oz. butter

1. Break the cauliflower into flowerets, trim off excess stems, and steam about 10 minutes. Or cook 8–10 minutes in barely enough boiling salted water to cover. Watch carefully to see that cauliflower does not become soft. Drain.
2. In the top of a small double boiler beat the egg yolks and cream hard. Blend in the salt, sugar, and paprika. Set over hot but not boiling water.
3. When this mixture is hot pour in slowly, beating constantly, the lemon juice. Keep beating until it has the consistency of thick cream.
4. Remove the whole double boiler from the heat and beat in the butter in small pieces. Remove the top part from the double boiler.
5. Beat the egg whites until stiff but not dry and fold into the sauce.
6. Arrange the cauliflower in a shallow casserole, pour the sauce over, and brown briefly under the grill. Serves 6.

CAULIFLOWER ALMONDINE

1 medium cauliflower
  Boiling salted water
1 tin cream of mushroom soup, undiluted

2 oz. blanched and split almonds
1 tablespoon butter melted
2 tablespoons bread or cornflake crumbs

1. Cook cauliflower in the water until barely tender. Drain and arrange in a small casserole.
2. Heat the soup and stir in the almonds. Pour over the cauliflower.
3. Top with butter and crumbs mixed. Bake 10 minutes in a 325° oven. Serves 4.

CELERY ALMONDINE

1 lb. celery sliced in thin diagonals
  Boiling water
2 tablespoons butter or margarine
2 tablespoons flour
¾ pt. chicken broth

¼ pt. cream
  Salt and pepper
3 oz. chopped blanched almonds
2 tablespoons grated Parmesan cheese
2 tablespoons bread or cornflake crumbs

SPLIT, sliced, or chopped almonds can be used with a number of vegetables, but they seem to do more for celery than for any other one.
1. Parboil the celery; that is, barely cover it with boiling water and let it come to a boil again. Drain.
2. Make a white sauce by melting the butter, blending in the flour, and gradually adding the chicken broth and cream.
3. Season to taste, stir in the almonds, and pour over the celery in a medium casserole.
4. Combine the cheese and crumbs to make a topping.
5. Bake 20 minutes in a moderate oven, 375°, or until browned and bubbling. Serves 4–6.

COGNAC CARROTS

1 lb. carrots sliced diagonally very thin
2 tablespoons butter
4 tablespoons good cognac

4 tablespoons water
Salt and pepper
1 tablespoon minced parsley

MELT butter in medium casserole. Stir in remaining ingredients, except parsley, keeping salt and pepper on the light side. Cover tightly and bake in a slow oven, 300°, 20 minutes, or until carrots are tender and liquid absorbed. Sprinkle with parsley before serving. Serves 5–6.

CALIFORNIA CARROTS

1 lb. shredded or coarsely grated carrots
2 tablespoons butter or margarine
1 medium onion minced

Salt and pepper
¼ pt. dry white wine

MELT the butter in a medium casserole and stir in the carrots and onion. Sprinkle lightly with salt and pepper and pour the wine over. Cover the casserole and bake in a moderate oven, 350°, 25–30 minutes. Uncover the last 5 minutes. Serves 4.

CARROTS ALMONDINE

¾ lb. grated raw carrots
1½ tablespoons butter or margarine
2 eggs well beaten
8-oz. tin evaporated milk

½ teaspoon salt
½ teaspoon sugar
3 oz. coarsely chopped almonds

MELT the butter in a small casserole. Mix the remaining ingredients and stir into the casserole. Bake 30–40 minutes in a moderate oven, 350°. Serves 4.

CARROT SOUFFLÉ

12 oz. mashed cooked carrots
½ oz. butter or margarine
½ oz. flour
¼ pt. warm milk

½ teaspoon salt
3 oz. grated almonds
4 eggs separated

1. Melt the butter in a saucepan, blend in the flour, gradually add the milk, season, and simmer 5 minutes or so.
2. Stir in the carrots and almonds.
3. Remove from the heat and stir in the well-beaten yolks. Cool to lukewarm.
4. Fold in the egg whites beaten until stiff but not dry.
5. Pour gently into a small greased soufflé dish or casserole and bake in a moderate oven, 350°, 50–60 minutes, until soufflé feels firm at the centre, or until a knife inserted in the centre comes out clean. Serves 6–8.

BACON AND SWEET CORN PUDDING

2 6-oz. packets frozen sweet corn, cooked,
   or 2 medium tins whole-kernel sweet corn
3 eggs well beaten
3 tablespoons thin cream
1 teaspoon salt

Dash pepper
2 tablespoons minced onions
¼ teaspoon baking powder
  Thinly sliced Cheddar
3 slices bacon cut in 1-inch squares

Mix the sweet corn, eggs, cream, seasonings, onions, and baking powder. Pour into a greased medium casserole. Cover with cheese, cut to fit, and then with bacon squares. Bake 40–45 minutes in a moderate oven, 350°, or until firm. Serves 6.

BAKED SWEET CORN OMELETTE

6 oz. drained tinned or cooked fresh or
  frozen whole-kernel sweet corn
3 eggs separated

½ teaspoon salt
¼ teaspoon paprika
3 tablespoons butter or margarine

1. Beat egg yolks until thick. Stir in sweet corn, salt, and paprika.
2. Beat the egg whites until stiff but not dry and fold into the sweet corn mixture.
3. Melt the butter in a small casserole and pour in the mixture.
4. Bake in a moderate oven, 350°, 25 minutes, or until a knife inserted in the centre comes out clean.

    Serve with a cheese sauce (a white sauce in which 2–3 oz. grated Cheddar or Canadian cheese is melted). Serves 4.

SWEET CORN-CHEESE TART

12 oz. cooked sweet corn cut from cob,
  frozen cooked, or tinned whole-kernel
2 oz. grated Swiss cheese
  Pastry for deep 9-inch pie
6 slices crisply cooked bacon

  Salt and pepper
5 eggs lightly beaten
¾ pt. thin cream
2 tablespoons grated Parmesan cheese

This 'pie' is hearty enough to serve as the main dish for a luncheon party or Sunday-night supper.
1. Roll out the pastry ⅛ inch thick and fit it into a deep pie plate. Crumble the bacon and spread on it.
2. Mix the sweet corn, Swiss cheese, and salt and pepper to taste. Spread over the bacon.
3. Blend the eggs and cream and pour gently over the sweet corn-cheese mixture.
4. Top with Parmesan cheese and bake in a hot oven, 400°, 15 minutes.
5. Reduce the heat to 350° and continue to bake 20–30 minutes longer, or until tart is firm in the centre, or until a knife inserted in the centre comes out clean. Serves 6.

DEVILLED SWEET CORN PUDDING

1 lb. whole-kernel sweet corn cooked,
  tinned, fresh, or frozen
3 tablespoons butter or margarine
3 oz. chopped onions
½ lb. diced cooked ham
1 teaspoon prepared mustard
1 tablespoon flour

1 teaspoon salt
½ teaspoon dry mustard
¾ pt. milk
2 eggs lightly beaten
1 tablespoon Worcestershire sauce
3 oz. soft bread crumbs
2 tablespoons melted butter or margarine

1. In a medium casserole melt 2 tablespoons of the butter and sauté the onions and ham. Stir in the prepared mustard.
2. In a saucepan melt the remaining tablespoon of butter, blend in the flour, salt, and dry mustard, and gradually add the milk. Stir constantly until thickened and smooth.
3. Add to the sauce the eggs, sweet corn, and Worcestershire sauce. Pour over the ham in the casserole.
4. Mix the soft crumbs with the melted butter and spread over the pudding.
5. Bake in a moderate oven, 375°, about an hour, or until the centre is firm to the touch. Serves 4–6.

PLANTATION SWEET CORN PUDDING

1-lb. tin cream-style sweet corn
¾ pt. milk
1 tablespoon butter or margarine
4 eggs slightly beaten
2 tablespoons chopped pimento

2 tablespoons chopped green pepper
2 tablespoons grated onion
1 tablespoon sugar
1 teaspoon salt

SCALD milk and melt butter in it. Combine sweet corn, eggs, pimento, green pepper, onion, sugar, and salt. Stir hot milk in gradually, blending thoroughly. Turn into greased medium casserole and bake in slow oven, 300°, 45–60 minutes, or until a knife inserted in the centre comes out clean. Serves 6.

SWEET CORN CASSEROLE WITH MUSHROOMS

¾ lb. drained tinned or cooked fresh or
  frozen whole-kernel sweet corn
2 tablespoons butter or margarine
2 tablespoons chopped onion

4 oz. sliced mushrooms
¼ pt. thin cream
  Salt and pepper
1 tablespoon chopped parsley

HEAT butter in a medium casserole and lightly sauté onion and mushrooms. Stir in sweet corn, cream, and seasonings. Cover and bake in slow oven, 325°, 20–25 minutes. Remove cover the last 5 minutes. Sprinkle with parsley before serving. Serves 6.

SWEET CORN AND ASPARAGUS CASSEROLE

16 oz. packet frozen sweet corn, cooked,
  or a 6-oz. tin whole-kernel sweet corn
1 6-oz. packet frozen asparagus stems or
  10-oz. tin all-green asparagus, cut up
$\frac{1}{4}$ pt. milk
1 tablespoon butter or margarine

1 tablespoon flour
$\frac{1}{4}$ teaspoon celery salt
1 tablespoon bread or cornflake crumbs
1 tablespoon grated Parmesan cheese
1 tablespoon chopped parsley

1. If you use frozen sweet corn and asparagus, cook them separately in 3 tablespoons boiling water, until barely tender. If you use tinned vegetables, drain them; in either case save the liquid.
2. Combine these liquids and measure out $\frac{1}{4}$ pt. Add the milk.
3. Melt butter in a saucepan, blend in the flour, cook briefly, and gradually add the liquid. Stir constantly until thick and smooth. Add the celery salt.
4. Spread the sweet corn in a shallow casserole and cover with the cut-up asparagus. Pour the white sauce over and top with mixed crumbs and cheese.
5. Bake in a moderate oven, 350°, 20 minutes, or until golden and bubbly.
6. Sprinkle with parsley before serving. Serves 6–8.

CUCUMBERS IN CREAM

6 medium cucumbers
  Boiling salted water
3 tablespoons butter or margarine
$\frac{1}{2}$ teaspoon sweet basil
$\frac{1}{8}$ teaspoon pepper

3 tablespoons minced spring onions
$\frac{1}{2}$ pt. thick cream
  Salt to taste
2 teaspoons chopped parsley

MOST people think of cucumbers as either a vegetable to be eaten raw or as the makings of pickles. However, cooked cucumbers have a delicate flavour and should be more widely served.
1. Peel the cucumbers, cut in quarters lengthwise, and scrape out the seeds, unless the cucumbers are really young. Cut them into 1-inch pieces. Cover with boiling salted water and simmer three minutes. Drain well.
2. Melt butter in a shallow casserole. Stir in the basil, spring onions, and pepper. Add the cucumbers and stir until they are well coated.
3. Bake in a moderate oven, 375°, 15 minutes, stirring two or three times.
4. Put the cream in a saucepan and boil it quite hard, reducing the $\frac{1}{2}$ pt. to $\frac{1}{4}$ pt. Season to taste. Stir it into the cucumber casserole, continue baking 4–5 minutes more, and sprinkle with parsley. Serves 4.

BAKED AUBERGINE

1 large aubergine
  Boiling water
1½ tablespoons salt
3 tablespoons salad oil or olive oil
1 onion chopped
1 medium green pepper cut in ¼-inch
  cubes
1 tomato skinned and chopped

½ teaspoon dried basil or 1 teaspoon
  fresh, chopped
½ teaspoon dried oregano or 1 teaspoon
  fresh, chopped
⅛ teaspoon pepper
2 oz. bread or cornflake crumbs
2 tablespoons butter

1. Wash the aubergine and cover with boiling water. Add 1 tablespoon of the salt and boil 20 minutes. Turn it several times to cook evenly, since it will float on top of the water. Drain and rinse it in cold water.
2. Peel the aubergine and cut in ¾-inch cubes.
3. Heat the oil in a frying-pan and lightly sauté the onion. Stir in the aubergine, green pepper, tomato, basil, oregano, remaining ½ tablespoon salt, and pepper.
4. Place in a greased medium casserole, cover with crumbs, and dot with butter.
5. Bake in a 350° oven about 30 minutes, or until well browned. Serves 4–5.

AUBERGINE SPECIAL

2 aubergines sliced ½ inch thick, unpeeled
3 tablespoons French dressing
1 medium onion sliced
1 tablespoon flour

½ teaspoon salt
¾ pt. milk
4 oz. grated Cheddar

1. Arrange the aubergine slices in a shallow casserole (cut them in half if very large). Cover them with French dressing and onion, using about half of the dressing. Let stand an hour and drain off any French dressing that has not been absorbed.
2. Bake about 15 minutes in a hot oven, 450°, or until the skin is black.
3. Heat the remaining French dressing in a saucepan, stir in flour and salt, and blend in milk. Stir until thick and smooth.
4. Add cheese and stir until cheese is melted.
5. Pour the cheese sauce over the aubergine and continue baking about 10 minutes longer, or until bubbly. Serves 4–6, depending upon size of aubergines.

AUBERGINE SOUFFLÉ WITH ALMONDS

2 medium aubergines peeled and cut in
  1-inch cubes
  Boiling salted water
2 oz. bread or cornflake crumbs
¼ pt. milk
2 tablespoons butter or margarine
  Salt and pepper

1 tablespoon onion juice or scraped onion
¼ teaspoon nutmeg (scant)
3 eggs separated
2 tablespoons buttered crumbs, bread or
  cornflake
2 tablespoons sliced or split toasted
  almonds

1. Cover the aubergines with boiling salted water and simmer until soft—8–10 minutes at most. Drain well and mash.
2. Cover the 2 oz. crumbs with the milk and let stand 2–3 minutes.
3. Mix the crumbs, butter, salt and pepper, onion juice, and nutmeg.
4. Stir in the aubergines and the well-beaten egg yolks. Cool to lukewarm.
5. Beat the egg whites until stiff but not dry and fold into the mixture.
6. Pour into a well-greased medium soufflé dish, sprinkle with the 2 tablespoons crumbs and almonds, and bake in a hot oven, 400°, 30 minutes, or until firm to the touch, or until a knife inserted in the centre comes out clean. Serves 4–6.

CREOLE AUBERGINE

2 medium aubergines cut in ½-inch slices,
  unpeeled
  Salt and pepper
  Boiling water
2 tablespoons salad oil or olive oil
1 small bay leaf

¼ teaspoon dried sweet marjoram or
  ¾ teaspoon fresh, chopped
3–4 spring onions cut up fine, both tops
  and ends
1 tablespoon chopped parsley
1 tin condensed tomato soup

1. Salt the aubergine slices and pile them up in the original shape. Let stand 15–20 minutes to draw out the bitterness this vegetable sometimes has. Wipe off the slices and cook them in boiling water 6–8 minutes, or until they begin to look transparent. Drain and arrange in a medium casserole.
2. Heat the oil in a small saucepan and cook the spring onions, marjoram, and bay leaf in it. Add the parsley.
3. Stir in the soup and simmer 3–4 minutes.
4. Pour over the aubergines and bake, covered, in a moderate oven, 350°, 10–15 minutes. Serves 4–6, depending on size of aubergines.

AUBERGINE WITH ANCHOVIES

2 aubergines cut in ¾-inch cubes, unpeeled
  Boiling salted water
3 rashers bacon diced and cooked crisp
4 oz. chopped onion
2 oz. chopped celery
6 anchovy fillets chopped

6 oz. peeled and diced tomatoes or small
  tin Italian tomatoes, drained
1 oz. chopped parsley
3 oz. bread or cornflake crumbs
1 egg
  Salt and pepper to taste
2 oz. grated Parmesan cheese

1. Cook the cubed aubergines in boiling salted water 4–5 minutes, or steam over boiling water about 10 minutes, until tender. Drain well.
2. When the bacon is crisp add the onion and celery to the frying-pan in which it is cooked, and cook until the onion becomes transparent but not brown.
3. Stir in the aubergines, anchovies, tomatoes, parsley, and half the crumbs. Mix lightly and add the egg.
4. Season with care—you may not need salt because of the anchovies.
5. Pour into a well-greased casserole and top with the cheese mixed with the rest of the crumbs.
6. Bake in a slow oven, 325°, 30 minutes. Serves 6.

AUBERGINE ARLÉSIENNE

1 or 2 aubergines (about 1½ lbs.) cut in
  ½-inch cubes, unpeeled
3 oz. minced onion
2 small green peppers seeded and diced
2 tablespoons salad oil or olive oil
2 medium tomatoes skinned and coarsely
  chopped
1 large clove garlic crushed

1½ teaspoons salt
¾ teaspoon dried oregano or 1 tablespoon
  fresh, chopped
⅛ teaspoon fresh-ground pepper
1 tablespoon drained capers
¼ cup coarsely chopped walnuts
  Strips pimento

1. Sauté the onion and peppers in hot oil 6 or 7 minutes.
2. Stir in the aubergine and sauté 3 or 4 minutes.
3. Add tomatoes, garlic, salt, oregano, and pepper. Blend well and arrange in a medium casserole, well greased.
4. Bake, covered, in a medium oven, 350°, 35–40 minutes, or until the aubergine is tender.
5. Uncover, stir in capers and walnuts, and bake 15–20 minutes longer, uncovered, or until quite dry.
6. Lay several strips of pimento on top before serving. Serves 6.

AUBERGINE, COURGETTES, AND TOMATOES

1 medium aubergine cut into $\frac{1}{2}$-inch slices, not peeled
2 thin courgettes cut in thin slices, unpeeled
2 large tomatoes skinned and sliced $\frac{1}{4}$ inch thick
2 medium onions sliced
$\frac{1}{2}$ teaspoon dried basil or 1 teaspoon fresh, chopped

3 tablespoons salad oil
$\frac{1}{2}$ teaspoon dried thyme or 1 teaspoon fresh, chopped
$\frac{1}{2}$ teaspoon dried rosemary or 1 teaspoon fresh, chopped
2 tablespoons chopped parsley
Salt and pepper
1 oz. grated Parmesan cheese or sliced Mozzarella cheese

1. Salt the aubergine slices and pile them up. Let stand about 30 minutes and wipe the slices with paper towels.
2. In a good-sized casserole arrange alternate layers of aubergine (cut to fit), onions, courgettes, and tomatoes.
3. Dribble a little oil on each layer and sprinkle each with a bit of each herb. Lightly salt and pepper all the layers except aubergine.
4. Sprinkle the top with Parmesan cheese or cover with slices of Mozzarella cheese.
5. Bake 45 minutes in a moderate oven, 350°, or until the top is browned and bubbly. Serves 6.

AUBERGINE AU GRATIN

1 large or 2 medium aubergines sliced $\frac{1}{4}$ inch thick
Boiling salted water

$\frac{1}{4}$ lb. butter or margarine
$\frac{1}{4}$–$\frac{1}{2}$ lb. thinly sliced Swiss cheese
Fresh-ground pepper

1. Soak the aubergine slices in cold water 20 minutes. Drain and cover with boiling salted water. Drain again and dry the slices on paper towels.
2. Melt the butter in a frying-pan and sauté the aubergine slices on both sides until delicately brown.
3. Arrange the slices of aubergine in a large shallow casserole, laying a slice of cheese over each. Sprinkle each layer with a bit of pepper.
4. Bake the casserole in a moderate oven, 350°, 30 minutes, or until the cheese is bubbling. Serves 6.

AUBERGINE NIÇOISE

2 medium aubergines peeled and cut in
  1-inch cubes
4 tablespoons olive oil or salad oil
1 clove garlic crushed
1 oz. minced onion
1 stalk celery chopped
2 small green peppers cut in 1-inch
  squares

12 pitted green olives
3 medium tomatoes peeled, seeded, and
  chopped
1 teaspoon capers
  Salt and pepper
3 tablespoons buttered bread or
  cornflake crumbs

1. Heat the oil in a large heavy frying-pan and sauté the garlic and onion lightly.
2. Add the aubergines, celery, peppers, and olives and simmer 10 minutes, stirring frequently.
3. Stir in the tomatoes and capers, and season to taste.
4. Spread in a medium casserole, sprinkle with crumbs, and bake in a moderate oven, 350°,
30 minutes, or until brown and bubbly. Serves 6.

CONTINENTAL CASSEROLE OF CHICORY

3 whole heads of chicory
8 oz. chopped chicory
3 tablespoons butter or margarine
3 oz. minced green pepper
  Salt
½ teaspoon sugar
2–3 outside leaves of lettuce

1 tablespoon lemon juice
3 tablespoons water
1 tin condensed cream of mushroom soup
¼ pt. milk
2 oz. bread or cornflake crumbs
2 tablespoons grated Parmesan cheese
2 tablespoons melted butter or margarine

THIS is a rather fussy recipe, but it makes a wonderful vegetable casserole to serve with a
plain meat.
1. Melt 2 tablespoons of the butter in a saucepan and stir in the chopped chicory, green
pepper, ½ teaspoon salt, and sugar.
2. Lay enough lettuce leaves over just to cover. Cover the saucepan and cook over very
low heat, without stirring, 15 minutes. Remove the lettuce leaves and discard.
3. At the same time, put the whole chicory heads in a saucepan with the lemon juice, the
remaining tablespoon of butter, water, and salt to taste. Bring to a boil and simmer,
covered, over the lowest possible heat until tender—25–30 minutes on each side. Drain.
4. Mix the soup and milk. Stir in the chopped chicory mixture. Spread in a greased shallow
casserole and top with a mixture of the crumbs, cheese, and melted butter. Bake 20 minutes
in a 350° oven.
5. Slit the whole chicory lengthwise and arrange the halves, cut side down, around the edge
of the casserole. Bake 10 minutes longer. Serves 6.

BRAISED CHICORY WITH WALNUTS

4 large heads of chicory
2 oz. butter or margarine
$\frac{1}{4}$ teaspoon dried basil or $\frac{3}{4}$ teaspoon fresh, chopped

Salt and pepper
$\frac{1}{2}$ pt. condensed consommé
2 tablespoons chopped walnuts
1 tablespoon butter or margarine

CHICORY makes a delicious cooked vegetable, though few people ever think of cooking it.
1. Cut the chicory heads in half lengthwise and let stand in ice water 15 minutes to crisp. Dry with paper towels.
2. Melt the 2 oz. butter in a shallow casserole and stir in the basil. Brown the chicory halves lightly on both sides and season very lightly.
3. Pour over about half of the consommé and bake in a moderate oven, 350°, 25–30 minutes, turning the chicory occasionally, and adding a little consommé as it becomes dry.
4. Brown the walnuts in the remaining tablespoon of butter and pour over the chicory before serving. Serves 4.

INDIAN LENTILS

1 lb. dried lentils
2 onions chopped
   Piece of ginger root the size of a small walnut
3 tablespoons butter or margarine

1 teaspoon turmeric
$\frac{1}{4}$ teaspoon chili powder
   Salt
$1\frac{1}{2}$ pts. water

1. Soak the lentils overnight in water to cover. In the morning drain them, rinse, and drain again.
2. Sauté the onions and ginger root in butter until the onions are golden, stirring frequently.
3. Add the lentils, turmeric, and chili powder, and cook until most of the butter is absorbed. Fish out the ginger root and discard.
4. Pour the lentil mixture into a medium casserole with salt to taste and water.
5. Cover and bake in a slow oven, 300°, 1–$1\frac{1}{4}$ hours, or until the lentils are tender and most of the water absorbed. Check once or twice, and add a bit more water if the lentils seem dry.
6. Uncover the last 10 minutes of the cooking time. Serve with wedges of lemon. Serves 4–5.

Paella

MUSHROOM PIE

2 lbs. mushrooms, washed, and trimmed if stems are long
5 tablespoons butter or margarine
1 teaspoon salt
½ teaspoon fresh-ground pepper
2 tablespoons lemon juice

2 tablespoons flour
¾ pt. chicken broth
⅛ teaspoon dried marjoram
¼ pt. dry sherry
¼ pt. thick cream
Pastry for 1-crust pie

1. If the mushrooms are large quarter or halve them.
2. Melt 4 tablespoons of the butter in a frying-pan and add the mushrooms, salt, pepper, and lemon juice. Cover and simmer 10 minutes over low heat, stirring occasionally. Skim the mushrooms out and arrange them in a shallow casserole.
3. To the juices remaining in the pan add the remaining butter, blend in the flour, and gradually stir in the chicken broth. Add the marjoram, correct seasoning, and cook until thickened, stirring constantly.
4. Remove the pan from the heat, stir in the sherry and cream, and pour over the mushrooms.
5. Roll out the pastry to ⅛-inch thickness and place over the mushrooms. If the casserole is small enough to be filled by the mushrooms, seal the pastry to the edge and slit several times to allow steam to escape. However, if casserole is not filled, cut the pastry to size and lay on top of the mushrooms.
6. Bake in a hot oven, 425°, 10–12 minutes. Reduce heat to 350° and bake 10–15 minutes longer, or until pastry is golden. Serves 6–8.

MUSHROOM CASSEROLE

1 lb. mushrooms, halved or quartered if large
4 oz. melted butter
1 teaspoon dried marjoram or 2 teaspoons fresh, chopped

½ teaspoon salt
1 tablespoon chopped chives
4 tablespoons chicken broth
2 tablespoons thick cream

1. Wash the mushrooms and cut off part of the stems where they are quite long. Arrange in a small shallow casserole.
2. Combine the melted butter, marjoram, salt, and chives and pour over the mushrooms. Stir well to be sure the mushrooms are all coated.
3. Mix the chicken broth and cream and pour over the mushrooms.
4. Cover the casserole and bake 20 minutes in a 375° oven. Uncover the last 5 minutes. Serves 4–5.

STUFFED MUSHROOMS TARRAGON

1 lb. large mushrooms
5 tablespoons butter or margarine
2 tablespoons chopped shallots or
  1 tablespoon chopped onion
1 egg beaten

1 tablespoon chopped fresh
  tarragon or 1 teaspoon dried
2 tablespoons brandy
2 oz. bread or cornflake crumbs
  Salt and pepper

1. Remove the stems from the mushrooms and chop fine. Sauté in 2 tablespoons of the butter with the shallots.
2. Add the tarragon, egg, brandy, crumbs, and salt and pepper to taste.
3. Sauté the mushroom caps in the remaining 3 tablespoons butter until golden.
4. Arrange cap side down in a shallow casserole, stuff them with the stems-crumb mixture, and grill them 4 inches from the heat 6–8 minutes, or until well browned. Serves 4.

STUFFED MUSHROOMS VERNON

1 lb. large mushrooms
4 tablespoons bread or cornflake crumbs
2 tablespoons minced parsley
$\frac{1}{4}$ lb. melted butter
1 teaspoon lemon juice

3 tablespoons minced shallots or
  2 tablespoons minced onion
Salt
Paprika

REMOVE the stems from the mushrooms and chop fine. Mix with the crumbs, parsley, shallots, melted butter, lemon juice, and salt to taste. Fill the caps with this mixture and arrange in a greased shallow casserole. Sprinkle with paprika and bake 5 minutes in a hot oven, 450°. Put under the grill for an additional 3–4 minutes. Serves 4.

ONIONS DE LUXE

3 lbs. small white onions peeled or
  3 16-oz. tins, drained
  Boiling salted water
$\frac{3}{4}$ pt. thick white sauce
  Salt and pepper
1 teaspoon dry mustard

$\frac{1}{4}$ teaspoon nutmeg
6 oz. chopped salted almonds or salted
  peanuts
1 small tin devilled ham (optional)
1 oz. buttered bread or cornflake crumbs

1. If raw onions are used cook them in rapidly boiling salted water until tender. Drain, and arrange half of them in a greased casserole.
2. Make the white sauce with $1\frac{1}{2}$ tablespoons butter or margarine, $1\frac{1}{2}$ tablespoons flour, and $\frac{3}{4}$ pt. milk, stirring until smooth and thick. Season to taste and add mustard and nutmeg.
3. Sprinkle half the nuts on the onions and cover with half the white sauce. Repeat the layers of onions, nuts, and white sauce.
4. Mix the bread or cornflake crumbs with the devilled ham and spread over the top.
5. Bake in a hot oven, 425°, about 25 minutes, or until brown and bubbly. Serves 6–8.

BAKED ONIONS WITH CREAM AND SHERRY

12 medium onions sliced
  Boiling salted water
¼ pt. thin cream
3 tablespoons dry sherry

½ teaspoon salt
  Fresh-ground pepper
3 tablespoons butter or margarine

1. Cover the onions with boiling salted water and cook until they are tender but still crisp—about 10 minutes. Drain and spread in a medium casserole.
2. Mix the cream, sherry, salt and pepper and pour over the onions.
3. Dot with butter, cover, and bake in a moderate oven, 325°, until tender, about 30 minutes. Remove cover the last 5 minutes. Serves 6.

SPANISH ONION CASSEROLE

2 Spanish onions sliced quite thin
  Salt and pepper
½ pt. sour cream

3 tablespoons buttered bread or cornflake
  crumbs
Paprika

SPREAD the onions evenly in a shallow greased casserole or pie plate. Season to taste, spread sour cream over evenly, top with crumbs, and sprinkle with paprika. Bake 35–40 minutes in a 375° oven. (The exact time will depend on the thickness of the onion slices.) Serves 4.

Note: You can substitute sweet cream, a thin white sauce, or consommé for the sour cream. If either of the last two, do not cover, and baste occasionally, adding more liquid if dry.

ONION CUSTARD

1 lb. small white onions peeled or 1-lb. tin
2 oz. butter or margarine
3 eggs well beaten
3 tablespoons thick cream

½ teaspoon nutmeg
  Salt and pepper
1 rasher of bacon shredded

1. Let the onions (if raw) stand in cold salted water an hour or so.
2. Slice them and sauté them lightly in sizzling butter, until they are soft but not coloured. Let them cool.
3. Combine the eggs, cream, nutmeg, salt and pepper. Stir in the onions and pour into a small greased casserole.
4. Scatter the bacon shreds on top and bake about 20 minutes in a moderate oven, 350°—until the custard is set and firm to the touch. Serves 4.

SCALLOPED ONIONS ALMONDINE

2 1-lb. tins tiny whole onions drained
1 tin condensed cream of mushroom soup

2 oz. grated Canadian cheese
2 oz. chopped or split toasted almonds

Mix the onions with the soup and pour into a small greased casserole. Top with the cheese and sprinkle with almonds. Bake in a 375° oven 30 minutes. Serves 6.

PEAS AND PASTA SHELLS

1 10-oz. tin petits pois
8-oz. packet pasta shells cooked
3 tablespoons salad oil
4 tablespoons butter or margarine
6 oz. onion chopped fine

2 small cloves garlic crushed
$\frac{1}{4}$ cup chopped parsley
$\frac{1}{2}$ teaspoon salt
 Grind of pepper

Heat the oil and butter and lightly sauté the onion and garlic. Heat the peas in their liquid and drain well. Put them into a small casserole and stir in the pasta, onion and garlic, parsley, and seasonings. Bake 15 minutes in a moderate oven, 350°, just long enough to heat it well. Serves 4.

BAKED POTATO PUDDING

6–8 large potatoes peeled and grated
1 small onion grated
3 eggs well beaten

$\frac{1}{2}$ pt. hot milk
6 tablespoons melted butter

Mix all the ingredients and pour into a well-greased medium casserole. Bake in a moderate oven, 350°, 1$\frac{1}{4}$ hours, or until firm. Exact time will depend on depth of potatoes in casserole. Serves 8–10.

BAKED SLICED POTATOES

1. Peel medium-sized potatoes. Hold them firmly and slice them medium thick, keeping the shape of the potato. Transfer potatoes when sliced to a well-buttered shallow casserole and press so that the slices fan out, overlapping slightly. Sprinkle with salt.
2. Mix grated Parmesan and grated Romano cheese and spread over the potatoes rather thickly.
3. Sprinkle over a generous amount of melted butter or margarine.
4. Bake the casserole 20 minutes in a hot oven, 500°, or 30 minutes in a 450° oven. Two potatoes will serve 3 people.

CREAMY SCALLOPED POTATOES

2½ lbs. sliced raw potatoes
1 tin condensed cream of mushroom soup

¼ pt. milk
1 medium onion minced

MIX the soup with the milk and onion. In a buttered medium casserole arrange alternate layers of potatoes and soup. Cover and bake 1 hour in a 375° oven. Uncover and bake an additional 15 minutes. Serves 6.

DEVILLED POTATO PIE

Crumb Part

2 oz. butter or margarine
1 teaspoon salt

2 teaspoons onion powder
12 oz. cornflake crumbs

Pie Part

5 oz. cornflake crumbs
2 tablespoons soft butter or margarine
1 lb. whipped cottage cheese
1¼ lbs. hot mashed potatoes

2½-oz. tin devilled ham
Salt and pepper
2 eggs slightly beaten

1. Mix the ingredients for the crumb part well and press two-thirds of the mixture on the bottom and sides of a buttered shallow casserole or deep pie plate. Build an edge on the rim of the crust, not on the plate.
2. Combine the pie ingredients, mix well, and spread carefully over the crumb shell.
3. Sprinkle the remaining third of the crumb mixture on top.
4. Bake in a moderate oven, 350°, 45 minutes, or until lightly browned. Serves 6.

PRINCESS POTATOES

6 medium-sized raw potatoes grated
4 oz. melted butter
7 oz. grated onion
1 oz. chopped parsley

4 oz. minced celery
2 teaspoons salt
½ teaspoon paprika

THE simplest way to prepare grated potatoes is to do them in a blender. Do these in 2 or 3 batches, and with the last batch add the onion, parsley, and celery. Mix everything together, put into a well-buttered 2-quart casserole, and bake 1 hour in a 375° oven. Serves 8.

218

HOT POTATO SALAD

8 medium potatoes, cooked, peeled, and
diced small
1 medium onion minced
2 oz. minced celery
2 tablespoons diced green pepper

1 teaspoon salt
¼ teaspoon fresh-ground pepper
3 tablespoons salad oil
3 tablespoons mild cider vinegar
4 slices crisp bacon crumbled

To be at its best, hot potato salad should always be made with freshly cooked potatoes.
1. In a medium casserole combine the potatoes, onion, celery, green pepper, salt, and pepper.
2. Combine the oil and vinegar in a small saucepan and heat to boiling.
3. Pour at once over the warm potatoes, mix well, stir in the bacon, and heat about 20 minutes in a moderate oven, 350°. Serves 6.

POTATOES FECHIMER

2 1-lb. tins white potatoes or 2 lbs.
potatoes boiled and peeled
1 oz. grated Parmesan cheese
Salt and pepper
Nutmeg

1½ oz. butter
1½ oz. flour
¾ pt. thin cream
1 tablespoon grated Parmesan cheese
3 tablespoons bread or cornflake crumbs

1. Chop the potatoes coarsely and toss them with the 1 oz. of grated Parmesan, salt and pepper to taste, and a dash of nutmeg.
2. Make a white sauce with the butter, flour, and cream, stirring until smooth and velvety.
3. Season to taste and stir in the tablespoon of Parmesan cheese.
4. Combine the sauce with the potatoes, spread in a buttered casserole, and sprinkle with crumbs.
5. Bake 30 minutes in a 375° oven. Serves 5–6.

HOT SWISS POTATO SALAD

2 lbs. cooked potatoes sliced
4 oz. Swiss cheese diced
2 oz. minced spring onions, including green
part
1 oz. minced fresh dill or ½ oz. dried
1 teaspoon salt (less if peanuts are salted)
2 oz. chopped peanuts

Butter or margarine
½ pt. sour cream
1 oz. grated Swiss cheese
2–3 tablespoons fine bread or cornflake
crumbs
2–3 tablespoons melted butter or
margarine

1. Toss lightly together the diced cheese, spring onions, dill, salt, and peanuts.
2. In a medium casserole arrange layers of potatoes, cheese mixture, dabs of butter, and sour cream to cover.
3. Repeat the layers, ending with potatoes.
4. Blend the grated cheese, crumbs, and melted butter together, and spread over the top.
5. Bake in a 375° oven 30–45 minutes, or until well browned. Serves 6.

QUICK LYONNAISE POTATO CASSEROLE

8 medium potatoes peeled and sliced
3 medium onions sliced
¾ pt. milk
  Salt and pepper

Dash ground cloves
Dash nutmeg
1 tin condensed onion soup
2 tablespoons chopped chives

1. In a saucepan cook the onions in milk about 10 minutes.
2. Season to taste and add cloves, nutmeg, soup, and potatoes.
3. Arrange in a buttered 2-quart casserole and bake in a moderate oven, 375°, uncovered, 30–35 minutes, or until potatoes are tender and liquid almost absorbed.
4. Sprinkle with chives before serving. Serves 6–8.

DIFFERENT SCALLOPED POTATOES

4 medium potatoes peeled and sliced thin
  Salt and fresh-ground pepper
  Flour

2 tablespoons butter
1¼ pts. chicken broth or condensed
  consommé

1. Place half the potatoes in a medium casserole. Sprinkle with salt and pepper and dredge with flour.
2. Add the remaining potatoes and sprinkle similarly with salt, pepper, and flour.
3. Dot with butter and pour the chicken broth or consommé over.
4. Bake, covered, in a moderate oven, 375°, 25–30 minutes.
5. Uncover and continue baking 10–15 minutes longer, or until potatoes are tender and liquid almost absorbed. Serves 4.

BAKED SWEET POTATOES WITH APPLES

1¾ lbs. boiled and sliced sweet potatoes
1 lb. apple slices ¼ inch thick·
2 oz. sugar
¼ pt. water

2 oz. brown sugar
6 tablespoons butter or margarine
  Juice 1 lemon

1. Boil sugar and water together 3 minutes, stirring until sugar is dissolved.
2. Drop apple slices into the syrup, a few at a time, and simmer gently, covered, until soft but not mushy. Skim them out with a slotted spatula or spoon. Save the syrup.
3. Sprinkle a little of the brown sugar in a medium casserole. Arrange a layer of potato slices in the casserole, then a layer of apples. Dot apples with butter and sprinkle with brown sugar.
4. Repeat the layers until the ingredients are used up, ending with potatoes, dotted with butter and sugar.
5. Stir lemon juice into the apple syrup and pour over the casserole.
6. Bake in a slow oven, 325°, 30 minutes. Serves 6.

ORANGE SWEET POTATOES

6 medium sweet potatoes cooked, peeled,
  and sliced
2 medium oranges sliced thin (unpeeled)
4 oz. brown sugar

5 tablespoons butter
3½ oz. strained honey
¼ pt. orange juice
1 oz. fine bread or cornflake crumbs

1. Build up layers, in a buttered medium casserole, of potatoes, sprinkled with brown sugar and dotted with butter, and then orange slices. Repeat until the potatoes and oranges are used up.
2. Heat the honey just enough to make it quite liquid, and mix it with the orange juice. Pour over the casserole.
3. Combine the crumbs with whatever butter and sugar are left and spread over the top of the casserole.
4. Cover and bake 30–40 minutes in a 350° oven.
5. Remove the cover after 15 minutes. Serves 6.

AUSTRIAN SPINACH PUDDING

2 1-lb. packets frozen chopped spinach
  cooked
8 eggs separated
4 oz. soft butter or margarine
1 oz. chopped parsley

4 slices white bread
  Milk
¼ pt. sour cream
  Salt and pepper
5 oz. dry bread or cornflake crumbs

1. Press all possible moisture out of the cooked spinach and purée it in a blender or food mill.
2. Beat the egg yolks lightly and stir in the butter. Combine with the spinach and parsley.
3. Soak the bread 3–4 minutes in enough milk just to cover and squeeze it dry.
4. Add the soaked bread to the spinach mixture, with the sour cream and salt and pepper to taste.
5. Beat the egg whites until stiff but not dry, dusting the bread crumbs over them towards the end of the beating. Fold into the spinach mixture.
6. Pour into a well-buttered large mould or soufflé dish, cover tightly (with foil if necessary), and place in a large pan, preferably on a trivet, and pour in enough boiling water to come halfway up the sides of the dish.
7. Cover the pan and steam 1¼ hours, adding more water as needed to maintain the level. Unmould if you have used a mould. Serves 8.

SPINACH MOUSSE

1 lb. cooked spinach or 1 packet frozen
  chopped spinach
2 eggs
1 egg yolk

$\frac{1}{2}$ pt. thick cream
$\frac{1}{2}$ teaspoon lemon juice
Salt and pepper
Pinch ground mace

1. Chop the spinach and then blend it in a blender for about 30 seconds, or put it through a food mill.
2. Beat the eggs, extra egg yolk, and cream together until thick.
3. Stir in lemon juice, salt and pepper to taste, and mace. Add the spinach, including liquid.
4. Pour into a well-buttered soufflé dish, casserole, or ring mould, set into a pan of hot water that comes about halfway up the dish, and bake in a moderate oven, 325°, 30–35 minutes, or until the mousse is firm to the touch in the centre. Serve at once. Serves 6.

Note: If you bake this mousse in a ring mould, invert it on a hot platter when ready, and fill the centre with creamed mushrooms, creamed sweetbreads, creamed chicken, or a mixture of the three.

PERSIAN SPINACH PIE

1 lb. spinach chopped or 1 packet frozen,
  thawed
10 oz. chopped spring onions
4 oz. chopped lettuce
6 oz. chopped parsley
2 tablespoons flour

$1\frac{1}{2}$ teaspoons salt
$\frac{1}{4}$ teaspoon fresh-ground pepper
3 oz. chopped walnuts
8 eggs well beaten
4 tablespoons butter or margarine
  Yoghurt (optional)

1. Drain the spinach well, pressing out moisture with a spatula.
2. Mix spinach, spring onions, lettuce, parsley, flour, salt, pepper, and nuts.
3. Stir in the beaten eggs.
4. Melt the butter in a large pie plate or large flat casserole and pour in the mixture.
5. Bake 1 hour in a 325° oven, or until the top is brown and crisp.
   Serve hot or cold, with yoghurt spread on top if desired. Serves 6.

SPINACH NOODLE PUDDING

2 lbs. spinach cooked or 2 packets frozen
   chopped spinach cooked
½ lb. fine noodles cooked
4 eggs separated

2 tablespoons grated onion
1 teaspoon salt
¼ teaspoon fresh-ground pepper
¼ teaspoon nutmeg

1. Beat the egg yolks and stir in the chopped spinach, onion, salt, pepper, and nutmeg.
2. Drain the noodles and blend them gently but thoroughly into the spinach mixture. Check seasoning.
3. Beat the egg whites until stiff but not dry and fold into the spinach mixture.
4. Pour into well-buttered casserole or soufflé dish and bake 25 minutes in a moderate oven, 350°. Serves 6.

SPINACH QUICHE

1 8-oz. packet frozen chopped spinach
   thawed
   Pastry for 9-inch pie shell
2 tablespoons minced shallots or
   1 tablespoon minced onion
2 tablespoons butter or margarine

¾ teaspoon salt
Dash of pepper
¼ teaspoon nutmeg (scant)
4 eggs
½ pt. thick cream
1 oz. grated Parmesan cheese

1. Roll out the pastry and line a 9-inch pie plate.
2. Sauté the shallots in butter until barely tender, and stir in the spinach, from which you have pressed out as much water as possible.
3. Put the spinach mixture in a blender with salt and pepper, nutmeg, and eggs. Blend 20 seconds.
4. Without stopping the blender pour in the cream and blend about 5 seconds more.
5. Pour into the pastry shell and sprinkle with the cheese.
6. Bake in a 375° oven 35–40 minutes, or until well puffed and firm in the centre. Serves 6.

BAKED MARROW

12 oz. cooked marrow, mashed, or 1 packet
   frozen, thawed
2 tablespoons butter or margarine
2 tablespoons brown sugar (generous)
2 tablespoons sweet or sour cream

½ teaspoon salt
Dash nutmeg
1 egg well beaten
2 oz. chopped toasted blanched almonds

SET aside about 1 tablespoon of the almonds and combine all remaining ingredients, blending thoroughly. Pour into a small well-greased casserole, top with the remaining almonds, and bake in a moderate oven, 375°, 30–40 minutes, or until brown and bubbly. Serves 4.

MARROW À L'AMÉRICAINE

1 2-lb. marrow
2 slices bread, crusts removed
4 rashers bacon diced and cooked crisp
2 tablespoons butter or margarine

1 medium onion minced
1 clove garlic mashed
2 eggs well beaten
2 tablespoons buttered crumbs

1. Cut the marrow into 1-inch slices, remove seeds, and boil in salted water 20–30 minutes, or until tender. Peel and mash.
2. Soak the bread in water to cover 3–4 minutes and squeeze dry.
3. Pour off half the fat from the bacon. To the remaining fat add butter and lightly sauté the onion and garlic.
4. Stir in the bacon bits, squeezed bread, eggs, and marrow.
5. Mix well, season to taste, and pour into well-buttered casserole.
6. Top with crumbs and bake in a hot oven, 400°, about 20 minutes, or until well browned. Serves 4.

STUFFED MARROW

1 2-lb. marrow cut in half lengthwise
    Salt and pepper
5 oz. bread or cornflake crumbs
$\frac{1}{4}$ pt. warm milk
3 oz. chopped blanched almonds

2 hard-boiled eggs chopped
2 oz. grated Cheddar cheese
1 tablespoon chopped parsley
3 tablespoons butter or margarine

1. Cut the marrow in half lengthwise and remove seeds. Salt the insides rather generously and place cut sides down on a baking sheet.
2. Bake 25 minutes in a moderate oven, 375°. Turn right side up and fit into a greased casserole.
3. To make the filling, combine crumbs, milk, almonds, eggs, cheese, parsley, and salt and pepper to taste. Mix well and fill the marrow, extending the filling to the edges.
4. Press the filling down very lightly and dot with butter.
5. Bake 25–30 minutes, or until the marrow itself is very tender. Serves 4.

BAKED TOMATOES STUFFED WITH MUSHROOMS

8 medium tomatoes, ripe but still very firm
½ lb. mushrooms coarsely chopped
  Boiling water
2 tablespoons butter or margarine
1 tablespoon flour
  Salt and pepper
¼ teaspoon dried basil or ¾ teaspoon
  fresh, chopped

¼ teaspoon dried oregano or ¾ teaspoon
  fresh, chopped
½ pt. milk
¼ teaspoon Worcestershire sauce
3 oz. soft bread crumbs
2 tablespoons grated Parmesan cheese
1 tablespoon minced parsley
2 tablespoons melted butter
  Anchovy fillets

1. Cover the tomatoes with boiling water, let stand 2 minutes, drain, and skin.
2. Scoop out the insides carefully, leaving shells. (Sometimes this is easier to do before skinning the tomatoes; then slip off the skin afterward.)
3. Sauté the mushrooms in butter and stir in the flour, salt and pepper to taste, basil, and oregano.
4. Slowly stir in the milk, continuing to stir until the sauce is thick and smooth. Add Worcestershire sauce.
5. Lay tomato shells in a shallow buttered casserole and fill with the mushroom sauce.
6. Mix the crumbs, cheese, parsley, and butter and top the tomatoes with the mixture.
7. Bake 15–20 minutes in a moderate oven, 350°.
8. Cross 2 anchovy fillets on each tomato before serving. Serves 8.

CHERRY TOMATOES WITH GARLIC

36 small ripe cherry tomatoes, stems
  removed
  Boiling water
1 teaspoon salt

3 tablespoons butter, margarine, or salad
  oil
1 small clove garlic crushed
¼ teaspoon fresh-ground pepper
1 tablespoon chopped chives

1. Pour boiling water over the tomatoes, let stand 20 seconds, drain in sieve, and slip skins off. Sprinkle with salt and spread on paper towels to dry a few minutes.
2. Heat butter in a shallow casserole. Add garlic and pepper.
3. Stir the tomatoes in, and continue to stir until they are well coated with the butter.
4. Put in a moderate oven, 350°, for just six minutes. Sprinkle with chives before serving. Serves 6.

TOMATO CASSEROLE

4 medium tomatoes sliced ½ inch thick
4 oz. grated Cheddar cheese
2 oz. thinly sliced onion

¾ teaspoon salt
⅛ teaspoon pepper
4 oz. crushed potato crisps

IN a small casserole arrange layers of tomato slices, cheese, and onion—2 layers of each. Sprinkle each tomato layer with salt and pepper. Top with the crushed crisps and bake ½ hour in a 350° oven. Serves 4.

AUBERGINE TOMATO BORDELAISE

2 large aubergines cut in ½-inch slices,
  unpeeled
  Salt and pepper
¼ pt. salad oil or olive oil
3 medium tomatoes skinned and sliced
  ½ inch thick
3 oz. sliced mushrooms

2 oz. chopped spring onions
1 large clove garlic crushed
1 teaspoon prepared mustard
1 oz. chopped parsley
2 tablespoons melted butter or margarine
3 oz. buttered crumbs

1. Sprinkle the aubergine slices with salt and pile them up in the shape of the aubergines, letting them stand 20 minutes. Wipe the slices with paper towels and sauté them to a golden brown in hot oil. Arrange in a good-sized greased casserole, in 2–3 layers.
2. Cover each layer with tomato slices.
3. In the oil remaining in the frying-pan sauté the mushrooms lightly.
4. Stir in the spring onions, garlic, salt and pepper to taste, mustard, and parsley.
5. Add the melted butter, blend well, and pour over the casserole.
6. Top with a thick layer of buttered crumbs and bake 20–25 minutes in a 400° oven. Serves 6.

COURGETTE-TOMATO CASSEROLE

6 small courgettes cut in ¼-inch slices (unpeeled)
4 medium tomatoes peeled and sliced
3 tablespoons salad oil
1 small clove garlic
¼ teaspoon dried oregano or ¾ teaspoon fresh, chopped

¼ teaspoon dried basil or ¾ teaspoon fresh, chopped
2 oz. grated Cheddar cheese
1 oz. grated Parmesan cheese
Salt and pepper
2 oz. bread or cornflake crumbs
2 tablespoons melted butter or margarine

1. Heat oil in a frying-pan and cook the garlic clove a few minutes. Skim out and discard.
2. Sauté the courgettes in the oil until lightly browned.
3. Combine the oregano, basil, and Cheddar and Parmesan cheeses.
4. Make alternate layers in a medium casserole of courgettes and tomatoes, sprinkling each layer with salt and pepper and cheese mixture.
5. Mix the crumbs and melted butter and spread over the casserole. Bake 20–25 minutes in a 350° oven, or until well browned. Serves 6.

COURGETTES ALLA PARMIGIANA

8 small courgettes, ends removed, and slit lengthwise (unpeeled)
1 tablespoon butter or margarine
6 tablespoons salad oil
½ small onion sliced thin
1 lb. tomatoes, peeled, seeded, and coarsely chopped

¼ teaspoon dried basil or ¾ teaspoon fresh, chopped
Salt and pepper to taste
1 oz. flour
2 tablespoons grated Parmesan cheese
½ lb. Mozzarella cheese sliced thin

1. In a heavy frying-pan heat the butter and 1 tablespoon of the oil. Sauté the onion until soft but not brown.
2. Stir in the chopped tomatoes, basil, and salt and pepper to taste. Simmer, uncovered. half an hour, stirring occasionally.
3. Coat the courgette halves generously with flour and sauté until brown in 4 tablespoons of the oil heated to sizzling. Drain on paper towels.
4. Use the remaining tablespoon of oil to grease a medium casserole. Arrange in it alternate layers of courgettes, tomato mixture, Parmesan cheese, and Mozzarella cheese, ending with Mozzarella cheese and tomatoes.
5. Bake 30 minutes in a moderate oven, 350°, or until the courgettes are tender. Serves 4–6.

NOTES

CHEESE, EGGS, CEREALS AND PASTA

BAKED CHEESE-MEAT SANDWICH CASSEROLE

9 slices white bread, crusts removed
2 tablespoons butter or margarine
1 lb. pork chipolatas cooked or 12 slices
   luncheon meat (tinned)
2 sliced tomatoes

4 oz. grated Cheddar cheese
4 eggs lightly beaten
1 quart milk (scant)
$\frac{3}{4}$ teaspoon salt
1 teaspoon dry mustard

1. Butter the bread and make 3 two-decker sandwiches, making the first layer the sausages, split, or 3 slices luncheon meat per sandwich, and the second layer tomato slices, topped with grated cheese.
2. Cut each sandwich diagonally in two and fasten with toothpicks. Arrange in a well-buttered casserole that holds them with just a little room to spare.
3. Combine eggs, milk, salt, and mustard and pour over the sandwiches.
4. Bake 1$\frac{1}{2}$ hours in a 325° oven, or until firm in the centre. Serves 3 generously or 6 lightly.

Note: If possible, make the sandwiches far enough in advance so that they can be refrigerated 2–3 hours before baking.

QUICHE LORRAINE

  Pastry for a 9-inch pie shell
8 slices bacon crisp-cooked
4 eggs
$\frac{1}{2}$ oz. flour (optional)
  Pinch nutmeg

$\frac{3}{4}$ pt. thin cream
1 tablespoon melted butter
4 oz. freshly grated Emmental cheese or
   half Emmental and half Gruyère cheese

THIS dish has become a most popular luncheon dish. It can be cut up in small squares and served with cocktails, and it is also a good choice for an after-theatre supper.
1. Make the pastry for a 9-inch shell. (It can be made well ahead of time, and chilled in its pie plate.)
2. Crumble the cooked bacon and sprinkle half of it on the bottom of the pastry.
3. Spread the grated cheese in the shell. It should nearly fill it.
4. Mix the remaining ingredients—the cream, flour, nutmeg, and the melted butter, or put them briefly in a blender and blend them for a moment. The eggs should be beaten—a whisk will do well for them—and added last.
5. Pour the egg-cream mixture gently into the pie shell, over the cheese. Sprinkle the remaining bacon over it. A sprinkling of grated Parmesan cheese on top will add to both the flavour and the appearance of the pie.
6. Put the pie in a 375° oven and bake it about 40 minutes. It is done when a knife inserted in the centre comes out clean. Serves 4 or 5.

Serve with sliced tomatoes and a mixed green salad. Hot rolls or hot French bread goes well with it too.

NEVER-FAIL CHEESE CASSEROLE

1 lb. Cheddar cheese coarsely grated
9 slices day-old bread, crusts removed
   Salt and pepper
1½ tablespoons dried minced white onion
1½ tablespoons dried minced green onion

4 eggs beaten lightly
1¼ pt. milk
1 teaspoon dry mustard
1 teaspoon Worcestershire sauce
2 tablespoons grated Parmesan cheese

1. Cut 3 slices of the bread to completely cover the bottom of a greased 2-quart casserole.
2. Sprinkle with salt and pepper, half of the white and green onion, and half of the cheese.
3. Make another closely fitted layer of bread and top with the remaining cheese, onion, and salt and pepper.
4. Top with the last layer of bread.
5. Mix together the eggs, milk, mustard, and Worcestershire sauce.
6. Pour over the casserole and refrigerate 3–4 hours or all day. Remove from the refrigerator 2 hours before baking, to bring to room temperature.
7. Top with grated Parmesan cheese and bake 50–60 minutes in a slow oven, 325°, or until firm in the centre. Serves 6.

DUTCH CHEESE PIE

Pastry

8 oz. flour
1 teaspoon salt
4 oz. firm butter or margarine

1 teaspoon caraway seeds
3 tablespoons ice water

Filling

1 tablespoon dry bread crumbs
1 tablespoon grated Parmesan cheese
¼ lb. minced ham or bacon
¼ lb. Edam or Gouda cheese shredded
2 whole eggs
2 egg yolks

½ teaspoon salt
½ teaspoon dry mustard
   Dash cayenne pepper
¾ pt. thin cream warmed
   Chopped parsley
   Grated Parmesan cheese

1. Make the pastry as usual, adding the caraway seeds before mixing in the water. Sprinkle the water over and mix quickly until a firm dough is formed. Knead lightly 4–6 times, wrap in foil or waxed paper, and chill 10 minutes. Roll it out on a lightly floured board to ⅛-inch thickness and line a 10-inch pie plate or a flan pan. Prick well, lay a piece of foil or brown paper on the bottom, and put in enough rice or beans, etc., to weight down the paper. Bake in a 425° oven 12 minutes. Remove the rice and paper and bake 5 minutes longer. Remove the shell from the oven and lower the heat to 350°.
2. Mix the crumbs and Parmesan cheese and spread on the pie shell.
3. Spread the ham or bacon on the crumbs, and the other cheese on top.
4. Beat the eggs and yolks together lightly and stir in salt, mustard, cayenne, cream, and parsley. Gently pour into the shell.
5. Top with grated Parmesan and bake 30–45 minutes, or until firm in the centre. Serve at once. Serves 6.

EGGS CONTINENTAL

4 hard-boiled eggs sliced
2 oz. soft fine bread crumbs
3 slices bacon chopped, cooked crisp, and
  drained
$\frac{1}{4}$ lb. mushrooms sliced

$\frac{1}{2}$ pt. sour cream
2 tablespoons minced parsley or chives
Salt
Paprika
2 oz. grated Cheddar

1. Spread the bread crumbs in a small shallow casserole or 8-inch pie plate.

2. Make a layer of egg slices over the crumbs.

3. Sauté the mushrooms lightly in the bacon fat.

4. Add the bacon, sour cream, parsley, and salt to taste.

5. Spread this mixture over the eggs, top with cheese, sprinkle with paprika, and bake 15–20 minutes in a 375° oven, or until cheese is melted and sauce bubbly. Serves 4.

EGGS DELMONICO

4 hard-boiled eggs sliced
$\frac{3}{4}$ pt. cheese sauce
2 tablespoons dry sherry

4 slices toast, crusts removed
Luncheon meat sliced
Grated Parmesan cheese

1. Make the cheese sauce with $1\frac{1}{2}$ oz. butter or margarine, $1\frac{1}{2}$ oz. flour, salt and pepper to taste, $\frac{1}{8}$ teaspoon dry mustard, $\frac{3}{4}$ pt. milk, and 6 oz. coarsely grated Cheddar. Stir in the sherry.

2. Lay the toast in a shallow buttered casserole or pie plate.

3. Lay slices of luncheon meat over the toast, and egg slices, overlapping, over the meat.

4. Cover with the sauce, top with grated Parmesan, and bake in a hot oven, 450°, 10 minutes, or until the sauce is bubbly and the cheese browned. Serves 4.

EGGS ORIENTALE

8 hard-boiled eggs
1½ tablespoons anchovy paste
2 tablespoons mayonnaise
6 ripe olives chopped
1 tablespoon lemon juice
2 tablespoons chopped walnuts or pecans
1½ oz. butter or margarine, melted

1½ oz. flour
¾ pt. milk or chicken broth
Salt and pepper
1 tablespoon Worcestershire sauce
¾ lb. cooked and coarsely chopped shrimps (optional)
½ lb. sliced mushrooms lightly sautéed

1. Cut the eggs in half lengthwise. Remove the yolks and mash.
2. Mix the yolks with the anchovy paste, mayonnaise, olives, lemon juice, and nuts.
3. Fill the egg whites with this mixture and lay the stuffed eggs in a shallow buttered casserole or pie plate.
4. Make a white sauce with the butter, flour, and milk or chicken broth. Season to taste and add the Worcestershire sauce.
5. Stir in shrimps and mushrooms and pour over the eggs.
6. Bake 15 minutes in a moderate oven, 325°.
7. Serve with spinach and noodles. Serves 8.

EGGS TETRAZZINI

6 hard-boiled eggs sliced
¼ lb. thin spaghetti cooked
1 small onion chopped
2 oz. butter or margarine
1½ oz. flour

16–17 oz. tin tomatoes or ¾ pt. rich milk
½ teaspoon salt
¼ teaspoon pepper
Grated Parmesan cheese

1. Drain the spaghetti and put in a rather shallow buttered casserole or deep pie plate.
2. Sauté the onion in butter until soft but not brown. Stir in the flour and gradually blend in either the tomatoes, chopped coarsely, or the milk. Stir constantly until sauce is thick and smooth. Season.
3. Mix a third of the sauce with the spaghetti and spread a little more of it on top of the spaghetti.
4. Arrange the eggs in an overlapping pattern on top of the spaghetti and cover with the remaining sauce.
5. Top with a rather heavy coating of Parmesan cheese and put 4–5 inches under the grill until well browned and piping hot. Serves 4.

Note: If you make this casserole well ahead of time, which can be done easily, bring it to room temperature (an hour) and bake 15 minutes in a moderate oven, 350°, before browning under the grill.

BAKED EGG CASSEROLE

6 hard-boiled eggs sliced
¼ pt. mayonnaise
¼ pt. ketchup

1 teaspoon lemon juice
3 tablespoons milk
½ teaspoon salt

ARRANGE the egg slices in a very shallow well-buttered casserole or pie plate, slightly overlapping them. Mix the remaining ingredients until smooth and spread over the eggs. Bake 15 minutes in a moderate oven, 350°. Serve on well-buttered toasted muffins or hot fluffy rice. Serves 4.

SWEET CORN BREAD

17-oz. tin cream-style sweet corn
4 oz. wholemeal flour
¾ teaspoon salt
¾ pt. milk, scalded

2 tablespoons butter or margarine
¾ teaspoon baking powder
3 eggs separated

1. Stir the wholemeal flour and salt into the hot milk over medium heat. Beat hard until it is the consistency of thick mush.

2. Blend in the butter and sweet corn and then the baking powder.

3. Beat the egg yolks well and beat into the mixture.

4. Beat the egg whites until stiff but not dry and fold in gently.

5. Pour the mixture into a well-buttered medium casserole and bake in a moderate oven, 375°, about 35 minutes, or until puffy and firm in the centre. Serve with butter. Serves 5–6.

POLENTA WITH TOMATO SAUCE

4 oz. fine oatmeal
¾ pt. milk
1 egg
2 oz. grated Parmesan cheese
1 teaspoon salt
⅛ teaspoon fresh-ground pepper
5 tablespoons salad oil

2 cloves garlic
2 oz. minced onion
1 tin condensed tomato soup
1 teaspoon cider vinegar
¾ teaspoon salt
¼ teaspoon fresh-ground pepper
3 tablespoons water
4 oz. Swiss cheese

1. Place oatmeal in a saucepan over very low heat and slowly stir in the milk. Keep stirring until the mixture thickens and comes to a boil. Let it boil about 3 minutes, stirring frequently.
2. Remove the pan from the heat, stir in the egg, and beat well.
3. Stir in the Parmesan cheese, salt, pepper, and 2 tablespoons oil.
4. Spread in a good-sized shallow casserole, well buttered. Chill until firm.
5. Cut the polenta into 2-inch squares and transfer them to a larger shallow casserole, leaving a little space between the squares.
6. To make the tomato sauce, heat 3 tablespoons salad oil, brown the garlic cloves a bit and discard. Stir in the onion, soup, vinegar, salt, pepper, and water and let simmer over very low heat about 10 minutes.
7. Pour the sauce over the polenta, top with the cheese, and bake 20 minutes in a hot oven, 400°. Serves 6.

GNOCCHI À LA GIOVANNI

½ lb. cream of wheat
1 quart milk
3 egg yolks

⅛ teaspoon salt
   Dash pepper
4 oz. grated Parmesan cheese
4 oz. melted butter

1. Bring the milk to a boil and slowly stir in the cream of wheat. Let it cook about 10 minutes over very low heat, stirring often.
2. Remove pan from the heat and add the egg yolks, salt, and pepper. Beat well and pour into a large shallow buttered casserole, patting it down to a depth of about ½ inch with the flat of your hand dipped into cold water. Chill until firm.
3. Cut the gnocchi into small circles with a biscuit cutter and lay them in a buttered shallow casserole, close together.
4. Cover with the cheese and butter and brown well under the grill. Serves 4.

GNOCCHI À LA FORUM

½ pt. water
2 tablespoons butter or margarine
½ teaspoon salt
¼ teaspoon cayenne
6 oz. flour

3 eggs
1 oz. grated Swiss cheese
½ teaspoon dry mustard
¼ teaspoon salt

Sauce

2 tablespoons butter
1 tablespoon flour
½ pt. milk
¼ pt. cream

4 oz. grated Swiss cheese
½ teaspoon dry mustard
1 egg yolk
3 tablespoons milk

1. Bring to a boil in a saucepan the water, butter, salt, and cayenne. Add the flour all at once and stir vigorously until it pulls away from the sides and forms a ball of dough.
2. Remove the pan from the heat and beat in the eggs well, one at a time.
3. Add the cheese, mustard, and salt.
4. Have a pan of gently boiling salted water ready. Put the gnocchi dough in an icing bag with a large plain tube and squeeze it out in long pieces into the boiling water. Cook until they rise to the surface, drain, and cut in pieces ½ inch long. Arrange the pieces in a shallow buttered casserole.
5. To make the sauce, melt 1 tablespoon of the butter in a saucepan, stir in the flour, and slowly add the milk, stirring constantly until it bubbles. Blend in the cream, half of the cheese, and the mustard. Cook about 5 minutes over very low heat.
6. Beat the egg yolk and milk together and stir into the sauce, stirring constantly until smooth and thickened.
7. Pour over the gnocchi, sprinkle with the remaining cheese, dot with the remaining tablespoon of butter, and place under the grill until golden brown and bubbling. Serves 6.

KASHA AND MUSHROOM CASSEROLE

½ lb. kasha (buckwheat groats)
4 tablespoons butter or margarine
1 egg
1 oz. minced onion

Salt and pepper
1½ pts. chicken broth
6 oz. sliced mushrooms sautéed lightly

1. Heat 1 tablespoon of the butter in a heavy frying-pan and stir in the kasha. Cook 10 minutes over a low flame, stirring constantly.
2. Break the egg into the kasha and stir vigorously until all the grains are coated and the kasha is dry.
3. Stir in the onion, salt and pepper to taste, the remaining butter, and the chicken broth.
4. Cover and cook over a very low flame 25 minutes.
5. Stir in the mushrooms. Add a little water if dry.
6. Turn the mixture into a buttered casserole, cover, and bake 30 minutes in a moderate oven, 350°. The kasha should be tender and moist. Serves 4–6.

ARMENIAN PILAFF

1½ lbs. washed and drained long-grain rice
4 oz. fine noodles broken up
5 oz. pine nuts or chopped walnuts
4 oz. melted butter or margarine
2½ pts. chicken broth or water

2 oz. currants (optional)
1 tablespoon salt
¼ teaspoon fresh-ground pepper
½ teaspoon allspice
Chopped parsley

1. Sauté the uncooked noodles and nuts in butter until golden, stirring constantly.
2. Add the rice, cooking and stirring 5 minutes more.
3. Add the chicken broth, currants, salt, pepper, and allspice.
4. Pour into a large casserole (or cook in the casserole from the beginning), cover, and bake 25–30 minutes in a slow oven, 325°, or until the rice is tender.
5. Stir carefully with a fork to let the steam escape, and sprinkle with parsley before serving. Serves 12.

BRAZILIAN RICE

8 oz. raw rice
1 tablespoon salad oil
1 clove garlic crushed
4-oz. tin mushroom pieces and liquid
1¼-oz. packet onion soup
    mix or 1 tin condensed onion soup

¾ pt. hot water
8 oz. peeled and chopped tomatoes or
    1 small tin Italian tomatoes
2 teaspoons salt
¼ teaspoon dried oregano or ¾ teaspoon
    fresh, chopped

1. Heat the oil in a heavy frying-pan and sauté the rice, garlic, and mushrooms until the rice begins to brown, stirring almost constantly.
2. Stir in the hot water and onion soup mix. (Reduce water to ½ pt. if canned soup is used.)
3. Add tomatoes, salt, and oregano and pour into a good-sized casserole.
4. Cover the casserole and bake 35 minutes in a moderate oven, 350°, or until the rice is tender and the liquid absorbed.

   Check at 25 minutes, and if there is still a good deal of liquid remove the cover. Stir with a fork to let steam escape before serving. Serves 6.

GREEN RICE

8 oz. cooked rice
½ pt. milk
4 oz. grated Cheddar cheese (scant)
2 oz. butter or margarine melted or salad oil
1 egg well beaten

2 tablespoons chopped onion
Salt and pepper
2 oz. minced parsley, chopped spinach,
    chopped chives, or any combination of
    these

COMBINE all ingredients, with salt and pepper to taste, in a well-buttered medium casserole. Bake 15 minutes in a 350° oven. Serves 5–6.

TANGY RICE WITH OLIVES

8 oz. cooked rice
6 oz. chopped stuffed olives
4 anchovy fillets chopped
1 tablespoon chopped capers
1 oz. chopped parsley
3 tablespoons chopped onion

$\frac{1}{2}$ teaspoon dried thyme or 1 teaspoon fresh, chopped
$\frac{1}{2}$ teaspoon dried basil or 1 teaspoon fresh, chopped
Salt and pepper
$8\frac{1}{2}$-oz. tin tomatoes chopped or 2 large tomatoes peeled and chopped
2 oz. grated Parmesan cheese

BUTTER a good-sized casserole and put in all the ingredients except the cheese. Stir well, top with cheese, and bake 30 minutes in a moderate oven, 350°. Serves 6.

GREEK RICE

12 oz. raw rice
1 onion minced
$\frac{1}{2}$ clove garlic crushed
2 tablespoons butter or margarine
4 leaves lettuce shredded
4 mushrooms sliced
4 medium tomatoes peeled, seeded, and chopped

3 sausages mashed
$1\frac{1}{4}$ pts. boiling chicken broth or water
Salt and pepper
1 tablespoon melted butter
4 oz. cooked peas
1 pimento diced small
3 tablespoons raisins sautéed in a little butter

1. Sauté the onion and garlic lightly in butter in a good-sized casserole.

2. Stir in the lettuce, mushrooms, tomatoes, sausage, rice, chicken broth, and seasoning to taste.

3. Cover the casserole and bake 20–25 minutes in a hot oven, 400°, or until the rice is tender and the liquid absorbed.

4. Stir in the melted butter, peas, pimento, and raisins, and leave in the oven just long enough to heat through—5 minutes or so. Serves 6–8.

POLYNESIAN MINGLE

12 oz. raw rice
 1 tablespoon butter or margarine
 1 oz. minced onion
 8 oz. celery sliced thin diagonally
1¼ pts. chicken broth

1 tablespoon soy sauce
1 teaspoon sugar
2 teaspoons salt
2 10-oz. frozen peas slightly thawed

1. Melt the butter in a heavy frying-pan and lightly sauté the onion and celery.
2. Stir in the rice and cook over low heat until rice is yellow, stirring constantly. Pour into a medium casserole.
3. In a small saucepan combine the chicken broth, soy sauce, sugar, and salt and bring to a boil.
4. Pour over the rice in the casserole and stir in the peas.
5. Cover the casserole and bake 30 minutes in a moderate oven, 375°.
6. Remove the cover, stir the rice with a fork, and continue to bake 15 minutes more. Serves 8.

RICE WITH VEGETABLES

1 lb. raw rice
1 small onion chopped
3 large tomatoes peeled and chopped or
  1-lb. tin drained
6 oz. cauliflower (fresh or frozen) chopped
  very coarsely

6 oz. peas, fresh or frozen
6 oz. runner beans, fresh or frozen
4 tablespoons salad oil
2 slices bacon diced
2 pts. chicken broth or consommé
  Salt and pepper

1. Heat the oil in a heavy frying-pan and cook the bacon and onion until the onion is transparent.
2. Stir in the rice and cook until it is lightly browned, stirring constantly.
3. Add tomatoes and broth or consommé, season to taste, and pour into a medium casserole.
4. Cover and bake 15 minutes in a moderate oven, 350°.
5. Stir in the vegetables, cover, and bake 20–25 minutes longer. Check seasoning when the vegetables are half cooked.
6. When rice is soft and liquid all absorbed, stir with a fork to release steam. Serves 8.

GOURMET WILD RICE

10 oz. wild rice
3 oz. butter or margarine
1 oz. chopped parsley
3 oz. chopped spring onions, both white and green parts
6 oz. diagonally sliced celery

1 tin condensed consommé
$\frac{3}{4}$ pt. boiling water
1 teaspoon salt
$\frac{1}{2}$ teaspoon dried marjoram or 1 teaspoon fresh, chopped
$\frac{1}{4}$ pt. dry sherry

1. Wash the rice well, in several waters, and let stand an hour before baking, covered with water. Drain thoroughly.
2. Melt the butter in a medium casserole and lightly sauté the parsley, spring onions, and celery.
3. Add the rice, consommé, water, salt, and marjoram.
4. Cover and bake about 45 minutes in a slow oven, 300°, or until the rice is tender and the liquid all absorbed. Stir with a fork two or three times while baking.
5. Stir in the sherry and continue to bake about 5 minutes longer. Serves 8.

WILD RICE WITH MUSHROOMS

8 oz. wild rice
1 tin condensed consommé
Salt and pepper

1 tablespoon butter or margarine
$\frac{1}{2}$ lb. mushrooms sliced and lightly sautéed in butter

1. Wash the rice in several waters and if possible let it soak an hour in cold water before cooking.
2. Drain the rice and put into a small casserole.
3. Pour the consommé over, add salt and pepper (about 1 teaspoon salt), cover, and bake 30 minutes in a moderate oven, 350°.
4. Stir in the butter and mushrooms, and add a little water or more consommé if the rice seems rather dry. Check seasoning. Cover again and bake 15–20 minutes more.
5. Remove the cover the last 5 minutes. Stir with a fork to let steam escape. All liquid should be absorbed by this time. Serves 6–8.

WILD RICE WITH NUTS AND HERBS

6 oz. wild rice
½ teaspoon salt
1¼ pts. cold water or chicken broth
1 medium onion chopped fine
1–2 oz. minced celery
1½ tablespoons butter or margarine

3 oz. broken walnuts, split almonds, or
 pine nuts
1 tablespoon chopped parsley
½ teaspoon dried rosemary or 1 teaspoon
 fresh, chopped
¼ teaspoon marjoram dried or ¾ teaspoon
 fresh, chopped

1. Wash the rice in several waters and let soak in water an hour or so. Drain.
2. Place in saucepan with salt and water or chicken broth. Bring to a boil and simmer, covered, until tender but not mushy.
3. Drain and place in buttered medium casserole.
4. Sauté the onion and celery in hot butter until tender.
5. Add nuts and herbs and stir lightly into the rice. Check seasoning and add salt if needed.
6. Bake 15 minutes in a slow oven, 325°, covered.
   Stir with a fork to release steam. Rice should be fluffy and somewhat moist. Serves 6–7.

BAKED MACARONI AND AUBERGINE

½ lb. elbow macaroni cooked until barely
 tender
2 medium aubergines peeled and diced
 small (½-inch)

2 tablespoons salad oil
8-oz. bottle tomato sauce
 Salt
 Mozzarella cheese

1. Sauté the aubergines in hot oil until golden brown.
2. Arrange alternate layers of macaroni, aubergine, and tomato sauce in a medium casserole, well buttered. Salt aubergines generously.
3. Cover the top with slices of cheese and bake 15–20 minutes in a moderate oven, 350°, or until browned and bubbly. Serves 4–6.

MACARONI WITH WINE

1 lb. cooked macaroni
1 medium onion minced
2 medium tomatoes, sliced
2 tablespoons minced green pepper

2 tablespoons butter or margarine
2 hard-boiled eggs, sliced
½ lb. Cheddar cheese coarsely grated
3 tablespoons dry sherry

1. Melt the butter in a large frying-pan and cook the tomatoes, onion, and green pepper lightly, not browning them at all.
2. Gently stir in the eggs and macaroni and pour into a medium casserole, well buttered.
3. In the top of a double boiler, over boiling water, melt the cheese, stirring occasionally.
4. When the cheese is melted blend in the sherry and pour over the macaroni.
5. Bake in a moderate oven, 350°, 30 minutes. Serves 4–5.

244

Chicken Teriyaki

MEXICAN MACARONI

8 oz. elbow macaroni cooked barely tender
1 lb. pork sausage meat
4 oz. chopped onion
4 oz. chopped green pepper
1 lb. tinned tomatoes coarsely chopped
¾ pt. sour cream

1 tablespoon sugar
1 teaspoon chili powder
 Salt to taste
¼ teaspoon dried oregano or ¾ teaspoon
 fresh, chopped

1. Cook the sausage meat in a large heavy frying-pan, with the onion and green pepper, until the meat is somewhat browned, breaking up the sausage into small chunks. Drain off the fat.
2. Stir in the tomatoes, sour cream, sugar, chili powder, salt, oregano, and well-drained macaroni.
3. Pour into a large casserole, cover, and bake 35–40 minutes in a moderate oven, 375°, until macaroni is well done.
4. Remove cover last 10 minutes. Serves 4.

EGG AND NOODLE CASSEROLE

6 hard-boiled eggs
8-oz. packet wide noodles, cooked and
 drained
1 tablespoon chopped parsley
1 tablespoon minced onion
4 tablespoons mayonnaise

1½ oz. butter or margarine
1½ oz. flour
¾ pt. milk
 Salt and pepper
½ lb. Cheddar, sliced or chopped
 Soft bread crumbs

1. Cut the eggs in half lengthwise, remove the yolks, and mash them.
2. Mix yolks with parsley, onion, and mayonnaise. Fill whites with the mixture.
3. Make a white sauce with the butter, flour, and milk, and season to taste. Stir in the cheese and continue to stir until melted.
4. Mix the noodles with half of this sauce and arrange them in a good-sized buttered casserole.
5. Lay the stuffed egg halves on the noodles.
6. Pour the remaining sauce over and around the eggs and cover with crumbs.
7. Bake in a moderate oven, 350°, 20 minutes, or until the crumbs are brown and sauce bubbly. Serves 6.

Bœuf en daube Niçoise

SPAGHETTI WITH ANCHOVIES

1 lb. thin spaghetti broken up and cooked
2-oz. tin anchovy fillets drained and
chopped
¼ pt. salad oil

1 clove garlic crushed
1 tablespoon chopped capers
3 tablespoons chopped onion
2 oz. grated Parmesan cheese

SAUTÉ the anchovies in hot oil for a minute or two. Stir in the garlic, capers, onion, and well-drained spaghetti. Top with cheese and bake in 375° oven 15 minutes. No salt is needed except in the water in which the spaghetti is cooked. Serves 6.

NOODLES WITH MUSHROOMS

8-oz. packet medium noodles broken up and
cooked
3 oz. sliced mushrooms or 4-oz. tin drained
1 medium onion chopped
1 small green pepper chopped
1 oz. chopped stuffed olives

3 tablespoons salad oil
½ pt. chicken broth
1 tin condensed cream of mushroom soup
Salt and pepper
2 tablespoons grated
Parmesan cheese

1. Sauté the mushrooms, onion, pepper, and olives in oil.
2. Add chicken broth and soup and cook 2–3 minutes, stirring. Season.
3. Stir in cooked and well-drained noodles and pour into a greased medium casserole.
4. Top with cheese and bake 25 minutes at 325°. Serves 4.

CHEESE-SPAGHETTI CASSEROLE

4 oz. shredded Provolone cheese
4 oz. shredded Cheddar cheese
¾ lb. thin spaghetti cooked until barely
tender
¼ lb. bacon diced fine
1 medium onion chopped
1 lb. ground lean beef

2 8-oz. bottles tomato sauce
1½ teaspoons salt
⅛ teaspoon pepper
½ teaspoon garlic salt
1 teaspoon dried oregano or
1 tablespoon fresh, chopped
4-oz. tin sliced mushrooms

1. Crisp the bacon in a heavy frying-pan.
2. Add the onion and beef and cook until the red disappears from the beef.
3. Mix in the tomato sauce, seasonings, oregano, mushrooms and their liquor, and spaghetti.
Simmer 15 minutes, stirring frequently.
4. Pour half of mixture into a large buttered casserole.
5. Cover with half of the Provolone and half of the Cheddar cheese.
6. Add remaining spaghetti mixture and remaining cheeses.
7. Bake 20–25 minutes in a 375° oven, or until brown and bubbly. Serves 10-12.

NOTES

DESSERTS

APPLE RICE MERINGUE PUDDING

8 oz. long-grain rice (not converted rice)
1 pt. milk, scalded
6 tablespoons sugar
$\frac{1}{4}$ teaspoon salt
2 one-inch pieces vanilla pod or 1 teaspoon vanilla extract
1 tablespoon butter or margarine

3 eggs separated
$\frac{3}{4}$ pt. water
$\frac{1}{2}$ lb. sugar
Juice $\frac{1}{2}$ lemon
6 medium tart apples peeled, cored, and halved
6 oz. confectioners' (or icing) sugar

1. A gluten rice is best for this delicious pudding. Wash it in cold water, cover with more cold water, and bring to a fast boil. Remove from stove and let stand 5 minutes. Drain and rinse in cold water.

2. Return to saucepan and add milk, the 6 tablespoons sugar, salt, and one piece of vanilla pod. Bring to a boil, add butter, and simmer over very low heat 30 minutes, or until rice is tender.

3. Stir the rice with a fork to separate the grains.

4. Beat the egg yolks well and stir into the rice. Spread on a well-buttered flat casserole or large pie plate.

5. Make a syrup of the water and $\frac{1}{2}$ lb. of sugar, adding the second piece of vanilla pod and the lemon juice.

6. Stew the apple halves gently in this syrup until just soft. Lift them out with a slotted spoon, drain well, and arrange on the rice.

7. Beat the egg whites until stiff but not dry, fold in the confectioner's or icing sugar, and heap the meringue over the apples.

8. Bake in a hot oven, 450°, 5–7 minutes, or until delicately brown. Serve warm or cold. Serves 6.

Note: If you want to dress this dessert up a little, make six fairly deep dents in the meringue, with the back of a tablespoon, before baking. Before serving put a teaspoon of red currant jelly in each depression.

BAKED BANANAS

6 medium bananas, peeled and
 quartered
¼ pt. orange juice

2 oz. brown sugar
2 tablespoons butter or margarine
2½ oz. grated coconut

Sauce

6 egg yolks
6 oz. sugar

8 fluid oz. dry white wine or Marsala wine
1 tablespoon rum or kirsch

1. Arrange the bananas in one layer in a large shallow casserole or in 2 layers in a medium, deepish casserole.
2. Mix orange juice and brown sugar and pour over bananas. Dot with butter, spread with coconut, and bake 12–15 minutes in a hot oven, 450°, or until bananas are soft and coconut a good toasty brown.
    Serve warm or cold, with or without sauce. Serves 6.

Sauce: Beat egg yolks and sugar well. Stir in wine and cook in a double boiler over boiling water until thick and creamy, stirring constantly. Remove from heat and stir in rum or kirsch. Serve warm.

BAKED FRUIT CASSEROLE

4 oz. oatcake crumbs
3 oz. chopped pecans
4 oz. brown sugar
3 tablespoons orange juice

1 tablespoon grated orange rind
3 oz. sultanas
2 apples peeled, cored, and sliced
2 peaches peeled and sliced

Mix all the ingredients lightly and spread in a rather shallow casserole. Bake 30 minutes in a moderate oven, 375°. Serve warm with hard sauce. Serves 4.

Hard Sauce: Cream together 2 oz. butter and 6 oz. brown sugar. Add 1½ tablespoons brandy flavouring, drop by drop, or to taste. Chill well.

BLACK CHERRY PUDDING

1-lb. tin black cherries
½ lb. sugar
5 oz. flour
1 teaspoon baking soda

1 egg beaten
1 tablespoon melted butter
6 oz. chopped nuts

Sauce

½ lb. sugar
4 oz. butter or margarine

¼ pt. cream
1 teaspoon vanilla

IF you like black cherries you will find this an outstanding dessert.
1. Mix the sugar, flour, baking soda, and the egg beaten with the melted butter. Stir in the cherries, well drained (but save the juice).
2. Add enough juice to the mixture to make a rather thick batter.
3. Add the nuts and pour into a shallow casserole or large pie plate, or, best of all, a Pyrex dish about 7½″ × 12″ and shallow.
4. Bake in a 350° oven about 30 minutes, or until it is firm to the touch.
   Serve warm with hot sauce or ice cream. Serves 7–8.

Sauce: Mix the sauce ingredients in the top of a double boiler and cook over boiling water until it thickens somewhat. Keep warm until serving. Or make early in the day and reheat in a double boiler at serving time.

BRAZIL NUT BREAD PUDDING

4 slices bread buttered, crusts removed
3 oz. sliced Brazil nuts
4 oz. sugar
¼ teaspoon salt

1 teaspoon vanilla
¾ pt. milk
2 eggs beaten slightly

1. Cut the buttered bread into squares or finger-shaped pieces.
2. Arrange them buttered side up in layers in a well-buttered casserole, sprinkling each layer with nuts.
3. Beat the sugar, salt, vanilla, and milk into the eggs and pour over the casserole.
4. Bake 1 hour in a slow oven, 325°. Sprinkle more nuts on top.
   Serve warm or cold, with plain cream, vanilla-flavoured whipped cream, or ice cream. Serves 6.

Note: To slice Brazil nuts easily, cover the shelled nuts with cold water, bring to a boil, simmer 4 minutes, drain, dry, and slice at once with a sharp knife.

CREAMY CHOCOLATE BREAD PUDDING

10 slices stale bread, crusts removed,
   cut in ¼-inch cubes
 3 pts. milk
1½ lbs. bitter chocolate
 1 teaspoon salt (scant)

6 eggs, 2 of them separated
14 oz. sugar
2 tablespoons vanilla essence
½ teaspoon almond essence

1. Heat the milk in a saucepan with the chocolate and salt until the chocolate is melted. Blend the mixture well with a beater.
2. Put the 4 eggs and the yolks of the other 2 in a large bowl and beat slightly, stirring in 12 oz. of the sugar.
3. Gradually stir in the chocolate milk and the vanilla and almond flavouring.
4. Stir the bread cubes into this mixture and let stand 10–15 minutes.
5. Pour into a large casserole, set in a pan with enough hot water to come halfway up the casserole, and bake 1 hour in a 400° oven.
6. When the pudding is almost done, beat the 2 egg whites until stiff but not dry, adding the remaining 2 oz. sugar gradually. Spread this meringue on the pudding and bake 5–10 minutes longer, or until the meringue is delicately brown. Serve warm or cold. Serves 10.

CHEESECAKE PIE

4 oz. fine oatcake crumbs
2 oz. sugar
2 oz. melted butter or margarine
1 lb. cream cheese softened
2 eggs

3 oz. sugar
¼ pt. evaporated milk
1 teaspoon vanilla
   Glacé cherries, peaches, strawberries,
   or pineapple

1. Mix the crumbs, 2 oz. sugar, and butter and press on the bottom and sides of a 9-inch pie plate. Build up the edge ¼ inch above the rim of the plate. Chill.
2. Beat the cream cheese in a mixer.
3. Beat in the eggs, one at a time.
4. Beat in the 3 oz. sugar, and continue beating until smooth.
5. Stir in the evaporated milk and vanilla and beat well.
6. Pour gently into the crumb crust and bake in a slow oven, 300°, 45 minutes.
7. When the pie is cool spread the top with glacé fruit and chill well. Serves 6.

DIPLOMAT CREAM PUDDING

2 dozen sponge fingers
6 oz. seedless raisins
2 tablespoons candied lemon peel minced

3 tablespoons candied orange peel minced
Kirsch
Apricot or peach jam

Sauce

6 oz. sugar
¾ pt. milk scalded

½ teaspoon vanilla
4 egg yolks well beaten

1. Soak the fruits in kirsch to cover.
2. Make the sauce first. Dissolve the sugar in the scalded milk, add vanilla, and cool to lukewarm. Pour over the yolks and blend well.
3. Spread one side of sponge fingers with jam and arrange close together, jam sides down, in the bottom of a small, deep, buttered casserole.
4. Sprinkle the sponge fingers with soaked fruit and pour over a little of the sauce.
5. Build up layers of jam-spread sponge fingers, fruit, and sauce until sponge fingers and fruit are used up. This should use up about half of the sauce.
6. Place the casserole in a pan of hot water and bake 1 hour in a moderate oven, 350°. Chill.
7. Cook the remaining sauce in a double boiler until thickened and serve hot with the pudding. Serves 5–6.

SOUR CREAM APPLE TART

2 lbs. sliced and peeled apples
¼ pt. sour cream
2 oz. butter or margarine
½ lb. sugar
8 eggs separated
2 tablespoons flour

1 lemon, juice and grated rind
½ teaspoon salt
Sugar
Fine bread crumbs
Blanched and shredded almonds
Cinnamon

1. Melt the butter in a large frying-pan and cook the apples, stirring frequently until tender.
2. Combine ½ lb. sugar, sour cream, egg yolks well beaten, flour, and lemon. Mix well and pour over the apples.
3. Continue to cook, over very low heat, stirring constantly, until the custard thickens. Pour into a good-sized casserole and cool.
4. Beat egg whites until stiff but not dry, adding salt when whites are foamy.
5. Fold into the cooled apple mixture.
6. Make a mixture of equal parts of sugar, crumbs, and nuts, stir in cinnamon to taste, and spread over the casserole.
7. Bake in a slow oven, 325°, 45 minutes, or until firm.
   Serve either hot or cold, with vanilla-flavoured whipped cream or ice cream. Serves 8–10.

TOFFEE DELIGHT

6 oz. crushed vanilla wafers
6 oz. chopped walnuts
6 oz. butter or margarine
4 oz. confectioners' or icing sugar

2 eggs separated
½ teaspoon vanilla
½ lb. unsweetened chocolate melted
¼ pt. thick cream whipped

1. Melt 2 oz. of the butter and mix it with the crumbs and nuts. Spread half of this mixture in a shallow casserole or large deep pie plate.
2. Cream the remaining 4 oz. butter and the sugar until light and fluffy, and beat in the egg yolks and vanilla.
3. Cool the chocolate slightly and blend into creamed mixture.
4. Beat the egg whites until stiff but not dry and fold into the chocolate mixture.
5. Fold in the whipped cream.
6. Pour this mixture over the crumbs in the casserole and cover with remaining crumbs. Chill for several hours or overnight.
   Garnish with more whipped cream when ready to serve, if desired. Serves 8.

HAZELNUT-APPLE CAKE

4 oz. shelled hazelnuts
4 apples peeled, cored, and sliced thin
2 day-old sponge or rice cake
3 oz. raisins
4 fluid oz. brandy

¾ pt. milk
4 eggs separated
½ lb. sugar
½ teaspoon vanilla
1 teaspoon grated lemon peel

1. Cut enough cake into thin strips to make 3 lbs. This can be bought sponge or rice cake. Spread the strips out on a tray and let them dry for a day, or at least overnight.
2. Cover raisins with brandy and let stand overnight.
3. Mix milk, lightly beaten egg yolks, 4 oz. of the sugar, and vanilla and pour over cake strips in a large bowl.
4. Toast hazelnuts 15 minutes in a slow oven, 250°, and rub vigorously in a coarse towel to remove the brown skins. Chop nuts medium fine or blend a few seconds in a blender.
5. Drain the cake strips, but save the egg-milk mixture. Handle the cake gently, so as not to break it up.
6. In a good-sized casserole arrange layers of cake, apples, drained raisins (save the brandy), and nuts, using half of these ingredients for each layer.
7. Pour over the casserole whatever is left of the brandy and the egg-milk mixture.
8. Sprinkle lemon rind on top and the 2 tablespoons sugar.
9. Bake the casserole in a moderate oven, 350°, about 30 minutes, or until golden.
10. Beat the egg whites until stiff but not dry, adding the remaining 4 oz. of sugar a tablespoon at a time.
11. Spread over the cake-pudding, dust with a little more sugar, and continue to bake another 10 minutes, or until the meringue is a delicate brown.
    Serve warm or chilled. Serves 8–10.

HAWAIIAN PUDDING

2 tablespoons butter or margarine
  softened
6 oz. confectioners' sugar
2 egg yolks

$\frac{1}{4}$ pt. thick cream whipped
8 oz. drained crushed pineapple
$1\frac{1}{2}$ oz. chopped walnuts
4 oz. fine oatcake crumbs

1. Cream the butter and sugar and beat in the egg yolks, one at a time.
2. Combine the whipped cream with the pineapple and nuts.
3. In a small round casserole spread a third of the crumbs.
4. Cover with the butter-sugar mixture and another third of the crumbs.
5. Spread the pineapple mixture on top and cover with the remaining crumbs. Chill several hours or overnight. Serves 4–6.

HONEY APPLE CRISP

$1\frac{1}{4}$ lbs. tart apples, sliced
2 oz. sugar
1 tablespoon lemon juice
7 oz. honey
$2\frac{1}{2}$ oz. flour

2 oz. brown sugar
$\frac{1}{4}$ teaspoon salt
$\frac{1}{4}$ teaspoon cinnamon
2 oz. butter or margarine

1. Spread the apples in a casserole and sprinkle them with the sugar, lemon juice, and honey.
2. Mix flour, brown sugar, salt, and cinnamon and cut in butter until the mixture is like coarse crumbs.
3. Spread evenly over the apples and bake in a moderate oven, 375°, 30–40 minutes, or until the apples are tender and the crust crisp and brown.
    Serve warm with cream or a scoop of ice cream. Serves 5–6.

PEACH-ALMOND PIE

4–6 large peaches, peeled and sliced
2 oz. blanched almonds
5 oz. flour
$\frac{1}{2}$ teaspoon cinnamon

$\frac{1}{4}$ teaspoon salt
$\frac{1}{2}$ lb. brown sugar
$\frac{1}{2}$ teaspoon almond essence
4 oz. butter or margarine

1. Sift the flour, cinnamon, salt, and brown sugar together.
2. Grate the almonds. Better, blend them 12–15 seconds in a blender, to pulverize them.
3. Mix almonds and almond essence with the sugar-flour mixture.
4. Cut in the butter thoroughly.
5. Arrange the sliced peaches in a medium casserole, cover with the dry mixture, and bake in a hot oven, 400°, 10 minutes.
6. Reduce heat to 350° and continue baking 25–30 minutes longer.
    Serve warm topped with scoops of ice cream, or cold with whipped cream. Serves 6.

LEMON PUDDING-CAKE

1½ tablespoons butter or margarine
6 oz. sugar
2 teaspoons grated lemon rind
3 eggs separated

3 tablespoons flour
3 tablespoons lemon juice
½ pt. milk
Pinch salt

1. Cream the butter and sugar and blend in the lemon rind.

2. Add the egg yolks and beat well.

3. Stir in flour alternately with the lemon juice and milk.

4. Beat the egg whites until stiff but not dry, adding salt when whites are foamy. Fold into the pudding mixture.

5. Turn into a small buttered casserole and bake 1 hour in a moderate oven, 350°, or until the top feels firm to the touch. The pudding will have a lemon sauce on the bottom.

　Serve warm or chilled. Serves 4.

PEACH-RICE CASSEROLE DESSERT

1 tin sliced cling peaches (1 lb. 13 oz.),
　well drained
8 oz. cooked rice
2 oz. sugar
½ teaspoon salt

1 pt. milk
2 eggs
½ teaspoon almond essence
2 tablespoons brown sugar

1. Combine sugar, salt, milk, and eggs in top of double boiler and cook over hot but not boiling water, stirring almost constantly, about 20 minutes, until somewhat thickened.

2. Remove from heat and add almond essence and rice.

3. In a buttered medium casserole make alternate layers of peaches and rice.

4. Top with brown sugar and bake about 30 minutes in a moderate oven, 350°, or until the custard is set.

　Serve warm or cold, with cream or topped with a scoop of ice cream. Serves 6.

BILBERRY PUDDING

1 lb. bilberries washed and picked over
½ lb. sugar
3 oz. butter or margarine
1 egg well beaten
6 oz. flour

2 teaspoons baking powder
¼ teaspoon salt
4 tablespoons milk
½ teaspoon vanilla essence

1. Cream 6 oz. of the sugar and the butter until fluffy and add the well-beaten egg.
2. Sift together flour, baking powder, and salt and add to the first mixture alternately with the milk. Add vanilla essence.
3. Carefully fold in 10 oz. of the bilberries, pour into a buttered casserole, and bake about 45 minutes in a 350° oven, or until firm. The exact time will depend upon the thickness of the pudding in the casserole.
4. Mash the remaining berries, add the remaining 2 oz. of sugar, and simmer 10 minutes over low heat. Strain and serve separately with the pudding, along with a jug of cream.

Serve the pudding either warm or cold. Serves 6.

QUICK HOT SPICED FRUIT CASSEROLE

1-lb. tin pineapple chunks
1-lb.-14-oz. tin peach halves
1-lb.-4-oz. tin apricot halves
2 oz. butter melted

6 oz. brown sugar
¼ teaspoon ground cloves
¼ teaspoon cinnamon
1 teaspoon curry powder, or to taste

DRAIN the fruits well and arrange in layers in a medium casserole. Combine the butter, sugar, and spices and sprinkle over the fruit. Bake 1 hour in a moderate oven, 350°.

Serve hot with a scoop of ice cream on each serving. Serves 8.

NOTES

INDEX

INDEX

HERBS	SOUPS	EGGS	CHEESE	FISH
BASIL *Annual* *Leaves* *used*	Tomato and others	Omelettes Stuffed eggs	Cottage cheese and others	In court bouillon Mackerel Fish sauces
BAY LEAF *Dried* *leaf of bay* *tree*	Fish Tomato stock		Cottage cheese	Boiled
CARAWAY *Biennial* *Seeds* *used*	Vegetable stock		Cream cheese and others	
CHERVIL *Annual* *Leaves* *used*	Asparagus Chicken Spinach Creamed	Any egg dish	Any cheese dish	Broiled Sauces
CHIVES *Perennial* *Stems* *used*	Bean Pea Vichyssoise	Omelettes	Cottage cheese Cream cheese	
DILL *Annual* *Leaves* *and seeds* *used*		Many egg dishes	Many cheese dishes	Broiled fish Shrimp
MARJORAM *Perennial* *Leaf* *used*	All stock soups Potato	Almost all	Many cheese dishes	All fish All stuffings All sauces
OREGANO *Perennial* *Leaf* *used*			Fresh in cream cheese	
PARSLEY *Annual* *Leaf* *used*	All soups	Omelettes Scrambled eggs	Many	Sauces Marinades
ROSEMARY *Perennial* *Leaf* *used*	Many meat base soups Many poultry base soups	Some egg dishes		
SAGE *Perennial* *Leaf* *used*	Most		Fresh in cottage cheese	Baked
TARRAGON *Perennial* *Leaf* *used*	Potato Tomato	Omelettes Many egg dishes	Many cheese dishes	Broiled Salmon Tartare sauce Fish sauces
THYME *Perennial* *Leaf* *used*	All stock soups	Many egg dishes	Some cheese dishes	Chowders Fried fish